The Shawshank Experience

Maura Grady • Tony Magistrale

The Shawshank Experience

Tracking the History of the World's Favorite Movie

Maura Grady
Ashland University
Ashland, USA

Tony Magistrale
University of Vermont
Burlington, Vermont, USA

ISBN 978-1-137-53213-8 (hardcover)   ISBN 978-1-137-53165-0   (eBook)
ISBN 978-1-349-95350-9 (softcover)
DOI 10.1057/978-1-137-53165-0

Library of Congress Control Number: 2016957786

Cover illustration: Ohio State Reformatory at Night. Digital photo by Scott Sukel, 2010

Printed on acid-free paper

This Palgrave Macmillan imprint is published by Springer Nature
The registered company is Nature America Inc., USA
The registered company address is: 1 New York Plaza, New York, NY 10004, U.S.A.

ACKNOWLEDGMENTS

The authors wish to acknowledge the assistance, encouragement, and direct aid of several individuals and institutions that contributed to making this book possible. First, our students at both Ashland University and the University of Vermont deserve more than just an appreciative acknowledgment, as we have both been teaching Darabont's film and King's novella for many years; most of the ideas in this book were born and refined in our university classrooms. University of Vermont colleagues and students read draft sections in manuscript form and provided crucial feedback for revision and further writing: Christopher Magistrale, Philip Baruth, Sarah Turner, Sarah Nilsen, Huck Gutman, Liz Paley, Dennis Mahoney, Hubert Zapf, Larry Bennett (and especially UVM alumni, Jess Slayton and Matt Muller, two outstanding students from The Films of Stephen King class, who offered new ideas that shaped and influenced Chap. 3). A section of this chapter initially appeared as "Robert Frost's Voice in *The Shawshank Redemption*," *Green Mountains Review* 28:2 (2015): 225–232; we thank the journal's poetry editor, Elizabeth Powell, for publishing it first. This project, which looks at Shawshank's film tourists, would not exist at all without Richard "Robby" Roberson, with whom this project began in 2013– his contributions extend well past ch. 4. In Ohio, April and Bill Mullen and Bob Wachtman lead a long list of *Shawshank* fans whose lives were forever changed by their direct contact with this movie and the subsequent preservation of its continued presence in the Shawshank Trail. We are grateful for their warmth, passion, and know-how. Thank you to Ashland University's Honors 390 students for the first Shawshank fan research project in 2013 and to *Almatourism: A Journal of Culture,*

Tourism and Territorial Development, which published the results of that study as "The Shawshank Trail: A Cross Disciplinary Study in Film Induced Tourism and Fan Culture" in 2015; portions of this research are reprinted in Chap. 4. We are indebted to the members of the Mansfield Convention and Visitors Bureau, especially Jodie Puster-Snavely and Lee Tasseff; the staff and tireless volunteers at OSR, particularly Mary Cabrera and Paul Smith, who opened their doors and gave so generously of their time; as well as Becky McKinnell who repeated our interview when recording devices failed. We are grateful to Amy Daubenspeck and the Ashland Convention and Visitors Bureau, Hilary Donatini, and Dawn Weber, for helping to get Tony to Ohio to deliver the Keynote Address at the twentieth anniversary celebration of the film's release. Thank you to Kathy Larsen, Lynn Zubernis, and Paul Booth for their work on fandom and helpful advice. Thanks are also due also to Sharleen Mondal, Emily Hess, Craig Hovey, Deleasa Randall-Griffiths, and Patty Saunders for reading early drafts of this manuscript. Thanks to Pippa, Ada, Cash, and Zoe for their patience and to the Johnson family and Pearce family for their support. But Ohio's biggest thanks go to Tim Johnson for reading every word and to Delia Roberson for absolutely everything. At Palgrave Macmillan, Shaun Vigil, our acquisitions editor, and Sowmiya Swamikannu, who served as the manuscript's production manager, were instrumental in bringing this book into existence and convincing us that Palgrave was the right place to publish it.

Contents

List of Figures

CHAPTER 1

Introduction

Over the course of Labor Day weekend, August 29–31, 2014, the community of Mansfield, Ohio, commemorated the twenty-year theatrical release of *The Shawshank Redemption*, a film that was shot in and around the city. Local events were planned to coincide with this tribute, including lectures about the film's making and meaning; tours of the Ohio State Reformatory (OSR), the retired former prison at the center of the movie; and a theatrical screening of *Shawshank* on Friday night in downtown Mansfield's Renaissance Theatre, the venue where the movie premiered on Tuesday, September 13, 1994, almost exactly twenty years earlier.

Fans of the film, both local and those traveling from out of town and state, were encouraged to indulge in a wide range of movie-related memorabilia. As an aid, they made use of the Shawshank Trail, a guide and roadmap to visiting fourteen of the actual shooting locations and major attractions associated with the film's production in Mansfield and its surrounding communities. *Shawshank* aficionados toured the Brewer Hotel (also known as the haunted Bissman Building) in downtown Mansfield where Brooks Hatlen and Red share the same apartment and the prison woodworking shop where Red and Tommy are employed, located in neighboring Upper Sandusky; drove out to the intersection of Snyder Road and Hagerman Road in Bellville, Ohio, where Red walked the highway to the hayfield in Buxton; met and took photographs with Renee Blaine (Linda Dufresne) and Scott Mann (Glenn Quentin) at the Pugh Cabin at Malabar State Farm, the log cabin where Mrs. Dufresne and her "golf pro lover" open the film; and paid homage to the famous oak tree (minus the rock wall leading up to

© The Author(s) 2016
M. Grady, T. Magistrale, *The Shawshank Experience*,
DOI 10.1057/978-1-137-53165-0_1

it, which was removed postproduction) where Andy asked his wife to marry him and later instructs Red to visit in his last conversation with Andy.

Fans following the Trail viewed artifacts from the film itself, such as Shawshank prison uniforms and badges, the actual prison bus that transported Andy and the fresh fish to Shawshank, the red pickup truck that gives Red a lift to Buxton, and the Trailways bus that Red rides to start his journey to Mexico, and before and after the screening of the film at the Renaissance Theater, they obtained autographs from and interacted with several of the actors who starred in *Shawshank*, including Scott Mann, Renee Blaine, the bank manager Andy visits on his way out of town (James Kisicki), Fat Ass (Frank Medrano), and Warden Norton (Bob Gunton). But Ohio State Reformatory, which served as the location for all the outside shots of Shawshank State Prison as well as Warden Norton's office, Red and Brooks' apartment, the corridor that Tommy mops, the room where *Gilda* is screened for the inmates, and Red's three parole board hearings was indubitably the biggest star of the weekend, the place fans most wanted to see and explore.

This book was born, appropriately, over the course of this anniversary weekend. It was conceived in response to a set of questions specifically relevant to the *Shawshank* experience: Why has this movie maintained such enormous popularity (its twenty-year anniversary commemoration was provided major publicity in the *New York Times*, *Pittsburgh Post-Gazette*, *Washington Post*, and on Cleveland, Columbus, and Toledo television stations)? Why does *Shawshank* resonate, over two decades later, as a work of art? Why does this film continue to draw such a diverse range of critical attention from musicologists, criminal justice experts, sociologists, film and cultural studies scholars, in addition to English and media studies teachers at both the high school and college levels? In what ways does Frank Darabont's authored screenplay and directed film differ substantially from the original Stephen King narrative, *Rita Hayworth and the Shawshank Redemption* (*RHSR*), published as the first of four short novellas[1] in the 1982 collection *Different Seasons?* What is the relationship between the real OSR and the fictional Shawshank Prison—where do their narratives intersect and diverge, and what insights, if any, do their respective histories provide about American penology? How accurately did the portrait of long-term incarceration in the movie reflect the experience in real life? Finally, how do we explain the fan phenomenon that this film engendered and still retains? Is it possible, and even prudent, to distinguish among the various fan bases—Stephen King's, *Shawshank*'s, and OSR's—that invariably intersect along the Shawshank Trail? Why did so many people wait in long lines to obtain autographs from the actors who starred in this film and to tour many of the actual location sites and artifacts featured on the Shawshank Trail? Fans traveled long distances with friends and family to visit the movie's filming sites on this special weekend. Was there something about the film itself that inspired these pilgrims to come in small groups or with at least another person, for we observed few visitors touring these sites alone? These are the main topics we have endeavored to address in this book. However, since so

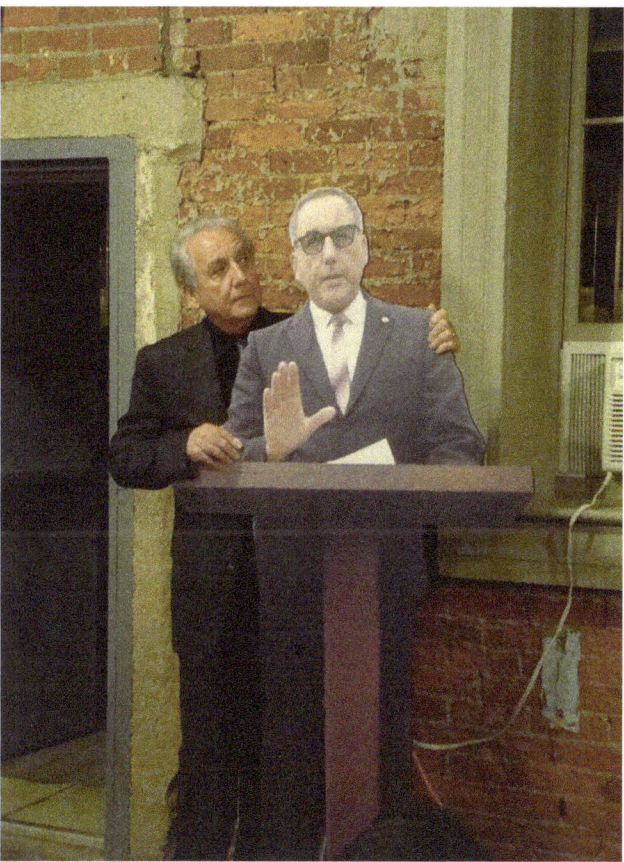

Fig. 1.1 Actor Bob Gunton introduces himself to Warden Samuel Norton (also Bob Gunton) during the cocktail party held at OSR during *The Shawshank Redemption* Twentieth Anniversary Event in 2014

many of these questions have their origins in Stephen King's novella, perhaps the most appropriate place to commence *The Shawshank Experience* is to discuss where *Rita Hayworth and the Shawshank Redemption* belongs in the prolific canon of America's storyteller (Fig. 1.1).

The King Corpus and *Shawshank*

The task of trying to categorize the career output of any author is made more difficult when that writer has been publishing over a book a year for nearly half a century. If we grant ourselves room to maneuver among some broad generalizations, the earliest Stephen King novels—including most of his fiction published in the late 1970s and the 1980s, the "first phase" of his writing career—were typically large tomes, epic in their narrative size and scope, and revolved around recognizable genre plots (sometimes conflating two or more into a single hybrid text): horror, dystopian technology, political paranoid thriller, epic fantasy, and the journey quest. *The Shining, The Stand, 'Salem's Lot, The Talisman, The Dead Zone, The Tommyknockers*, and *IT*, for example, present macrocosmic views of postmodern America, providing the reader with a journey to the center of a post-Watergate/Viet Nam heart of darkness. These are books solidly centered on the adventures of boys and men, while, in part because of the resulting criticism King received, in the late 1980s and throughout the 1990s his novels tended to focus more on women. Many of the books that appeared in this "second phase" of his career show evidence of King's ability to produce highly circumscribed, tightly wrought narratives bearing few of the epic tendencies we find in *The Dark Tower* or *The Stand*. If the novels from King's "first phase" can best be described as stories of epic proportion played out across a big screen to accommodate an interfacing with history, America's interstate highway system, the existence of multiple parallel universes, and a broad discussion of social-political dynamics, as each contains an enormous cast of characters and subplots, then books such as *Misery, Dolores Claiborne, Gerald's Game, Rose Madder*, and *Bag of Bones* are more like classical Greek dramas played out on deliberately circumscribed stages, employing consistent scenic backdrops, a narrow time frame, and a small cast of characters shaping a much more intimate storyline. In addition to being generally shorter and more compact, the work in the "second phase" of King's career is strongly feminist orientated, preoccupied with women's issues, forsaking supernatural monsters and replacing them with monster-husbands of everyday reality—domestic tragedies of entrapment, endurance, and survival.

King's most recent works, those novels and tales that have emerged in the new millennium, have tended to reflect many of the writer's earliest concerns—a return, for example, to an adult Danny Torrance and *The Shining* in *Doctor Sleep* (2013), the apocalyptic vision of *The Stand* revisited without any of its hopeful potentiality in *Cell* (2006), and strong female characters capable of self-rescue in the psychological terror tales "The Gingerbread Girl" in *Just After Sunset* (2008) and *A Good Marriage* and *Big Driver* from the collection *Full Dark, No Stars* (2010). Another element that characterizes King's writing during the post-millennium stage of his publishing also revisits a genre that has interested this novelist throughout his career: the detective story. Crime fiction has always occupied an important place in King's library,[2] since he is as a voracious reader who has frequently acknowledged publicly his affection for the stories of Ed McBain, Raymond Chandler, John D. MacDonald, Thomas Harris, and Cormac McCarthy; and as an author who utilizes crime elements to greater or lesser degrees in earlier novels as diverse as *The Dead Zone*, *Needful Things*, and *Dolores Claiborne*. More recently, *Mr. Mercedes* (which won the Edgar Award for best crime novel of 2014 from the Mystery Writers of America) and *Finders Keepers* are even more overtly indebted to the crime genre. In fact, King's typical narratological structure—with its emphasis on action-driven plots and protagonists who are forced to problem-solve their way out of threatening situations—is highly reminiscent of detective fiction; he even published a short story, "The Doctor's Case," that employed Arthur Conan Doyle's characters from the Sherlock Holmes series. The presence of actual detective-police characters in King's canon is, ironically, oddly rare; as in Hitchcock's films, King's archetypical protagonist-narrators, everyday working men and women who are often pulled into situations against their better judgment and will, come to operate in the role of the detective. As is often the case in crime fiction, the narrator-protagonists in the majority of King's post-millennium novels—*Joyland*, *11/22/63*, *Dr. Sleep*, *Mr. Mercedes*, *Revival*, and *Finders Keepers*—not only occupy central roles in the storyline, they also control the flow of the plot itself, leaving the reader to uncover events at the same time as the characters.

There are many places where gothic fiction and detective fiction interface. The detective crosses narrative space in multiple genres, as evident in role of Deckard in the cyborg-horror film *Blade Runner*. So, too, does the gothic infiltrate genres that appear at first glance to exist outside the realm of horror art in moments when boundaries are blurred that distinguish good from evil, health from perversity, monstrosity from normality, crime from punishment. *Shawshank* technically begins where most detective tales end: a double homicide has been commissioned; the criminal apparently responsible for the two murders has been apprehended, convicted, and now will serve time in a penitentiary without the possibility of parole. This is all the audience knows when the film and novella introduce us to Andy Dufresne, the "wife-killing banker" serving two life sentences in Shawshank Prison. The remainder of the narrative not only reveals Andy's innocence but also the paradoxical deepening of his character even as it descends into criminality, as he confesses to Red: "I had to come to prison to learn how to be a crook." Since it is only through Red's flashback narration that both the reader and filmgoer attain relief and insight into the true nature of Andy's wrongful convictions and escape, Red serves in the role of a quasi-detective, often an intentionally unreliable narrator, providing us with slices of information he has deliberately withheld and even used to mislead, and only eventually clarifies. Within both the gothic and detective genres, multiple interpretations are frequently embedded within a single text, as is the case with Robert Louis Stevenson's *The Strange Case of Dr. Jekyll and Mr. Hyde* (1886), and part of the experience for the audience comes from suturing together the individual parts that the narrative affords into a satisfying, or at least comprehensible, whole. Red may prefer checkers to chess, but he is an absolute master strategist/storyteller who remains in command of when and how the various plot twists of his first-person account unfolds. It is natural for readers and film audiences to overlook that Red is always in possession of Andy's complete history from the moment Red's voice initiates the narrative's presentation and, presumably, until the reunion of the two men in Mexico (or, in the case of the novella, Red's decision to commence the journey there). Only then does Red give up absolute control over the plot, abandoning the history of its telling to a "conclusion [that] is uncertain" (*RHSR*, 101) because its final unfolding will take place in Mexico and in "real time." Like Sherlock Holmes at the end of one of his mystery tales, Red alone is in possession of a complete knowledge, and the way in which he presents this information often resembles the detective's revelation of false leads that unfold into a final resolution of the case and an explanation of its various mysteries. In the case of *Shawshank*: the ultimate purposes of the rock hammer and those "big goddamn posters" up on Dufresne's wall, Andy's legal innocence and his choice to escape from Shawshank instead of using Heywood's rope to commit suicide, the change that occurs to Red as a result of his friendship with Andy, and Red's own decision to "break parole" in order to journey down to Mexico to join him, rather than commit a crime that would put Red back in Shawshank.

Many of the film's enthusiasts make a sharp distinction between *Shawshank* and those King novels and films that contain his "typical" scary subject matter that has largely been responsible for making him an international bestseller (even though *Shawshank* is not the only King narrative that eschews such material); indeed, in the more than two decades since the release of the movie, a surprisingly large percentage of its disparate fan base remains unaware that Frank Darabont's adaptation was based on a Stephen King novella. Within this percentage, there are those who are thoroughly shocked when they discover this fact, as many aficionados of the film disavow any interest in horror art—some claiming repugnance towards the entire genre. There exist people who have never read a Stephen King novel or watched a film adaptation of one of his books, and have no intention of ever doing so, but they have watched the film version of *Shawshank* twenty times. Rob Reiner, a founder and executive of Castle Rock Entertainment, the production company that has adapted several of King's novels, including *Shawshank*, into movies, "finds it interesting that two of the most talked-about film adaptations of Stephen King's work [*Stand By Me* and *Shawshank*] came from the same collection of novellas and don't rely on classic horror or supernatural elements of storytelling" (qtd. in Heidenry, par. 18). As George Beahm has argued frequently, "King's enduring popularity stems in part from his refusal to write only supernatural horror, in which the monsters are external. Those books can be highly entertaining fiction, and popular in their own right ... but the stories in which the monsters are mortal are often more frightening because they are *real*" (193). To continue this line of argument, further distinctions separate the King fictional world and *Shawshank*: there are no literal doorways leading to parallel universes or alternative realities; the story is a long-developing narrative featuring two men in the absence of women characters; both novella and film are low on action and high on sentiment; and while there is a fair amount of violence, particularly early on, *Shawshank* contains no gore and is quite discrete in how much of its violence actually takes place on either the page or the screen. In marketing the film, Castle Rock Entertainment, especially initially, avoided associating it with King's fiction and the rest of the King film-adaptation canon (as was also the case in marketing *Stand By Me*). The studio heads decided not to use King's name for fear that the writer's reputation would alienate mainstream filmgoers who would dismiss the film without giving it a fair viewing (Beahm 481).

These differences notwithstanding, *Shawshank* is actually a highly representative text within the King canon. In addition to resembling other King novels via its connections to crime fiction narratology, the novella also features a character who is the archetypical King protagonist: Andy Dufresne is an ordinary man who finds himself suddenly trapped in extraordinary circumstances; he must find a way, relying primarily on his wits and independent spirit, to survive. Several of King's most notable male protagonists harbor secrets that result in their undoing. Male secrets unify the plots of texts as diverse as *Pet Sematary, Apt Pupil, The Shining, 1408, Under the Dome*, and *A Good Marriage*. The males in these novels, however, are not representative King heroes; they are merely protagonists trapped by circumstances and compulsions beyond their capacity to control. Andy Dufresne in *Shawshank* maintains a secret hole in his cell wall that he keeps to himself for years, refusing to disclose it even to his best friend, Red. But unlike these other King males whose secrets eventually corrupt them—destroying the interpersonal bonds they have with others as well as their own sanities—Andy's secret, rather than inducing self-corruption, sets him free, completing his transition from victim into hero. As a King hero, Andy is unassuming and unassailable—most of all, he is best defined in terms of his indomitable spirit. Most of King's heroes and heroines are similar men and women who do not think of themselves as heroes, but nevertheless find themselves pitted against intimidating and corrupt forces and institutions. Andy's level of intelligence and fertile imagination puts him at a level that perhaps best resembles the writers who populate the landscapes of other King's narratives, those self-contained males who, like Ben Mears in *'Salem's Lot*, Bill Denbrough in *IT*, or Paul Sheldon in *Misery*, possess the imaginative capacities and self-discipline to overcome life-threatening adversity.

Although Andy is definitely better educated, cultured, and employed than the majority of King's blue-collar heroes and heroines, he still shares much in common with them as well, as they all communicate a strong element of the independent Yankee New Englander. "I have a very common nature," says King, "which is why my books sell. I am not capable of being fancy" (qtd. in Baxter 27). The King male hero stands apart from the crowd by virtue of his native (rather than an effete or even university-imparted) intelligence and self-reliance—most of them, like Andy, are unmarried—and their individuality is a big part of what makes them archetypically American. Andy can be distinguished from the other Shawshank prisoners around him, as Red is first to notice, insofar as he asserts his individuality in ever-increasing doses. While other prisoners succumb in varying degrees to the isolating forces of prison institutionalization, Andy finds a way to hold on to his inimitable identity. Red tells us he had "a walk and a talk that just wasn't normal around here." Maybe he stands out because of his comparative cultural sophistication, surrounded as he is with high school dropouts, evinced in his personal preferences for chess over checkers, Mozart over Hank Williams, the pursuit of geology over standing around idly smoking cigarettes, wall photographs of Einstein over sports figures, and fiercely independent and smart film starlets over bimbos. In the end, Andy's distinctiveness, his individuality, is a secure enough part of his personality that it never translates into an air of elite superiority—except when he calls Bogs an "ignorant fuck" and Warden Norton "obtuse"—and both of these men are deserving of their put downs. In fact, rather than lording his status as the most educated man in Shawshank, Andy uses his intelligence to teach men who for most of their lives were not teachable. He may have felt compelled for obvious reasons to help the guards and the warden do their taxes, but assisting fellow inmates to obtain their GEDs must be viewed as an act of altruism. While the typical King hero is fiercely independent, he is also loyal to his *ka-tet*—the small group of friends and fellow warriors so named in *The Dark Tower*—but this is a concept also present in many other King novels. We see this level of commitment present especially in Andy's relationship with Red, a friendship bond that is as strong as any to be found in the King canon.

Further, Dufresne is as much a portrait of the American hero as any to be found in King's canon. When Dufresne decides to tunnel out of Shawshank, he is traveling in the footsteps of generations of American cinematic rebels, from James Dean and Steve McQueen to Sylvester Stallone and Clint Eastwood. Standing against odds that are not in their favor and clearly demarcated in terms of good embattled against evil almost to the point of allegory, the outcomes of the narratives in which these men appear hinge on the choices they make. At some point in nearly every one of the various films that feature these actors, they must confront the same "simple choice: to get busy living or get busy dying" that Andy faces in *Shawshank*. Perhaps most important, Andy follows in the line of these other American everymen insofar as he will not sacrifice his individuality in the face of dehumanizing forces that seek to break him. Not surprisingly, these are also the American antiheroes who have inspired many of the core male protagonists in King's own fiction, the fiercely iconoclastic and desperate characters from the Bachman books and *The Stand*, certainly, but also Roland Deschain from *The Dark Tower* who provides the keystone to the rest of King's canon as the archetypical western hero of a grand narrative whose task is nothing less than to save the world from impending destruction.

While Dufresne emerges as a prototypical King hero, there are various other elements that tie *Shawshank* to the larger King corpus. The argument can be made that *Shawshank*, like the majority of King's other film adaptations, bears important similarities to the postmodern horror film. Just as King's brand of horror frequently exposes the terrors beneath the placid surfaces of everyday American life—the abject intrusions of violence against the body, the imminent threat of death, the feebleness of human will in the face of events beyond our ability to control—*Shawshank* presents a similar recreation of terror that assails Andy as well as the viewer. Although *Shawshank* is technically not a horror film, Darabont reveals again his appreciation for and understanding of the genre in which he has spent most of his Hollywood career as either a screenwriter or director by creating an audience experience where fear and pleasure commingle.[3] He has established a Hobbesian world, brutal and unstable, where prisoner bodies and psyches are always in danger of violation, where paranoia prevails, and where the audience experiences terror bounded by the tension between proximity and distance, reality and illusion. As we will examine at various points elsewhere in this book, *Shawshank* employs many elements typically associated with the horror genre: a haunted gothic space (OSR), that is cavernous at the same time that it is claustrophobic and subterranean; horror monsters (Bogs and the sisters, and later, Warden Norton and Captain Hadley); a besieged horror protagonist in Andy who the film frequently genders female; and, most importantly, an atmosphere of instability and dread where characters and viewers alike are forced to undergo moments of stress and panic that simulate the physical and emotional thrills experienced in a horror film. The relief the filmgoer feels at the conclusion of other King adaptations, when, for example, Paul Sheldon (*Misery*) or Wendy and Danny Torrance (*The Shining*) triumphantly escape peril, is similar to how we feel after Andy's successful flight from Shawshank; indeed, simply escaping from this prison is an impressive feat, but the feeling of exultation the audience feels when Andy finally pours himself out of the sewage pipe and into the creek is more directly relevant to the horror of the claustrophobic underground journey itself, a staple of the horror genre. In the horror film, the audience's relief in the survival of the protagonist is always proportional to the level of terror from which he or she has escaped.

Shawshank features Manichean forces in opposition against one another, and there likewise exists a strong level of perverse sexual violence that is closely aligned with the film's moral divisions. This sexual divide is present in other King novels, such as *The Stand, The Dark Half, Rose Madder, Lisey's Story,* and *Doctor Sleep.* Sexuality in King's universe is either cloyingly romanticized—mired in the sentimental domain of white, bourgeois heterosexuality, as in *Bag of Bones, 11/22/63, Lisey's Story,* and *Mr. Mercedes*—or it goes in the opposite direction, sinking to the level of vulgar masculine appetite in the form of brutal rape assaults, both heterosexual and homosexual. In the King canon, definitions of healthy sexuality are delineated (and constrained) by normative sexual practices aligned with the writer's heroes and heroines. The range of limited sexual activities that are not coded deviant in his fiction, however, is so traditional that they are reminiscent of the 1950s, King's own childhood reference point. As a corollary, there is no tolerance for alternative behavior in the bedroom, even if shared between consenting heterosexual couples. Bondage and sexual role play (which are in turn linked to incest and child molestation) in *Gerald's Game,* the indulgence of fetish wear, oral sex, and male masturbation in *The Stand,* male-to-female transvestitism in *'Salem's Lot,* and just about anything else remotely at the edge of kink is viewed harshly by the writer as psychologically perverse and signaling metaphorically an avenue for personal corruption.[4] These sexual constellations are fixed points in King's universe, and as deviant sexual practices become more frequent and intense in each of his books, the participants' affiliation with evil strengthens proportionately. At the Overlook Hotel in *The Shining,* for example, the various sexual acts that are proffered to Jack Torrance bring no real fulfillment or interpersonal bonding, providing only the tease of eroticism without accompanying satisfaction. The full range of the Overlook's powers are expressed in acts of sexual sadism and Jack's descent into the hotel's corruption is signaled in part by his lack of interest in Wendy and arousal in the company of a costumed ghost woman wearing "a small and sparkly cat's-eye-mask ... dressed in clinging white satin ... smooth-and-powdered naked under her dress" (350). Sexuality at the Overlook becomes a thinly veiled disguise for manipulation and personal humiliation, motivated by a derisive mean-spiritedness that is always on the cusp of violence.

Homosexuality is particularly exaggerated and odious throughout his fiction and signals the complete degeneration of an individual who has lost his moral bearings. While King appreciates the value of same-sex friendships—they are, in fact, some of his most compelling fictional portraits of both men and women—he steers clear of investing them with any kind of homoerotic charge. His male-bonding permutations, like Andy and Red, are intensely intimate, but never sexual. Indeed, homosexuals submit to the worst possible stereotyping in King's fiction, often crossing over into pedophilia, and some of the most perverse human monsters in King's world share the bond of male homoeroticism (e.g., Dussander and Todd in *Apt Pupil*, Henry Bowers in *IT*, Sunlight Gardner in *The Talisman*, Horace Derwent in *The Shining*, The Kid in *The Stand*, Wild Bill in *The Green Mile*, and Gasher in *The Dark Tower*, to name the most egregious homophobic examples). Bogs and the sisters in *Shawshank* are labeled "bull queers," embodying the type of sadistic male violence that King has linked to homosexuality throughout his career. Accordingly, throughout his fiction, there is little evidence of positive gay or lesbian characters portrayed as mature, morally responsible, or loving, but there exist plenty of examples of homosexuality as a metaphor for tyranny, personal as well as political, psychological maladjustment, and primal cruelty—and this is exclusively the case in the context of adult male homoeroticism. Although their predatory nature leads Red to acknowledge in the film that the sisters "have to be human first" to qualify as homosexuals, the fact that both the novella and film define the sisters solely in terms of their sexuality works as an implicit indictment of their homosexual acts; their violence cannot be separated from their sexuality. Since the release of the film, Darabont has tried to distance himself from charges of homophobia by insisting that the sisters are not gay but rapists who substitute the subjugation of men when women are unavailable ("The Buzz" 70). But as Edward Madden counters more convincingly, "the rapists, however, are still labeled 'queens' or queers: they remain marked as homosexual" (192), while the heroes of the film, Red and Andy, both avow heterosexual desire exclusively, as aligned in their overt sexual response to Rita Hayworth and the other highly sexualized posters of women who share space on Andy's wall.

DARABONT AND KING FILM ADAPTATIONS

At this writing, the King film canon contains 59 adaptations of his work, encompassing TV movies, miniseries, three long-running televised programs, and 36 Hollywood theatrical films over a period of roughly forty years. It's a prolific assemblage; no less impressive than the literary canon the writer has assembled over the past five decades. Using writer credit references from the Internet Movie Data Base, Forrest Wickman discovered in 2011 that King was fourteenth (with 127 "writer credits") on a list of authors whose work has been adapted into film. At the time of Wickman's survey, he ranked behind William Shakespeare (831), Charles Dickens (300), Edgar Allan Poe (240), and The Brothers Grimm (212), but in front of Mark Twain and Ian Fleming. However, King remains the only living writer on the list of the top 24 authors (Wickman). It should therefore come as no surprise that in dealing with such a prodigious body of work, some of these films are difficult for an adult to watch, much less appreciate. Films such as *Dreamcatcher*, *Children of the Corn*, and *Maximum Overdrive* are little more than cinematic embarrassments and only serve to support the denigration of detractors such as Harold Bloom, who views Stephen King's contributions—filmic adaptations as well as literary authorship—as lacking "any aesthetic dignity ... an image of the death of the Literate Reader" (3). Unfortunately, many viewers and critics have unfairly repudiated the entire King canon after viewing one or two of these celluloid disasters.

We would prefer to emphasize instead the number of artistically successful adaptations that have occurred since *Carrie* was released in 1976, a body of film art that has drawn together some of the world's major directors, screenwriters, and a range of the most accomplished actors and actresses working in Hollywood. Frank Darabont's reputation now resides among the best of them; in fact, if Darabont were to stop writing, directing, and producing any further work for Hollywood, his "prison" films adapted from Stephen King—*Shawshank*, *The Green Mile*, and *The Mist*—have already immortalized his filmic career. If Kathy Bates retains the unofficial title of the archetypal actress for a Stephen King film, then Frank Darabont may be the ultimate King screenwriter/director, as he has now directed and authored the screenplays for four Stephen King adaptations. The first of these, *The Woman in the Room* (1983), an early tale from King's first collection of short stories, *Night Shift*, and Darabont's directorial debut, impressed King tremendously. When Darabont again sought to take advantage of the novelist's innovative approach to selling the property rights to his work for one dollar in return for five percent of the box office receipts (see Magistrale, *Hollywood's* 7; although some sources claim that Darabont actually paid $5000 for the rights in the form of a check that Stephen King purportedly never cashed, see *Shawshank: Redeeming*), King sold him the permission rights to *Rita Hayworth and the Shawshank Redemption*, and the film's pre-production began in January 1993. Darabont had no trouble selling the script he had authored to Rob Reiner, who at the time was operating as one of the chief executives for the production company Castle Rock Entertainment, and Reiner was immediately astounded by the quality of the screenplay (both Morgan Freeman and Tim Robbins continue to cite the quality of *Shawshank*'s screenplay as the reason they were likewise drawn to the film). However, since he was a virtual unknown in Hollywood at the time, only sharing screenwriting credits on the 1980s' remake of *The Blob* and *The Fly 2* (the regrettable sequel to David Cronenberg's *The Fly*), Darabont faced a more arduous task in convincing Castle Rock to grant him permission also to direct *Shawshank*. According to Ernie Malik, who served as the production publicist for *The Shawshank Redemption*:

> Frank owned this script for five years. He wrote it in eight weeks. He brought it into Castle Rock. One of the heads of Castle Rock at that time was Rob Reiner. Rob Reiner had just finished directing *A Few Good Men*, which hadn't come out in theaters yet. He read the script, and the story I heard was that he pushed a check across the table to Frank for 1.75 million dollars. And he said, "Frank, this is the best script I have ever read. Thank you very much. I am going to direct it." Frank Darabont tore the check up in front of Reiner and said, "No, I am going to direct it." And Reiner wanted Tom Cruise to play Andy Dufresne. (*Shawshank* Panel)

Although tempted by the role, Cruise would take the job only if Reiner served as the film's director. Despite the latter's efforts to convey his confidence in Frank Darabont and assurances that he, Reiner, would be closely involved in all stages of the production, Cruise ultimately passed on the opportunity. Tom Hanks was likewise considered for the role, but was already committed to filming *Forrest Gump*, and at various points Nicolas Cage and Kevin Costner were also attracted to movie because of the script's quality. Tim Robbins was therefore not the first choice, although it is now hard to imagine anyone else playing Andy Dufresne.

Castle Rock and Rob Reiner, who King later credited with saving "my film-associated reputation from the scrap-heap" (*Shawshank: Redeeming*), ultimately rolled the dice in allowing Darabont to direct his first feature film. Any other Hollywood production company would have never taken such a risk, a testament to Rob Reiner's ability to recognize quality and talent, his faith in the script, personal clout at Castle Rock, and the studio's courageousness. But it is also a sign that Castle Rock and Reiner sensed early on that they had a "hot property" in their hands and felt compelled to provide Darabont with their unwavering confidence. As the director has acknowledged gratefully, "I had Castle Rock's complete trust and support... If I'd had standard studio interference and meddling on that movie, if I'd spent my time battling to defend my film against executives who wanted everything different, Lord knows how that movie would have turned out" (qtd. in Beahm 492).

Stephen King possesses deep insight into the anxieties, violence, and other horrors that belie the placid surface of bourgeois America. Future cultural historians will likely remember King for his portraits of end-of-the-century and twenty-first century men and women struggling to endure in an America that is slowly rotting from the inside out, surrendering whatever elements of decency and virtue it once possessed, and lost in the effort to understand how it managed to stray so far from its own original values. King has written well and often about the anomie that haunts postmodern America. For the past fifty years, he has had his finger on the pulse of American cultural life; the patient has often appeared in critical condition, the prognosis less than optimistic, but King has always appreciated the resiliency of the patient's spirit, his ability to find a way to survive in spite of bad odds. That spirit is as "American" as the immediately recognizable horrors that beset King's protagonists, making them attractive figures for Hollywood filmmakers looking for appealing storylines with empathetic characters. And these elements, sometimes at the risk of being pressed to sentimental hyperbole, have drawn Frank Darabont into the King universe. In a sense, Shawshank prison is a microcosm of America; it is an emblem not just of the failure of the criminal justice system but also a metaphor for all the American institutions that have proven unworthy of the people they were meant to serve. And as we will discuss in forthcoming chapters, there is not an American institution that Stephen King has failed to examine; in each case, they are found to be either corrupt or woefully inadequate. When Andy's hard work at self-rehabilitation through a growing acceptance of personal responsibility, perseverance, and a Protestant work ethic are undermined by a murderous institution and broken system, which all run counter to the vision of America and its Dream, Andy risks it all for a final bid to get "that hotel, that boat." Ironically, Andy must go to Mexico in order to obtain the things he believes "are not too much to ask." Nothing in life is fair. Sometimes it takes nineteen years in prison to learn this truth. But armed with this sobering knowledge the resilient individual toughens himself and carries on. Covered in shit and on his own, hoping that the future will be better than the past, hoping that someday his loneliness might be abetted when his soul mate joins him for endless games of chess under a warm blue sky that has never known New England snow, the sound of ocean surf keeping rhythmic time in the not so distant background. Who doesn't share a stake in such a dream?

Like King, Darabont appreciates the slow unfolding of a dense, emotionally charged plot that deliberately confounds an audience's first impressions of its protagonists and the harrowing situations in which they are cast. The capacity to triumph over the madness of despair and disappointment with special emphasis on vulnerable and sympathetic males trapped in situations that threaten them physically and especially psychologically are the quintessential themes that connect King and Darabont. In an interview conducted in 2002, King supplied his own observations on several of these concerns as they pertain specifically to the film adaptation of *Shawshank*:

> It's a terrific piece of work. It's a film about human beings—and human beings are not secondary to the theme of horror. That's an important thing to remember: You cannot scare anyone unless you first get the audience to care about these make-believe characters. They have to become people with whom you identify. We go to the movie with the understanding that we are watching people who are not real. But if we come to like them, and we recognize that the things they are doing are also part of our own lives, if they are reacting the way in which we would react under similar circumstances, then we become emotionally invested. (Magistrale, *Hollywood's* 12–13)

We see here evidence of the importance King places on character development; he and Darabont understand the value inherent in making an audience "care about make-believe characters." And this helps to explain why *Shawshank* keeps its focus firmly centered on Andy and Red. When Red's narrative continues after Andy's escape, Red is never really alone; Andy is still central to his life and the remainder of his story. The narrator remains connected to Andy's memory, which supports Kermode's argument for reading this film in religious terms: Red tracks Andy's progress to Mexico via a postcard from Fort Hancock, envisions him driving along Mexican coastal roads, perpetuates his legacy in retelling stories at the dinner table with other inmates, and cannot escape being haunted by the absence of his lost friend as he tends the soil in OSR's potter's cemetery. Post-parole, he fulfills his promise to Andy by following his path to the oak tree in the Buxton meadow, and Andy's letter—literally, his voice in Red's head—is there waiting for him, providing gentle encouragement and guidance, although Andy will not appear again physically until the final minutes of the film.

It is not only in *Shawshank* where Darabont strives to create an "emotionally invested" picture. In *The Green Mile*, a similar bond is established between death-row guard Paul Edgecomb and convicted prisoner John Coffey that draws the audience into their respective characters and the unlikely intersection of their histories. *The Green Mile* reprises many of *Shawshank*'s central themes—male-centered bonds, racial and class relationships, the redemptive power of love and art, the onerous burden of human interconnectedness, and the shifting and blurring perimeters of criminality, punishment, and moral responsibility. Confined to the microcosm of prisons, both narratives allow King and Darabont the opportunity to examine male behavior under a microscope: how they handle stress, the emotive and psychological bonds they are capable of forming with other men, the nexus of suffering and friendship that serve as universal connecting points crossing race and class, the shifting power dynamics that occur between the oppressed (inmates) and the oppressors (their guards), and to approach the topic of gender from a unique angle because both films are nearly exclusively male domains, either excluding women or referencing them only metaphorically. Moreover, the plots of these two films are closely aligned insofar as they feature major characters that undergo unlikely and radical spiritual and behavioral transformations as a result of close contact with a protagonist whom they initially misjudge. Red and Paul initially underestimate both Dufresne and Coffey—Red thinks Andy's a snobby elitist while Paul wonders if Coffey is mentally incompetent—and they certainly fail to anticipate how profoundly their own lives will be impacted in each of these life-changing associations. If *Shawshank* can be interpreted as a religious film in terms of its pursuit of transcendent themes, *The Green Mile* is even more so; the worlds of *Shawshank* and *The Green Mile* surprise their audiences by gradually extending their obvious affinities beyond the prison film genre to become intense explorations of spirituality.

The two films likewise share similar narrative structures that draw filmgoers into their dynamic story lines. Important moments in both *Shawshank* and *The Green Mile* occur in misleading flashbacks where the remainder of each film is spent systematically undercutting the viewer's false impressions of Andy and John Coffey as plausible murderers. The audience is pulled into an identification with Edgecomb's perspective just as it is with Red's: our understanding of Andy and Coffey likewise moves from a naïve (and, in Coffey's case, racist) acceptance of their guilt to a more profound awareness of the complexities that motivate their actions. Ironically, in both these films, something of the filmgoer's first impression turns out to be accurate: John may not have slain the little girls for whom he "tried to take it back," just as Andy may not have killed his wife, but each comes nevertheless to assume a level of accountability or responsibility—something akin to a shared universal guilt over the experience of human suffering—for the respective murders with which they are wrongly convicted. In turn, the audience is made to appreciate the slipperiness of human justice when confronted with degrees of moral ambiguity. Our level of sympathy rises correspondingly as we realize that Dufresne and Coffey are really men of goodness rather than predators; in spite of their constricted physical states, we are drawn to their commitment to helping alleviate suffering, their willingness to engage self-sacrifice, and their ability to inspire others. King restates this point most eloquently in *Danse Macabre* where he supplies an interpretative key to understanding the secular religiosity that buoys *Shawshank* and *The Green Mile*: "I believe that we are all ultimately alone and that any deep and lasting human contact is nothing more or less than a necessary illusion ... but feelings of love and kindness, the ability to care and empathize, are all we know of the light. They are efforts to link and integrate; they are the emotions which bring us together, if not in fact then at least in a comforting illusion that makes the burden of mortality a little easier to bear" (25–6).

In the context of this effort to "link and integrate," the alienating acts of sacrifice in *The Mist* pose a far less uplifting vision than what is presented in *Shawshank*, nor do they inspire the same level of audience involvement in the complicated ethics of shared suffering that Coffey transfers to Edgecomb at the end of *Green Mile*. Darabont himself recognizes that there are "some people who hate [*The Mist*] ... they got a bleak, nasty movie that kicked them in the stomach and said some deeply negative things about humanity they weren't prepared to hear" (qtd. in Beahm 168). There is a deliberately metatextual moment at the beginning of *The*

Mist where the main character, art designer David Drayton, appears in his studio flanked by canvas artwork perhaps depicting other potential Stephen King book cover art or film posters, as he applies the finishing touches to a large painting of Roland the Gunslinger. Roland is pictured in a framed portrait standing in front of one of the many wormhole-doorways that connect the multiverses of *The Dark Tower*. Outside, a storm rages that drives the Drayton family down into their basement. The storm slams a treetop through the Drayton front window, and the film thus opens with its important emphasis on "windows" that serve as portals to other dimensions. The poster painting of Roland and a threshold from *The Dark Tower* foreshadows Drayton's imminent imprisonment in the Food World supermarket where he and his son will be beset by flying creatures that have entered our world through a "window" or doorway-wormhole opened by the ill-fated Arrowhead Project. *Shawshank* employs a similar motif of a doorway-mirror-wormhole appearing in the form of the various movie starlet posters with which Andy identifies and that hide the tunnel he will use to travel into another world. The difference between these two sets of symbolic portals is that Andy's portal points the way to freedom, while *The Mist*'s many windows, including those found in the supermarket itself, serve as tunnels for the monstrous.

Moreover, although the hero of *The Mist* is similar to Andy Dufresne (and Roland Deschain) insofar as they are men of action, Drayton's choices only complicate the situation inside the imperiled supermarket, while Andy's choices point the way out of danger. All of the problems that Drayton attempts to remedy in *The Mist* are made worse by his choices—particularly his ultimate escape plan that results in the film's tragic and unnecessary ending—and probably would have resulted in less disastrous consequences had Drayton simply done nothing. He leads a group into a pharmacy to acquire medicine to aid the injured, but ends up only getting more people killed. In pursuit of an explanation about the origins of the monsters attacking the supermarket, Drayton interrogates a soldier about the Arrowhead Project. Subsequently, word gets out in the supermarket that army experimentation had something to do with releasing the mist and the monsters, and this gets the soldier killed in a sacrificial ritual led by Mrs. Carmody, a religious fundamentalist. Panicked runners are typically the first to die, while survivors know when to hold back and do nothing. Perhaps this is the major reason why *The Mist* is a less compelling and less popular film than either *Shawshank* or *The Green Mile*: the characters in the supermarket "enact a pop-culture version of a Hobbesian struggle"

(Briefel 156) and the filmgoer is never encouraged to establish quite the same bond with David Drayton that occurs with Andy and Red, Coffey and Paul.

TRACKING *THE SHAWSHANK EXPERIENCE*

The pages that follow—especially Chap. 2—will delve to greater or lesser degrees into fundamental aspects of the American criminal justice system, exploring the history of the Ohio State Reformatory as well as the fictionalized rendition of prison life as it is portrayed in *Shawshank*. The thesis "thread" that unifies this book is OSR itself: saved from demolition because of its role in the movie *Shawshank*, the prison offers a potential source for revisiting issues relevant to American penology, past and present. While existing scholarship has explored separate aspects of the reformatory, this book presents OSR's story in a more comprehensive fashion relying on archival material that has never before been part of any published record. Additionally, OSR and *Shawshank* are juxtaposed in the context of prison tourism, specifically detailing the relationship that exists between a film that has become many people's *favorite* movie and its "cathedral of punishment" setting that remains as intriguing as it is intimidating. Those moments when the penal experience at OSR paralleled—and also diverged from—the rendering of inmate life at Shawshank are important parts of Chapters 2 and 3. This book recognizes and celebrates the fact that both OSR's history and Darabont's film are similarly layered, complex texts. Our most ambitious intentions here are ultimately to contribute to the existing scope of scholarly knowledge available on Darabont's nuanced movie, King's critically neglected novella, OSR's labyrinthine past that spans parts of three separate centuries, and the type of fan response exclusive to only a selective number of Hollywood movies.

This book commences appropriately with the history of OSR, and its picture is featured on the cover because the facility is such a core part of this book. Our goal is to present an accurate and coherent view of the institution's past and present: its inmate populations and the conditions they endured, guards and administration, its purposes as a reformatory and, eventually, a maximum-security prison, and the actual building itself—both as a functioning facility and in its current status as a historical monument, tourist attraction, and its past and contemporary place within the central Ohio community. This opening chapter also addresses why OSR represented the perfect locale for *Shawshank* and explores the semiotic range of its penal design. Aside from the prison's castle-like exterior, its century and a half-year past is an illustration of good intentions leading to system failure, particularly when the Ohio Department of Corrections complicated the facility's mission in the middle of the twentieth century, recalibrating its purpose from a reformatory to a repository for adult felons as part of the larger Ohio penitentiary system. Chapter 2 tracks the history of the reformatory through extensive interviews with current OSR historians and personnel and in mission statements from former superintendents. There are also many surviving inmate documents, such as letters and diaries, that attest to the humanity and power of endurance that early OSR prisoners summoned during their incarcerations; certainly a major reason for *Shawshank*'s popularity is its ability to inspire similar hope in the midst of an inhumane penal environment. The history of OSR and the plot of *Shawshank* are thus suggestive of the numinous experience as described by Rudolf Otto in *The Idea of the Holy* insofar as both offer oppositional constructions of terror and transcendence, art and horror, hope and despair. The inmates at Shawshank Prison share a lot in common with the unfortunate fates of many who found themselves incarcerated at OSR throughout the twentieth century: existing in a numinous world that overwhelms the individual, causing fear in the subject, a paralyzing sense of being overpowered, of being dependent, of having their identity challenged (via institutionalization). But as was the case for many of the young reformatory inmates at OSR during its early years at least, the film and novella also embrace another part of the numinous presence in the human spirit's capacity not only to endure but also to transcend the paralysis that incarceration instills. Just as Andy's love of art and music help shape and sustain his humanity while a prisoner at *Shawshank*, young inmates at OSR built beautiful furniture, clocks, and metalwork that brought them a sense of pride and self-worth. *The Shawshank Redemption* likewise presents its own study of American penology—sometimes accurate, sometimes exaggerated—and this forms the basis of the chapter's comparative design.

Chapter 3 continues the critical work initiated in this introduction by connecting *Shawshank* to those gothic elements, especially the haunted house, more typically associated with Stephen King's oeuvre. While the chapter's primary focus is on Darabont's cinematic adaptation, it also compares, whenever appropriate, the King novella to Darabont's film: typically, how the latter simultaneously drew from, reconfigured, and enriched the original source text. The topic of penal institutionalization, for example, is of paramount significance to the film, but less important to King's novella.

Brooks and Andy represent the two extreme responses to institutionalization; Red is caught fluctuating between them, and his decision finally to embrace Andy's perspective essentially saves his life. Red may be the "guy who can get it for you" in Shawshank, but Andy is the one who gets Red his freedom by providing an alternative to the despair that earlier dooms Brooks. Dufresne's own redemption, however, owes a great deal to Red as well; the latter provides Andy with the rock hammer he uses to create his tunnel, the large posters that disguise his escape hatch, the opportunity for Andy and Captain Hadley to meet during a work detail, and a friendship that Andy trusts enough to express his complicated guilt over the death of his wife and the necessity for his escape.

This chapter further engages the implications associated with the interracial bond between Andy and Red, a bond that became immediately relevant when Darabont cast Morgan Freeman in Red's role, thereby highlighting social constructions that were less germane to King's use of the sixties time context. This chapter likewise contextualizes *Shawshank* in light of the various Hollywood genres that it manages both to inculcate and subvert: melodrama, the prison film, film noir, and the interracial male buddy movie. Lastly, Chap. 3 also analyzes the specific allusions that Andy makes to a broad spectrum of art often underappreciated by film scholars and movie fans alike, but that holds critical relevance to the meaning of the film. *Shawshank*'s various cinematic, literary, and musical allusions—either initiated by or linked directly to Andy—are not haphazard references, but instead produce an intertextuality that is crucial to a true understanding of the film. It is not only that Andy employs artistic references that baffle those who live and work in the prison; conversely, *Shawshank* is enhanced for the viewer who can trace and connect to Andy the various musical and filmic references with which he is associated. Although *Shawshank* is a narrative of men in prison, its subtext also reveals a great deal about women, and the fluidity of gender. Each of the actresses featured in Andy's poster art is a powerful, nontraditional representation of the feminine. In fact, all of Andy's artistic citations in the film are transgressive; they parallel Andy's challenge to the hegemony of the prison both in terms of what the art itself signifies as well as how Andy chooses to deploy and display it (e.g., using the posters to disguise the mouth of his escape tunnel and commandeering the prison PA system inside the warden's office). Andy's affiliation with female artistic representations, an issue which is so much more developed in the film than it is in the novella, actually links him to the most powerful female characters found in King's canon:

Dolores Claiborne, Jessie Burlingame (*Gerald's Game*), Rose Madder, and Susannah Dean in *The Dark Tower*. The females in these novels possess highly impressive levels of inner strength and independence, and they are situated at crisis points where they must either rise above their oppression or capitulate to it entirely. As such, these fictional characters have much in common with the female actresses (and their cinematic roles) who are disguising Andy's escape hatch: women who emerge in possession of a fierce will to survive, to triumph over the adversity men have placed in their way by undercutting patriarchal dominion and traditional definitions of gender. Andy establishes an unarticulated identification with the women who adorn his cell wall; he comes to share more in common with their subversive personalities and the strategies they employ in their respective film roles for dealing with oppressive men and institutions than he does with the male inmates he encounters every day. Moreover, each of these women is a representation of artistic beauty, of the power of art to restore and reinvigorate—elements that likewise distinguish Andy's character and eventually help to transform Red's. One of the first things Dufresne does when he becomes Brooks' assistant in the prison library is to pursue funds and donated books and musical recordings to convert the prison's existing shabby and limited book and magazine repository into a *real* functioning library. As Red informs us, "Andy built a library," arguably the most enduring part of his legacy at Shawshank, but also a reminder of art's potential to function as more than just entertainment. The same thing can be said about the various women artists with whom Andy is associated throughout the film. In a subtle, almost unconscious association, the Shawshank wall we see knocked out to make way for Andy's expanded library finds a parallel in the escape tunnel Andy is carving within the wall of his cell. Andy's personality, similar to the three character actresses featured on the respective posters that disguise this tunnel, is all about breaking down walls, literally and especially metaphorically.

Shawshank's fan base is so enthusiastic and prolific that it has inspired the creation of the Shawshank Trail, in addition to multiple fan-generated websites devoted to further study and discussion of the film, OSR, and other set locations. While *Shawshank* saved OSR from the wrecking ball, it also brought renewed public and scholarly interest to the prison's own historical eras. The fandom phenomena associated with the film and OSR in Chap. 4 can be viewed as separate subjects, but they are likewise interconnected experience because popular interest in OSR's history expanded exponentially as a result of *Shawshank*'s success. The Shawshank Trail has brought together the unique stories of a prison, a community, and the film that employed them as its backdrop in creating a work of art that has now become a part of the world's cinematic pantheon. This final chapter considers the experience the Trail provides for fans and how it fits into current fandom theory—exploring its nexus to state and local tourism, fan identification with the film, and the Trail's affect on fans by stimulating various personal and emotive levels of nostalgia. The Shawshank Trail may be viewed as an illustration of Matt Hills' position that "fans engage with reiterated, mediated narratives of production ... which despite the fact that they may not have personally experienced ... entwine with their sense of self [so] that they become 'prosthetic memories'" (30). This chapter further describes the origins and proliferation of the Trail itself; how it represents a community's celebration of arguably the most celebrated event in its history, but also how the Trail continues to encourage a working relationship between area businesses and the tourism industry that was spawned as a result of *Shawshank*'s success. The existence of common, central locations for the film's setting highlighted in the Trail helps to explain why this film has gained a fan base that extends into cyberspace, well beyond state and local interest, and has inspired many from that base to undertake pilgrimages to central Ohio. *Shawshank*'s audience has developed a commitment to it that is more intimate and rarefied than it is for the typical Hollywood film—including *Forrest Gump*, *Speed*, *The Lion King*, *The Mask*, *Dumb and Dumber*, and *Pulp Fiction*—which, as we will discuss, were all produced the same year as *Shawshank* and at the time of their release appeared destined for far greater levels of success.

NOTES

1. The other novellas, in addition to *Rita Hayworth and the Shawshank Redemption*, are: *The Body*, *Apt Pupil*, and *The Breathing Method*. *The Body* (*Stand By Me*) and *Apt Pupil* were adapted into movies in 1986 and 1997, respectively.

2. In the *Playboy* interview from 1983, King admits to being fascinated as a child with the serial killer Charles Starkweather:

   I used to clip and paste every new item I could find from him, and then I'd sit trying to unravel the inner horror behind that ordinary face. I knew I was looking at big-time sociopathic evil, not the neat little Agatha Christie-style villain, but something wilder and darker and unchained. (qtd. in Underwood and Miller 41)

3. Frank Darabont's first job in the movies was as a production assistant in the 1981 low-budget horror film, *Hell Night* (1981), starring Linda Blair. His first writing credit was on the 1987 horror film, *A Nightmare on Elm Street 3: Dream Warriors*. In addition to his directorial and screenwriting efforts on cinematic adaptations from Stephen King, Darabont has also been involved with several other projects in the horror genre, such as screenwriting for *The Blob* (1988), *The Fly 2* (1989), *Mary Shelley's Frankenstein* (1994), and serving as the creator and writer for the zombie television series, *The Walking Dead* (2010–).

4. Susie Bright offers this spot-on summary analysis of sexual practices in King:

> *Gerald's Game* is an ugly stereotype about how sexual desire leads [wo]men into the blackest of holes ... When did letting go of responsibility in sex become a psychological crime? Chalk up another one to the puritan army ... Why is semen—more than blood, pus, and sewage put together—the most grotesque bodily fluid in American literature? The King James Bible seems to be our companion reader to every Stephen King novel. (52, 54)

CHAPTER 2

In the Belly of the Beast: Ohio State Reformatory and *The Shawshank Redemption*

I left Mansfield Reformatory more than forty years ago, and have been "clean" ever since, acquiring very little wealth in the interim but a great deal of respectability, a wonderful family, and friends who would never dream I'd passed in and out of a prison. "The Field" we called it[1] ... on the streets of Cleveland's eastside. Tough guys ... Cagney, Bogart ... then getting out of the police car in front of OSR and looking up at that looming monstrosity of gothic architecture, Poe's "House of Usher" gone awry. The only thing missing was that proverbial inscription, "Abandon Hope All Ye Who Enter Here!" (Inmates)

Welcome to *Shawshank*!

Though it isn't the location that opens the film, the historic Ohio State Reformatory (OSR) is arguably the most indelible image in *The Shawshank Redemption* and its evocative impression is perhaps as menacing as Dante's inscription visible to those entering the Gates of Hell or Poe's crumbling symbol of Freudian repression at the conclusion of "The Fall of the House of Usher." As this former inmate tells us, the foreboding limestone fortress situated in a low plain had the power to humble those who had previously fancied themselves "tough guys" consigned to serve their state-mandated time there. Literary allusions aside, this inmate's description of both the guys and the prison are straight out of the movies. The obvious references are to classic gangster and crime films of the 1930s and 1940s,[2] but the other allusions—despite seeming more literary than cinematic—also have connections to Hollywood. *The House of Usher* (1960) starred Vincent

© The Author(s) 2016
M. Grady, T. Magistrale, *The Shawshank Experience*,
DOI 10.1057/978-1-137-53165-0_2

Price in a smoke-drenched set punctuated by violet costumes contrasted against a decaying lofty gray stone mansion[3] and Spencer Tracy starred in an evocative, Expressionist adaptation of *Dante's Inferno* (1935) that also featured a young dancer named Rita Cansino, before she changed her name to Rita Hayworth.[4]

Standing in for Shawshank State Prison, the imposing Ohio State Reformatory seems to live and breathe in the film as much as Andy, Red, and the warden. The building's majestic, gray limestone façade's symmetry has a lot to do with that, but so does the atmosphere created by what Mark Kermode calls "the awesome landscape in which this drama will be played out" (18). The building and grounds served as "the defining character" (Kermode 18) for the filmmakers, cast, and crew, infusing the film's performances and mise-en-scène with an authenticity impossible to fabricate out of whole cloth. It is impossible to say how the reformatory influenced the actors' performances—but it undoubtedly had some effect—especially since in several scenes the building appears to be looming behind Bob Gunton (Warden Norton), "like the lair of some vampiric count" (Kermode 46).

Stephen King invented a history for Shawshank State Prison, as he does with many fictionalized Maine locations in his work. But whatever the associations with Hollywood that OSR evokes, this location is not merely a backdrop created for Hollywood. While this real building undoubtedly influences the film's look and character, OSR's own complex, complicated, and often disturbing history needs to be understood if we are to understand its full impact on the film. But what history? Whose history? It might be more accurate, when speaking of OSR, to talk of "histories," since before it was finally closed in 1990, the Ohio State Reformatory had housed 135,000 inmates in 100 years of operation and consistent accounts of conditions on the inside are at best challenging to find. The documented "official history" of the institution, variously called the Intermediate Penitentiary, the Mansfield Reformatory, and the Ohio State Reformatory, is sparse and usually drawn from the perspective of state and prison officials. For an institution as storied and imposing as this one, it may at first seem surprising that so little official history exists. Many of the records are scattered—buried in dusty filing cases at the State Library in Columbus, the capital of Ohio, at the homes of private citizens, and in the building itself. The reasons for this disparate record-keeping vary, but chiefly come down to the gap between the abandonment of the building by the State of Ohio in 1990 and the reclamation of its care by the Mansfield Reformatory Preservation Society in 1994. During these intervening years, the building was unsecured and curious members of the public (including former guards and inmates) were able simply to walk in and help themselves to anything that had been left inside the abandoned prison. This is one of the reasons an air of mystery still hangs over OSR.

Some might argue that its indeterminate history is part of the building's mystique. Paranormal enthusiast Sherri Brake, author of *The Haunted History of the Ohio State Reformatory*, notes that three things draw visitors to the reformatory: "the grand architecture, the history, and the ghost stories" (12), but we suggest that Brake's position is not sufficiently ambiguous, that the gaps in the history of the building and its inhabitants create a mystery and a sense of the unknown that complicates efforts to understand what occurred over time on the grounds of this building. According to several sources, including Brake, the ghost stories pre-existed the building of the reformatory's structure itself. Brake refers readers to the violence of the frontier and settlement of the Mansfield, Ohio area as European immigrants committed uncounted acts of murder and other brutal crimes against the indigenous population of Native Americans before taking possession of the land. She details many notorious acts of violence thought to have resulted in the area's hauntings, including murders of Indians who were then not given proper burial. Tales of Indian displacement and their inevitable reactions in the form of raids and more killing occupy the 60 years between early settlements and the start of the Civil War, when the plain on which OSR now stands became a Civil War soldier training camp. The land was likely chosen because of the freshwater spring located there and was named Camp Mordecai Bartley, after the eighteenth governor of Ohio (1844–1846), a politician devoted to abolition.

Camp Bartley was then renamed several times—first to Camp Buckingham and then to Camp Mansfield (Brake 26). Historical accounts indicate death rates at camps like this one were very high, with soldiers dying from diseases such as smallpox, mumps, measles, whooping cough, scurvy, malaria, typhus, scarlet fever and dysentery, as well as venereal diseases. Since an estimated two-thirds of Civil War casualties resulted from disease and infection, and the majority of those soldiers died far from home, students of the paranormal have good reason to speculate that a great number of those spirits have failed to find peace and remain on or near the grounds of OSR. Brake details several stories of ghosts seen by soldiers during training and attributes the public's willingness to believe these tales to the prevalence of Spiritualism in the late nineteenth century. Stories of ghost sightings at the location began as early as 1861.

Brake explains: "Paranormal researchers and ghost hunters speak often of imprinted energy, and it is possible that this condition exists upon the land itself as a result of the military training conducted there during the Civil War" (31). These stories exemplify the ways in which the ground where OSR was built is a layered repository of restive energies from successive generations, extending to include the prison itself. This is the stuff, of course, of horror myths, but in the case of OSR, paranormal enthusiasts have cast back to historical-based acts of violence and infamy that have not remained exculpated.

While there were no state-sanctioned executions performed at the reformatory during its time as an operational prison facility, there were many deaths—violent, tragic, and mysterious—on the grounds and inside the building itself. In an email interview, Susan Guiher, who taught college writing courses to inmates at OSR in the 1980s, recalls a tragic accident connected to her own family: "My grandfather, [OSR guard] David Brown, his wife, Jenny, and their eight-year-old son, Ellsworth, met their deaths on the reformatory grounds at the railroad crossing one September day in 1926. It was his day off and they were crossing from [Routes] 545 to 13 to visit my mother at the farm, and he did not see the train. My grandfather was a guard for the work crews that worked along the roadsides, digging ditches, planting and mowing. The men regarded him highly as he was very kind. They wrote poems and letters to him which my mother passed on to me" (Guiher). The sorrowful nature of these and other deaths lend an air of melancholy to the building's history. A growing subculture of paranormal enthusiasts has gravitated towards OSR, along with other sites in the Mansfield area, as a popular location for "ghost hunts." The haunting of several *Shawshank* locations[5] has been featured on television in series such as: *Ghost Hunters, Ghost Adventures, my ghost story, Scariest Places on Earth, Scariest Stories on Earth,* and *Ghost Hunters Academy.* The vast size of the building and lack of artificial light doubtlessly contributes to ghost hunters' fascination, as does the horror evoked by the building's neo-gothic architecture, which we discuss later in this chapter. Several critics have referred to Shawshank Prison as a "purgatorial space" (Fiddler 9; Kermode 23) and ghost hunters likewise see OSR as a spiritual way station that has trapped the souls of prisoners, guards, and others who perished there and refuses to let them go.

Until now, this kind of unofficial history has been the best information available for those interested in the building, although a fair amount is known from public records about the funding for, design of, and initial construction of the prison, which we will also discuss later in this chapter. But due to the lack of access to state records on prisoners, many questions remain for historians now trying to piece together a picture of OSR during the time of its operation as an active prison. Who passed through OSR's doors? How long did they stay? How did they live? How were they treated? What happened to them after they were released? There is, as of yet, no single source which answers these questions. As Rebecca McKinnell, historian at the Mansfield Reformatory Preservation Society (MRPS), and Nancy Darbey (MRPS board member and author of the 2016 "Images of America" book *The Ohio State Reformatory*) have told us, the history of the reformatory is only now being written. Access to inmates' records, internal documents detailing day-to-day operations of OSR, and other pertinent information often exists in fragments and therefore resists authentication and accurate conclusions. But by 2015, after years of careful and painstaking work by the Preservation Society, OSR's story is finally being assembled, published, and displayed, taking its rightful place in the official history of the state. Facilitating this process was the August 2014 announcement that OSR is to be the home of the official Ohio Corrections Museum, displaying artifacts, records, documents, and other historical materials from prison facilities in all of the state's 88 counties. The museum will be housed in the administration building portion of OSR, which featured prominently in *Shawshank* as the warden's office, the parole board hearing room, the stairwell, the prison library, the hallway where Tommy is mopping floors just before the warden summons him, the interior of Brooks' and Red's room at the Brewer Hotel, and other scenes. After the building ceased operations in 1990, these areas were neglected and suffered extensive weather-related damage and vandalism. The crew of *The Shawshank Redemption* had to perform significant repairs prior to filming in 1993, but following the conclusion of filming, the building was once again left on its own. Without heat during the long Ohio winters or cooling during the hot, humid summers, the internal drainpipes froze and flooded the building, damaging internal walls, floors, and ceilings. The Preservation Society's work has therefore been more in the nature of rebuilding and restoration than preservation. The Preservation Society is a 501 (c)(3) incorporated in October 1994, though it began earlier as an organization of locals interested in saving the building. In the past 20 years, the building's restoration has been funded almost entirely through private means, namely, the money raised from tours of the building, ghost hunts, and special events.[6] Cared for by dedicated volunteers, the building has many passionately devoted supporters and has been steadily increasing its number of visitors in the last five years. In 2013, there were 80,000 visitors to the region, with OSR and the Shawshank Trail contributing an estimated $3–$10 million in tourism the Mansfield area (Schulz). By 2015, the estimated number of annual tourists to OSR exceeded 110,000 (Kennard), and competition to become a volunteer worker and/or guide at OSR remains fierce.

The reasons these visitors and volunteers are drawn to an old prison are diverse, but everyone involved agrees on one thing—"without *Shawshank*, we couldn't have saved the building. The fate of the historic Ohio State Reformatory is now inextricably linked with *The Shawshank Redemption*, since almost everyone coming here ... has seen *Shawshank*" (McKinnell, Interview). Fueled by enthusiasm generated by the film, OSR has been able to expand its offerings and the Preservation Society has correspondingly stepped up the pace of renovations. A lot is owed to *Shawshank*, not only by OSR but also by the entire Mansfield area. In 2014, prior to the twentieth anniversary Labor Day events, we spoke with Mansfield Convention and Visitors Bureau (CVB) President Lee Tasseff about the economic impact he's seen on the area because of the influence of *The Shawshank Redemption*. CVBs are not-for-profit organizations tasked with the promotion of business and visitor travel, advertising all the historical and entertainment sites as well as restaurants and hotels at a given locale. Through trade associations, advertising, promotional materials, direct sales, and other hospitality initiatives, a CVB is less dedicated to advocating individual attractions, than to promoting the region where these attractions are located. Tasseff, who became President of the Mansfield CVB in 1990, received personal thanks in *Shawshank*'s end credits for his help with the early stages of production when the filmmakers chose Mansfield as the central location for the film. Tasseff explains that the CVB connected the 1993 production's location scouts with realtors, hotels, and to various chambers of commerce, noting "the [Mansfield] chamber president at the time was the one who found us the warehouse" in which to build and house the enormous multi-tier cellblock set. The CVB began actively promoting *Shawshank* tourism around the fifteenth anniversary of the film, as we discuss in Chap. 4. Tasseff reflected, "This is a smaller area. We don't have [only] one thing to promote ... We used to be known [chiefly] for Miss Ohio [pageant]. Now we're known for this [*Shawshank*] after only five years" of marketing film tourism (Tasseff).

In a story straight out of Hollywood lore, the production was first "sold" the Ohio location by the then-Ohio film commissioner Eve Lapolla at a "large convention of film producers" in Los Angeles. Lapolla recalls she "had pictures of the prison at the time [but] unfortunately it was Murphy's Law day and I couldn't find the pictures" when Frank Darabont's people stopped by Ohio's booth to chat with her. As they walked on, Lapolla said she thought she would send the pictures through the mail but worried about losing Darabont's attention, so she counted herself lucky when, as she recalls, "Five minutes after Frank left, I found the pictures and I ran down the aisles searching for him and I finally caught up with him" (*Shawshank* Panel). Tasseff informed us "the [production] location was contingent on where the prison was" so a suitable-looking prison was the first requirement for Darabont and Castle Rock Entertainment and "the second question they asked was: 'can you find us a warehouse? If you can, we're coming'" (Tasseff).

Tasseff recounted this sequence of events to us in 2014 during a conversation after a meeting of the Shawshank Trail Organizing Committee in the formal dining room at OSR. During the facility's operational years, in this room superintendents (i.e., wardens) hosted formal dinners for government representatives and dignitaries from across the state. Looking around the now-restored wood-paneled room complete with period furniture, Tasseff remarked: "That's tourism. It's got to be authentic. It's got to be a place where people can step inside. Unless you have a green screen and can recreate [*Gone with the Wind*'s] Tara and you can step into it—[maybe] that's the future ... but until then, this is history, this is real." The Mansfield community has embraced the irreplaceable asset they have in this building; both as a historic site and as a site of pilgrimage for *Shawshank* devotees who long to connect in a material way with the film they love. The location, far from simply serving as a setting, also seems to have influenced the filmmakers and performers through what locals call its "presence." Bob Gunton, *Shawshank*'s warden, explained that although filming did not occur in the main cellblocks at OSR, the mood of those spaces affected his performance. Gunton felt that OSR "became an unspoken character. It was always looking over our shoulder, standing in our way. Breathing the history of all the lifers that had walked in and never walked out." Gunton reported how the cellblocks created an impression he found hard to shake: "I walked through some of the old cell blocks and I saw the stains, the scratches, and the indentations. That and the potters' field out back with numbers on the gravestones [affected me]. It just was a place of desolation and it was very daunting ... I got the heebie-jeebies" (*Shawshank* Panel).

In the 10-year anniversary DVD feature "Hope Springs Eternal: A Look Back at *The Shawshank Redemption*," *Shawshank* production designer Terence Marsh concurred that in deciding where to house the film's production, "the challenge was finding the prison basically. And I think we found it, and the prison is a main character, or one of the main characters, and works in its strange dreamlike way" ("Hope Springs"). Stephen King, in the same documentary, commented: "When the set decoration is good—when it's right—when they get the sense of the book through what's between the lines or what's behind the lines, even—then it becomes like walking into your own head" ("Hope Springs"). This comment from King is interesting, considering there is very little physical description of the Shawshank State Penitentiary in his novella. It is therefore remarkable that the choice of OSR felt *so* right to King that he implies OSR is what he had pictured all along while writing. The Maine coastal setting described in the novella is not matched by Mansfield's farm-like acreage of low plains, and the individual locations within the prison for most of the film's scenes have no reference points in the novella's text. Therefore, King's relatively sparse descriptions of Shawshank's physical characteristics were not inconsistent with Darabont's imaginative use of the evocative settings in Central Ohio. King's remarks also invoke again the power of OSR as a building: once someone connects with its presence as a prison, it is impossible to disassociate it from King's descriptions. It is probable that the film has so shaped King's own perspective that he now views Shawshank in the shape of the OSR. King's focus in the novella, however, is more on developing Red and illustrating his emotions and observations than on crafting any atmosphere based on a physical description of the prison building and grounds, but the novelist does offer descriptions of specific locations that became sites of key character interactions. For example, early on in the story, King describes the yard at Shawshank where Andy and Red speak for the first time, when Andy arranges for the purchase of the rock hammer. This is a significant plot point (as it introduces this key physical object) and King distinguishes the scene by offering far more description than in any previous scene. Red remembers that "it was on a Sunday" and that he had "just finished speaking with Armitage" (*RHSR*, 11). Although this minor character, like many in the novella, is never fully developed—merely serving as background, appearing and then disappearing from the narrative text—Armitage helps to illustrate that this prison is populated with other human beings besides Andy and Red. King provides a rare description, in this case of the yard: "The east side is a thick stonewall full of tiny slit windows. Cellblock 5 is on the other side of that wall. The west side is Administration and the infirmary. Shawshank has never been as overcrowded as most prisons, and back in '48 it was only filled to two-thirds capacity, but at any given time there might be eighty to a hundred cons on the yard—playing toss with a football or a baseball, shooting craps, jawing at each other, making deals" (*RHSR*, 11).

A visual parallel with OSR coincidentally exists on this point. Though it has since been torn down, a stone wall originally surrounded OSR—it was called the "Whisky Wall," due to its funding source—a special tax on whisky implemented by Ohio lawmakers after construction stalled due to lack of funds around ten years after the OSR cornerstone had been laid. Originally, the Ohio legislature anticipated funding to come from "the Scott law," a tax on saloons for sales of alcoholic beverages, but the law was overturned by the Ohio Supreme Court before OSR could collect its 10%—a subsequent whisky tax on consumers was a way around this, and construction resumed 10 years after it had first begun. The phases of construction can actually be observed in the building itself. As Nancy Darbey explained, visitors to OSR can still see the so-called whiskey line on the prison building, where larger bricks were replaced by smaller, less expensive ones once construction was re-started after the tax was implemented. The funding dispute delayed construction and was the reason that the prison was still incomplete when it welcomed its first inmates in 1896 (Meyers and Meyers 96–7). When these original inmates arrived, they were sent to live in the "West Block": six tiers of cells with two ranges on each tier and 36 cells per range. There was also a four-man cell and one one-man cell on each side. The remaining cells were meant for two men, giving a total capacity of 876 men in the West Block (Meyers and Meyers 98) (Fig. 2.1).

The first superintendent, W.D. Patterson, previous head of the Cleveland Workhouse, allegedly handpicked the first 150 inmates at OSR and "they were probably the best of the worst" (Sukel). To these first inmates were added the intended population for the reformatory, youthful first-time offenders each entering with 18 months on his sentence and a guaranteed parole review at the end of that period: "[Whether] you got out after that 18 months all depended on your behavior while you were in there. That's the way it was from opening day until the flip to max [security]" (Sukel). The reformatory's early goals to educate and reform inmates ran

Fig. 2.1   View from top floor of Ohio State Reformatory central cellblock

into practical restrictions almost immediately: the facility faced immediate overcrowding in cells meant for one man. King's novella offers this description of the inmates' living conditions at Shawshank: "The one-man cells in Cellblock 5 were only a little bigger than coffins" (*RHSR*, 11), which is echoed in Fiddler's description of OSR where he notes "the contrast between the cathedral-like exterior and the coffin-like cells" (Fiddler 197). Though King doesn't specify how large Shawshank's cellblocks are in the novella, this passage implies there are at least five of them, perhaps contributing to inmate anonymity. OSR has two cellblocks while Terence Marsh's set in the film only has one (with tiers of cells facing each other), contributing to the feeling in the film that every inmate in the prison knows (or at least can recognize) each of the other prisoners. By contrast, McKinnell observed that those incarcerated at OSR generally knew very few of their fellow inmates—this was a survival tactic—to "keep your head down and not draw any attention" (Interview).

King uses description sparingly in order to draw attention to key plot points. When descriptions about locations are provided, the scenes nearly always contain significant expository details. This structure emphasizes the progression of Andy's acquisition of the tools that will facilitate his escape as King gives further descriptions of the yard and the "auditorium during a movie show" (*RHSR*, 18), as well as the succession of posters in Andy's cell, with references to the starlets, their clothing, and their poses. Because *all* moments in a film must be physically located, our attention is far less drawn to these central cinematic locations when they appear in written form. However, King's use of more specific locations signals something special—as descriptions of Andy's window and the relative locations of Andy and Red's cells (*RHSR*, 14, 6) indicate. None of the other prisoners' cells are described. So, from the general sparse description that King offers, the filmmakers of *The Shawshank Redemption* created a lived-in, believable world, no doubt aided by the atmosphere already generated by the historic reformatory. However, while we admire the cinematic effect created by the use of this indelible location, it is important to keep in mind that there is a real history behind it.

OSR's History: From Reformatory to Maximum-Security Penitentiary

The chief architect of OSR, Levi Scofield (1842–1917), and his stone sculptures and buildings are well known in Ohio, but his fame outside the state is limited. He was born in Cleveland, the son and grandson of builders, and was a talented sculptor who served in the Corps of Engineers during the Civil War. His first professional commissioned work was a prison in Raleigh, North Carolina, perhaps inspired by the need to rebuild the state after the bloody conflict (Moser). The Central Prison in Raleigh was commissioned in 1869 by the state's General Assembly. The structure was to be "a grandiose and imposing castellated complex," meant to replace the "log huts" that had previously housed black and white prisoners. The inmates, with bricks they themselves manufactured, essentially constructed the facility. By 1875, a block of 64 cells had been completed and the entire complex was finished by 1884. The *North Carolina Architects and*

Builders Biographical Dictionary notes that Scofield's first construction was typical of its time, describing it as a "large and imposing public facility, visible from the public thoroughfares and the railroad, meant to display the state's investment in public safety. The castellated architectural style also evoked a popularly understood sense of protective, militant architecture" (Bishir).[7]

Many Ohioans are familiar with Scofield's work, including the Kimpton Scofield Hotel in Cleveland and the striking Cuyahoga County Soldiers' and Sailors' Monument in downtown Cleveland. The latter monument (partly financed by Scofield) features a 125-foot Quincy granite column surrounded by sculptural groupings (crafted by Scofield himself) depicting the four branches of the Union Army.[8] Scofield also designed the Athens (OH) Lunatic Asylum (later: The Ridges). The Asylum opened in 1874 after 10 years in construction and was designed after the principles outlined by Dr. Thomas Story Kirkbride. More than a dozen facilities were constructed following Kirkbride's vision for more humane and effective mental health care—a now obsolete method called the "Moral Treatment"—emphasizing "a healthy environment and … sense of respectable decorum" (www.kirkbridebuildings.com). The "Moral Treatment" offers a close parallel to the philosophy of reform that guided the core principles of the OSR. The presence of extensive gardens, healthy activity (such as farm work), and calm surroundings in a majestic setting were believed to have a positive effect on patients' mental health and recovery; some of these principles likewise found their way into daily operation at the reformatory. In addition, the turrets, detailed finishes, stunning woodwork, and intricate tile and stained glass windows of the Athens Asylum most likely inspired the work Scofield would later contribute to the reformatory.

The home of OSR, Richland County, Ohio, was settled in the early 1800s, a violent and uncertain time in America's history. The draw for settlers was the rich farming soil (the origin of the county's name), with the city of Mansfield founded in 1808 as the county seat. Named for the surveyor general of the United States, Jared Mansfield, the city grew from 20 houses in 1817 to 2330 residents in 1846, and 13,473 by 1890 ("Mansfield, Ohio"), four years after the cornerstone of OSR was laid down on a 30 acre plot just over two miles north of the city center. In 1884, the state legislature approved funds for the building of the prison. The city of Mansfield celebrated with ceremonies drawing 15,000 denizens who cheered the long work of business and political leaders who had successfully lobbied and fundraised to build the prison in Mansfield, beginning after the Civil War. The day construction began (November 4, 1886) was feted by a headline in the *Richland Shield and Banner* as "Mansfield's Greatest Day," and the list of important visitors in attendance did a lot to bolster that claim. Former U.S. President Rutherford B. Hays (born in Delaware, Ohio), Senator John Sherman, Ohio Governor J.B. Foraker (1886–1890), and prison campaign leader General Roeliff Brinkerhoff were all present at the dedication ceremony (Futty).

Initial construction of the more than 250,000 sq. feet building was completed in 1896, with the first inmates finishing much of the work on the building, finishing work on the sewer system and, some accounts say, on the 25-foot stone wall which once surrounded the prison buildings (Futty).[9] The East Cell block was not complete until 1908 (Meyers and Meyers 97). The reformatory was intended to house inmates on their first offense or who were young but still too old for the juvenile facility (the Boys Industrial School) in Lancaster and too young or inoffensive for the Ohio Penitentiary in Columbus, which held the state's most dangerous convicts (Futty). The emphasis on distinguishing and separating younger prisoners was part of the movement of prison reform taking place at the end of the nineteenth century, when it was thought that the right rehabilitative approach applied to the right class of prisoner could yield positive results.

A system in need of reform was how OSR Superintendent Dr. James A. Leonard (1901–1918) characterized penal institutions in general. For centuries, the common model had been "imprisonment in a general place of confinement, into which all the weak, wicked, or broken offenders were cast without reference to age or character of the offense committed." Little thought was given either to the nature of individual crimes or the value of rehabilitation. "These great prisons," wrote Leonard, "necessarily became schools of vice, from which men and women, with less of conscience but more of cunning, went forth to prey again upon society" (Meyers and Meyers 93). OSR was designed, at least initially, to show a better way—that the conveyance of education, religion, and vocational training could salvage a wayward citizen and make him a benefit to, rather than a burden on, society.

In nineteenth century Ohio, it was former inmate-turned-legislator Allen O. Meyers who was largely responsible for positive changes to prison conditions in creating the reformatory. Meyers had been incarcerated as a youth, but later became a newspaper reporter before being elected as a

Democrat to the Ohio State House of Representatives. As a state representative, Meyers helped shepherd a series of proposals into law, including the elimination of "contract employment,"[10] the authorization of indeterminate sentencing, the creation of a parole system, harsher (cumulative) sentences for repeat offenders, and the call to construct the "intermediate penitentiary" that would become OSR. (Meyers and Meyers 93). The importance of reform, instead of only punishment, distinguishes OSR's history, even when tough times, more hardened inmates, and tighter finances made these goals more difficult to achieve.

The founding of Ohio State Reformatory reflected a general optimism in the field of corrections—a commitment to viewing rehabilitation as a vital part of prisoner incarceration for the first time in the history of penal institutions. Some of the first experiments with what was called "indeterminate sentencing" (imprisonment with the possibility of parole) had been conducted at Elmira (NY) Reformatory in 1877. Even before OSR construction was completed, the Ohio legislature began to get cold feet in response to the mounting costs of building the facility. The original appropriations made by the legislature to fund construction were inadequate and at times the work of building stopped altogether. Mansfield-area politicians responded by raising funds for the "entire legislative body" to visit the New York State Reformatory in Elmira. That reformatory, opened in 1876, was founded on the principles of practical training through "rewards and appeal to the prisoners' self-interest," and was a model for OSR and others. The goals of reform by institutions such as these led to the implementation of "individual treatment, the indeterminate sentence and parole [which were] universally embraced and would not be seriously questioned until the 1970s" ("Elmira"), when OSR had transitioned into a maximum-security prison.[11] Following their visit to New York, the Ohio legislators returned to Ohio with "a new idea and a new vision" and agreed to grant $180,000 in appropriations for OSR—a happy ending, it would seem. In its first 30 years of operation, OSR was praised for its rehabilitation success rates, a result of its goal to "develop the good in its subjects" (Jenkins, T.C.). In the 1930s, state correction employees at OSR published these "philosophical points" relevant to the reformatory's goals:

> OSR is the intermediate step between reform schools and penitentiaries. It seeks not only to discipline, but to reform the men who come within its jurisdiction. It attempts, also, to rehabilitate the men who leave its doors; to help them find new places for themselves in the social structure outside

the high grey walls. The first constitution of the state of Ohio (1803) had these prophetic words written into it: "The true design of all punishment being to reform and not to exterminate mankind ..." Reform, rather than punishment, is the ultimate objective of the Ohio State Reformatory; and education, according to the penologists of the day, is the basic step toward reform. Therefore, one of the most important units in this "walled-in city" of the reformatory is its school system. Every boy and man who leaves the reformatory may not be a reformed character, but he most certainly is better prepared to fight his battle than before, by reason of a better education and, in many cases, a practical trade. (qtd. in McKinnell, *Ohio* 5–7)

While there is very little surviving information from the inmates' perspective during this period, what records there are seem to indicate that OSR compares favorably with other, more stringent penitentiaries in the early decades of the twentieth century. The "official" statement highlights a level of success—success measured in experiments emphasizing education, religious obedience, and practical skill building within an environment of reward and positive reinforcement. In a turn-of-the-century report summarizing the early years of the reformatory, Superintendent Leonard notes that "Commissioners from the German government, after visiting the OSR, have published in English and German very complimentary statements, and the German reformers who are endeavoring to introduce reformatory methods into German prisons have taken the Ohio State Reformatory as a model" (qtd. in McKinnell *Ohio*, 10).

A 1934 report issued by T.C. Jenkins—another of OSR's earliest long-serving superintendents—is an enthusiastic account of the accomplishments of the facility, its inmates, and its staff. The report begins with a valedictory Foreword written by the then-governor of Ohio, the Honorable George White: "An examination of the reports herein of the reformatory work at Mansfield in behalf of our better grade of prisoners, must convince the most skeptical of the great value of this State institution. The management is in competent hands and the original intent and purpose of the school are being faithfully carried out. We have many features worthy of consideration by other states" (Jenkins, T.C.). Was the report's audience (other members of the State Department of Corrections? The Governor? Taxpayers?) reassured that after less than 40 years of operation, the "better grade" of prisoners was hard at work enacting OSR's "original intent and purpose"? If the information presented in the report can be relied upon, OSR was efficient and cost-effective. Jenkins outlined the payroll costs at $174,700, food and clothing at $115,000, gas and coal at only $39,000, and the last significant expense of $40,000 paid out to the dependent children of inmates.[12] The inmates on the farms and gardens overseen by the institution produced all food and any surplus was sold at market value to benefit the reformatory (Jenkins, T.C. 11). Of the 3372 total number of inmates at the time, 1626 attended classes at the middle and high schools on site, where they were taught by a team of 16 teachers (Jenkins, T.C. 15). By 1928, classes were offered in steam engineering, plumbing, steam fitting, electrical mechanics, and welding. The report notes, "one hour each day is given to class room study on these subjects, and seven hours to practical experience in the shops." Of the 27 student-inmates who sat for state exams in "stationary engineering and firing," 25 passed (Jenkins, T.C. 30).

In later years, education up to college was offered, with professors from nearby Ashland University (then Ashland College) contracted to teach in a variety of subjects. In an email interview, Susan Guiher, now retired, described her teaching stint during the 1980s:

> Every time I entered the "castle" I touched the same copper doorknob, engraved with the Seal of Ohio, that my grandfather, whom I never knew, touched when he opened that same door when he came to work as a guard there in the 1920s.
>
> I taught speech a couple times as well as English I and II. There were five of us who taught on the same evening, with me the only female. We were quite a crew, and when classes were delayed because the inmates were in "count down" we sat in the intake hall (main room that's in several movie scenes) and joked and smoked cigarettes. After the inmates were accounted for in our classrooms, we were escorted by guards through the end of one of the adjoining cellblocks, down steps beside the cells, to the yard outside and into Fields School building. I'll never forget my first class. I closed the door, and Mr. Bledsoe, sitting in the front seat, said, "Aren't you afraid to be shut in here with all of us convicts?" A reply just popped into my head: "I don't see any convicts. All I see are students." He became the best writer in the class, and a few years later some of his poetry was published.

Beyond enjoying the creative outlet the courses offered, the inmate-students also benefitted by gaining more "applied" skills. As Guiher recalled: "One of the activities I had the students do in the speech course (later called communications) was to role play" parole board "where those who had 'been up' before made up the board members and those who were 'going up' presented to the board. I learned a great deal anyway! In general, the men were appreciative of being able to take college courses"

(Guiher). Since Sue Guiher was teaching at the reformatory after it had become a maximum-security facility, it's safe to assume that earlier generations of (lower-security) inmates were also appreciative of the opportunity for free schooling. The education provided by OSR was obligatory in the early days, but by the 1960s it was voluntary. The prison high school was called "Fields High School" to avoid causing embarrassment to inmates presenting their transcripts post-release. Those not prepared to complete high school could get up to an eighth-grade education. The piecemeal approach to schooling featured in the film, with Andy pictured as the sole teacher preparing fellow inmates for their GED exams, was not an accurate reflection of the historical reality at OSR: "Andy tutors the one kid. They had a school here [at OSR] that would have taught [inmates]. There were teachers; they had classes" (McKinnell, Interview).

Twenty-first century readers may need to be reminded that the educational opportunities OSR offered throughout the twentieth century were a core element of its reformation plan for incarcerated boys and men. Subsequent research has shown that education increases the potential for post-parole inmate success in the world outside of prison, which, in turn, reduces the rate of recidivism and benefits the greater public good. Moreover, educational programs such as those at OSR presented evidence to prisoners of a world that existed beyond the penitentiary walls, of the "opportunity to acquire a degree of skill or to master a trade along industrial lines which can be applied to earning an honest living upon release" (McKinnell, *Ohio* 8), and to aspire to lives beyond criminality. The opportunity for education represents one of the great hallmarks of prison reform; to the degree that this still remains an issue under debate in the American penal system today illustrates how far advanced OSR was in recognizing and employing it as part of the reformatory's rehabilitation design.

Jenkins' 1934 report, in addition to singing the praises of the educational and vocational programs at OSR, gives us some indication of the routine (daily and otherwise) at the institution. It provides a detailed account of the initiation process for new inmates, with a tone of foreboding (for inmates) and reassurance of severity (to tax-payers and politicians). Describing the central guardroom (used for the cafeteria scenes in *Shawshank*), the report notes: "[I]t is here that men hear the first clang of steel bars behind them; and here that they lose their identity as citizens. Here they cease to be names and become merely numbers. It is here in this room, sitting on the 'mourners' bench,' facing the steel cage, that men begin to realize the seriousness of a prison sentence" (Jenkins, T.C. 9). Though perhaps meant as a caution, one can't help but be struck by empathy for the inmates, even as Superintendent Jenkins does his best to impart a warning to would-be offenders and to reassure those reading this report that a properly stern tone is being taken with those whose errors in judgment had landed them behind OSR's walls.

This chilling set-up is then followed by a matter-of-fact accounting of the prisoner intake procedure at OSR, with great effort to humanize the guards and staff, often at the expense of the inmates. (1) A prisoner is first brought to the information desk, "which is presided over at present by Mr. Forsythe"; his commitment papers are registered and he is led upstairs to the guard room, "where he faces for the first time, the grim, forbidding barred door" which then swings shut behind him. (2) Next, "P.A. McClure, day captain of the guard, receives him" and all the personal belongings are catalogued before he takes his place on the "mourners' bench" and waits until the captain has determined that he has spent sufficient time contemplating that "the way of the transgressor is a difficult one" (9). Next, (3) the prisoner's religion is determined through questioning, "so that he may worship as he chooses while in prison." (4) Prisoners are sent to the bathhouse to receive their uniforms—whether the cold shower and delousing procedure depicted in *Shawshank* was followed is omitted—and prisoners then meet the chaplain and are "fingerprinted and photographed" (Jenkins, T.C. 9). How prisoners are led to their cells is not divulged, nor is the response of the more seasoned inmates to new prisoners' arrivals. First-person accounts indicate taunting and shouting by veteran inmates was standard, which suggests that the arrival of the fresh fish in *Shawshank*, while perhaps exaggerated, was at least an occurrence that was expected and tolerated by the prison authorities. It is, however, noteworthy that Jenkins makes no mention of such behavior in his description of prisoner introduction procedures at OSR (Fig. 2.2).

At the end of the report, Jenkins comments that words like "penology," "sociology," and "psychology," do "sound fine and maybe I'll go in for them sometime when I have more time—but right now, all I can do is look after this job here." The report attributes the reformatory's success to this attitude, noting it "may be one reason why the Mansfield Reformatory isn't in the headlines with wholesale prison breaks, dining room riots, and prison corruption" (42). Indeed, the reformatory did maintain a relatively clean reputation for a considerable time, but it is disconcerting that inmates' psychology was not considered in Jenkins' report. In fact, his dismissive attitude towards penal studies and theory would suggest a strong

Fig. 2.2 The central guard room at OSR

anti-intellectual bias and a conservative attitude in suggesting further advances in prison reform, viewing as it does penitentiary life in strictly practical, get-the-job-done terms. OSR volunteer guide and photographer Scott Sukel describes his impression of Jenkins in this way: "You knew where you stood with him, he was fair but very strict. During the Jenkins years, it was a non-smoking facility. Inmates, officers, administration—*no one* smoked." Jenkins was reportedly influenced by his predecessor and mentor, Dr. Leonard, who had "tried to make it a better system. That's what [Jenkins also] wanted to do. Seeing as how that's the way Leonard wanted it to be, his 'understudy' Jenkins carried that on. That place was a good place and they were always striving to do better" (Sukel).

During the Depression, budgets were squeezed, yet the language of reform was not abandoned. Jenkins noted that the reformatory's ethos was aligned with the State of Ohio's first constitution: "The true design of all punishment being to reform and not to exterminate mankind" (Jenkins, T.C. 4). But, as Jenkins further opined, the state's will to put those words into practice was not always strong. Jenkins glossed over funding difficulties in his report, choosing instead to focus on the achievements at OSR as of 1934, noting: "Under the provision of the State-Use System, the Ohio

State Reformatory now turns out, with inmate labor, all of the furniture used at other state institutions, much of the men's clothing, shoes, tin buckets, and other articles" as well as farm products (Jenkins, T.C. 56). As is typical in Jenkins' prose, by emphasizing the tangible, measurable output of the inmates, he avoids the more nebulous question of conditions affecting well-being, both physical and spiritual.

Jenkins does acknowledge that by 1934, OSR's inmate population was "dangerously overcrowded" at 3529 (Jenkins, T.C. 7, 56) in a facility originally built to house 1800 (Brake 48). Even in this early report in the first decades of the reformatory's operation, we can see the danger of the state exploiting OSR. In a solid parallel with *Shawshank*'s fictional Maine legislature, a body that Norton believes is only interested in funding "more walls, more bars, and more guards," Ohio strained OSR's space and resources from this early date. By 1958, the State of Ohio would begin to shift this facility into one very different from its original intention, signaling the end of the penal experiments in reform, a lack of optimism for humanity and the spirit of rehabilitation, and a decision to re-emphasize punishment over reform.

What had happened to this "good place" between OSR's auspicious beginnings and 1978, when a federal lawsuit was filed on behalf of OSR's 2200 prisoners by the Counsel for Human Dignity? The lawsuit claimed that conditions at OSR were "brutalizing and inhumane" and therefore violated the prisoners' constitutional rights. Ike Webb, a former Captain of the Guards at OSR in the 1950s and 60s, perhaps reflects best the changed nature of both the reformatory's philosophy and the treatment of its inmates as OSR transitioned into a maximum-security facility:

> Now you have your reformers, ACLU and do-gooders as I call them—crying about cruel and inhumane punishment, forgetting the fact that these men were sentenced for committing crimes against humanity and most after receiving probation more than once… So until prisons are run in such a way as to throw the fear of God into anyone instead of being soft in fear of public opinion, these youths will keep on committing crimes, each one progressing in violence until a death occurs. Then an innocent victim will suffer. The prisons should be allowed to do the job the families and schools were unable to do and that is to teach discipline and respect through fear if necessary and let the do-gooders find some other project to crusade for. Granted there will always be crime, but with stricter prisons it may make the young ones think twice and take the burden off the taxpayers who are paying the bill. (qtd. in McKinnell, *Ohio* 13)

By 1983, the lawsuit was resolved in favor of the inmates and prison officials had agreed to improve conditions and later to close the prison, but it would take another seven years until all prisoners were located to new, modern facilities constructed directly behind OSR ("The Ohio State Reformatory"). This transition is not easily understood nor concisely described in the official record. According to historians, guards, and inmates, attempts to delineate this period in OSR's history vary widely depending on who is doing the telling. For nearly a hundred years, the prison operated with at least an ostensible attempt to live up to its ethos of inmate reclamation. But as with many lofty goals, it very often fell short in practical application for many of the men incarcerated there. A clear picture of actual conditions at any time is still difficult to ascertain, since authorities' official records and prisoners' accounts vary so wildly. The oral histories that OSR has on record belong primarily to medium-security West Block inmates who were incarcerated from the 1950s–1980s. As McKinnell explains: "Most of the inmates I've talked to ended up in West cellblock which meant that was medium security prison which means they were *not* troublesome. They had slightly better jobs" (Interview). The decision to convert OSR from a reformatory to a maximum-security institution occurred in 1958, coincidentally the year before the death of well-respected Superintendent Art Glattke died (the superintendent from 1939–1959). At that time, the state determined that while a reformatory was a valuable institution, the needs of the criminal justice system were for "higher security inmates" and this commenced a twelve-year transition of OSR to maximum-security. According to Sukel, "they just kept bringing harder and harder-core criminals in" until in 1970, when the transition was completed and institution abandoned the hopeful philosophy and practices that had helped "wayward boys" (Sukel) find redemption. Locals, OSR volunteers, and historians generally view this change with sadness (Fig. 2.3).

Overcrowding was a problem almost immediately for OSR. In a speech given in the 1910s, Superintendent Leonard noted that the prison was already beyond its intended capacity. The Depression brought more overcrowding, as men down on their luck were often drawn into crime and, once in prison, many prisoners refused parole knowing they faced even harsher living and working conditions on the outside. McKinnell told us: "A lot of inmates said, 'I might as well stay [in prison].' This happened across the country ... not just here. It was nationwide. Prisons were *heavily* overcrowded during the Depression. And it's because a lot of guys

Fig. 2.3   One of the two-person cells at OSR

turned down parole and said, 'what have I got to go out to? I read the papers. I know what it's like out there. Family come and tell me what it's like. Shoot, I might as well be in here!'" (Interview). A fire at the Ohio State Penitentiary on April 21, 1930 contributed to the problem of overcrowding, since some displaced prisoners from "the Pen" located in Columbus were transferred to OSR. An eyewitness described the Ohio Pen fire in dramatic terms: "We're sitting on top of a living volcano here. There have been rumblings right along … when the cry of fire went up Monday night, and the yard was filled with smoke, I knew the volcano was loose" (Meyers, Walker, and Dailey, Jr. 79). At the time of the fire, there were 4900 inmates packed into a facility designed for 1500. In many ways, it's remarkable that only 322 inmates died in what has been called the worst prison fire in U.S. history. Indeed, the relatively low number of fatalities can be partially attributed to inmate bravery and selflessness, as opposed to the rather sadistic action of the warden, who delayed calling in the fire brigade because he thought the fire had been set by inmates trying to escape. There were many inmates who rushed back into the building to carry out others. One inmate, Narcissa Gaeta, carried over fifty men from the fire to safety (Meyers, Walker, and Dailey, Jr. 94). Not every inmate was so selfless, of course, and some inmates seized the opportunity to set additional fires in the Catholic chapel and the woolen mills (99).[13]

The impact of the fire on the remaining prison facilities in the state was immediate—nine days after the fire, 600 inmates were transferred to the London (Ohio) Prison Farm and about 300 inmates were transferred to OSR. These 300 were described years later by OSR tour guide and pastor Ron Puff as "really rough people" (Sciullo). There is no record of how well the Pen transfers fit with the already-resident population of younger and lesser-offending inmates but by 1934, the prison population's makeup seems to have stabilized, with a majority of OSR inmates serving their first sentence (2211 out of 3372). The second largest category of inmates—676—consisted of those who had previously served at the Industrial School that pre-existed OSR (Jenkins, T.C. 52).[14] These statistics are evidence that the reformatory kept to its mission of admitting younger and less-dangerous offenders as its primary population. Even after 1958, when the plan to transition OSR into a maximum-security penitentiary was announced, the official policy was still to serve younger, lower security inmates. In his 1962 thesis for the Ohio State University's Masters in Social Work program, Robert Ernest Titko commented on the gap between OSR principles and reality: "No one may be sent to the Ohio State Reformatory unless he is over sixteen years of age and under thirty years of age. He must never have committed a previous adult felony for which he was incarcerated in a penal institution. The last statement is much more complicated than it might first appear" (Titko 6). Titko explains that various caveats might enable an inmate to serve time at OSR, such as having committed (and served time for) crimes as a youthful offender, or as a member of the military, or if he had previously been paroled for one of these crimes. Consequently, the majority of the population at OSR consistently fell into the categories of first-time offenders and juvenile (first-time and repeat) offenders.

Writing about the issue of prison escapes, Titko notes that while blame for recidivism by paroled felons generally falls on state authorities, "escape is strictly an institutional problem." Titko cites that during 1961, 32 men (or less than 1% of the incarcerated population) "escaped from the various honor camps operated by the Ohio State Reformatory" (1). This was still "one of the nation's lowest escape rates during 1961 for major penal institutions" (2). Of these 32, all but one was returned to OSR—the 31 recaptured men served as the demographic for Titko's Masters' study. King's Red takes great delight in regaling readers with tales of multiple prison escapes from Shawshank Prison and, in doing so, seemingly responds to Titko's thesis that determining a prisoner's reasons for escape is essential for determining whatever "went wrong" (2) that led to desperate action. Titko interviewed each of the 31 escapees to determine "reasons (1) for initially considering escape, and (2) for finally deciding to escape" (Titko 3). Could discovering these reasons be used to direct policy changes to reduce future escapes? Were there parallels with Andy's reasons for escaping *Shawshank*, which happened to occur within the time frame of Titko's study? Darabont omits any reference to other prisoner escapes, leading the viewer to wonder if Andy's effort may be unique within the annals of Shawshank Prison. But then again, Shawshank was a maximum-security penitentiary, and when inmates were at work outside the prison walls, they were always "properly supervised" with guards or the warden always in sight of the working party. *Shawshank*'s lottery-type drawing for the plate factory roof resurfacing job—a "special detail [which] carries with it special privileges"—belies the notion that such privileges were typically earned by model prisoners. This event in *Shawshank* appears rigged because of Red's shady relationship with the guards and minus a sense of a structural division of labor within the prison determined through an official process.

Titko found that prisoners with strong family ties on the outside were far less likely to attempt escape, as were those who expected favorable rulings from the parole board. *Shawshank*'s characters all declare blithely their certainty that they will never be paroled: "I'm up for rejection next week," but Dufresne has greater reason than any other inmate to be pessimistic about his chances since he is serving *two* life sentences. Especially after the warden not only tells him "nothing stops or you will do the hardest time there is" but is likewise willing to become an accessory to murder in order to make sure Andy remains in Shawshank, Andy has cause for low expectations. The warden follows up on his threats by putting Andy into solitary confinement. At OSR, as in most prisons, time in solitary confinement was what is known as "dead time," or time *not* counted towards the completion of a prisoner's sentence. Could we put it past the fictional Warden Norton to punish Andy Dufresne beyond the actual record of 43 years that Albert Woodfox spent in solitary before his release in 2015?[15] As one of Titko's participants related, "as my parole hearing got nearer, I got more convinced that they wouldn't give me a parole. The pressure kept building up; I left" (Titko 39). The most frequently reported reason for escape was unmet familial obligations that the inmate felt could be solved only through personal contact. Andy's marital problems are discussed at length immediately preceding his escape—Andy and Red have what Darabont calls "essentially the most candid conversation that they've ever had" (*Shawshank: 20th Anniversary DVD Commentary*) about Andy's wife, his marriage, and what he finally has acknowledged as his role in driving his wife away. Obviously, his marital problems cannot be resolved by his escape. So, the reasons shared by OSR's escapees in Titko's study that best approximate Andy's justification for his own escape are probably the following: "policy objections" and "assignment dissatisfaction." The other top reason is "reaction to confinement," but in the time between the end of his torment by the sisters and Tommy's revelation, Andy seems (at least outwardly) content with his place at Shawshank. Some of this is undoubtedly the distraction work his escape tunnel provides, but his friendship with Red and other inmates also appears to supply Andy with a stability that is often missing in Titko's interviews. After Tommy's murder, however, Andy's focus appears to darken, turning more desperate; his level of disillusionment with the penal system is perhaps best summarized when Andy supplies Red with what will prove to be the clearest explanation for his escape: "I didn't shoot my wife, and I didn't shoot her lover. Whatever mistakes I made, I paid for them and then some." Tommy's murder forces Andy to recognize several important things: (1) the warden will never sanction a review of Andy's case; (2) that Andy is never going to leave Shawshank or cease work on the warden's illicit financial operations; (3) that even though Andy is aware he has already paid a severe price for two murders he did not commit, a dysfunctional criminal justice system will go on punishing him indefinitely; and (4) that because of this heightened awareness of his situation, Andy feels he has nothing to lose. His escape choice thus becomes an act of calculated desperation wherein he decides to take matters into his own hands even at the risk of his life or deepening severity of punishment if he is caught.

Inmates were segregated by race until relatively late in OSR's history. A former OSR convict reminds us that "back in 1958, blacks and whites did not cell together. Very few of us worked together. The jobs were very discriminated. Blacks celled in the back of the Range and whites celled in the front" (qtd. in McKinnell, *Ohio* 18). Black inmates were also denied the opportunity to access the same educational and vocational training resources as white inmates until Bennett Cooper, a fascinating and important figure in criminal justice history, desegregated the inmates' working conditions. A Cleveland native born in 1921, Cooper is assumed to have been the "first Negro appointed as Superintendent of a State Correctional Prison" when he achieved the position in 1966 (Cooper). As a young man, Cooper completed three years of college before serving in the (then-segregated) U.S. Army and reaching the rank of Sgt. Major. Cooper then began working for the U.S. Postal Service while attending Western Reserve College (later Case Western Reserve University). Cooper earned a Bachelor's Degree in Psychology in 1949 and a Master's in Psychology in 1952. By 1956, Cooper had decided to leave the Postal Service for a career in corrections. His first position was as the Chief Psychologist at OSR in 1957 and he was promoted to Associate Warden of Treatment in 1963. As Cooper recalled in 2006: "As Associate Warden, I was responsible for treatment, programming, education, social services, vocational schools, inmate groups, condition of confinement and management of department heads. Racial segregation was everywhere in job assignments, training, food services, cell assignments and other places. I disagreed with the segregation policies of the administration, officers and inmates" (Cooper). Cooper's account notes that while the Visiting Room was not segregated, the cafeteria was, as were as the cell blocks and work details: "I kept noticing that only black inmates worked shoveling coal on the coal piles. Coal was the way we fueled the prison and farms. Working on the coal pile was considered an undesirable and dirty job, but [should not be done] only by black inmates." As Cooper elaborated: "I advised staff and inmates that all inmates need to be assessed for education and skills then assigned to a job to reinforce that training and skill so that they can get a job upon release" (Cooper). He also oversaw a peaceful and relatively smooth desegregation of the cells and all other areas of the prison beginning in the late 1960s (McKinnell, Interview).

In contrast to what we see in *The Shawshank Redemption*, OSR's system of assigning labor is fairly well documented, and until the 1970s, jobs were assigned based on an inmate's level of education as well as his race. Literate inmates and those with usable professional skills, such as typing, were given office jobs (if they were white). But under OSR's reformatory model, all inmates were trained in a vocation and given an education. This model emphasized the rehabilitation and reform of inmates in most senses of the word and held sway until the late 1950s when OSR morphed into an institution centered on the punitive system of punishment that dominated American corrections by the end of the 1970s. The film indicates that there are "trusties" who work in the infirmary (Hadley summons them after his beating of Fat Ass early in the film) without explanation of how this status is earned. At OSR, inmates were granted work detail in "trusty" positions (e.g., administrative building, superintendent's living quarters, chaplain's living quarters) and at the "honor camps" only after careful assessment of their crimes, sentences, and psychological profiles. While some of the "honor" detail was located on or near OSR (for example, the adjacent "Honor Farm," which supplied food for OSR), many camps were further afield and might prove to be closer to the OSR inmate's home-town. "Honor Status" was a coveted position, not just because the work was more pleasant and the living conditions less restrictive (dormitories rather than cells), but because prisoners with this designation were often looked on more favorably by parole boards (Titko 16).

PROJECTING THE PRISON: IMAGE VERSUS REALITY

For the most part, King kept images of the physical structure at Shawshank in his "own head," that is as described through Red's narration—he did not put them down on paper for us to visualize—but they seem to be in our heads, nonetheless. Are readers shaped by our collective mental images from prison films, the same images that may have shaped King's writing as well? Or are we influenced by archetypal nineteenth-century images of actual prisons as gothic castles? McKinnell notes:

> If you look at most of the older prisons, you look at East Alleghany Lunatic Asylum, Ohio Penn, you look at us [OSR]—not so much Alcatraz because that was such a unique site—but those others that I've mentioned, almost every one of them has this gothic, castle-like exterior. It could be that they're all this Richardson Romanesque, big blocky huge stone exterior that was so prevalent in public architecture. Which came first? [The reasoning that] the castle-like look is appropriate for prisons? Or [that] it was this type of architecture the prisons were built at this time when that style was in vogue? The building is *meant* to be intimidating and every guy who came here said this building scared the death out of them ... scary, scary place. (Interview)

OSR was founded on a well-intentioned reform ideology that was con-tradicted by its architecture, the latter what Michael Fiddler calls in his essay "Projecting the Prison," a "visual sleight of hand" that manages to "embrace the grotesque and make it stand for the prison as a whole" (204). The public expected prisons to resemble the "look" of the gothic in the nineteenth century, while also insisting, "such buildings be cam-ouflaged and hidden from view" (Pratt 56). OSR definitely embodies the iconography affiliated with nineteenth-century prisons, the era when it was conceived and constructed: a gothic façade that was deliberately situated several miles outside of Mansfield's city center, surrounded by miles of unpopulated fields and adjacent land where a large farm once was. OSR resembled other prisons from this epoch insofar as it was a place local citizens knew existed—they needed only to drive by it—but the facility was also sheltered from their daily view—an unobtrusive reminder of what awaited the wayward tempted to stray into criminality. The spaces where contemporary facilities are built, in contrast, are no longer found at the margins of city centers, but have become more a nondescript part of the urban landscape, and new prisons have become increasingly indistinguishable from their surroundings (Fiddler 194). So, OSR highlights some of the contradictions highlighted in Fiddler's assessment of penology: like a gothic cathedral, its façade inspired terror even as its interior workings encouraged spiritual reformation and inmate preparation for reintegration into society. But OSR serves to illustrate Fiddler's thesis only so long as it promoted actual penal reform despite its gothic appearances; once it was forced to relinquish its goal as a reformatory and transitioned into another maximum-security prison, part of the larger Ohio penitentiary system from 1958–1970, it came to resemble a gothic dungeon inside as well as out.

The tension between the realities of prison life and *Shawshank*'s ability to "cannibalize existing images and meanings of the prison to produce its own willful nostalgia" also creates for Fiddler a false perception of penal life (203). Because the concept of a prison as depicted in movies such as *Shawshank* is a simulacrum, Fiddler argues that cinematic renditions of penitentiary life provide a distorted portrait, a facsimile of the gothic façades from the nineteenth-century that "project a disturbing image while concealing the modern, rational disciplinary processes within" (204). Consequently, while Michelle Brown remains critical of *Shawshank* in her book *The Culture of Punishment* for its failure to provide a more realistic examination of penology, Fiddler objects for opposite reasons: that the film has become part of a long cinematic history that unfairly equates prisons with the brutality of dungeons. For Fiddler, modern prison reform is elided by the building's severe gothic exterior, and the outside of prisons such as OSR project a particularly sinister visual message for a movie audience: "façades designed to suggest 'places of real terror' were exactly that, façades, observing a different penal philosophy" (204). As these remarks reveal, Fiddler is far too comfortable downplaying the continuance of the very real horrors that define penal existence, past and present. By stressing advances in penology that have rendered "the gothic prison into a 'spectral memory'" (194)—i.e., a projection of Hollywood that precludes an accurate approximation of prison culture–Fiddler fails to acknowledge that what went on inside those nineteenth-century structures actually did and still does resemble accurately the terror symbolized by their façades. By overemphasizing the "visual codes" represented by the gothic prison façade while at the same time understating the failure of most prison reform, especially at the level of the maximum-security penitentiary, Fiddler would corset the horror continuum of prison life into a strict Victorian construction that is no longer viable. A report published in 1993 by criminologists Charles Logan and Gerald Gaes of the Federal Bureau of Prisons, however, argues convincingly that despite various reform movements since the Victorian era, "Meta-analysis of research on rehabilitation has not yet established that any particular method of treatment is significantly and reliably effective. We still do not know what 'works' in correctional treatment, but it wouldn't matter even if we knew, because the fundamental purpose of imprisonment is not the correction but the punishment of criminal behavior" (246). Unfortunately, agents of authority haven't made changes in the way inmates continue to be incarcerated; this failure reflects either a willful ignorance of reformist criminal justice scholarship or a skepticism towards and rejection of the very concept of rehabilitation. As Foucault discusses in *Discipline and Punish*, the old form of punishment may have begun with a torturer extracting a confession from his victim, but in "modern, more rational" times, psychologists probe the minds of prisoners with a scientific rigor that Foucault equates with just a different kind of torture. Logan and Gaes remind us that the real business of prisons has always been the punitive punishment of offenders, not their rehabilitation.

The speciousness of Fiddler's argument is highlighted further in Frances Robinson's report on existing penal facilities in Europe. Built in the first decade of the twentieth century, many of Europe's prisons resemble closely the gothic façade of OSR, yet inmate treatment has not advanced very far in the century since their construction. The fortress-like structure of Forest prison in Brussels built in 1910 to house 360 inmates currently holds 600. In two of its four wings, three prisoners are held in cells designed for one; they eat there and share a toilet. In the other two wings of Forest Prison, "prisoners have individual cells but no running water. They must relieve themselves in a bucket that can go unemptied for 48 hours" (Robinson A8). In the United Kingdom, where Fiddler writes and resides, an official report on London's Pentonville Prison found "significant, easily visible vermin infestations" in space that was built for 913, but holds 1303. And Korydallos Prison in Athens was meant to hold 840 people, yet held 2300 in April 2013. Hugh Chetwynd, director of the Council of Europe's Committee for the Prevention of Torture, concluded that overcrowding means "staff struggles to keep proper control, so they resort more to excessive force" (Robinson A8).

American jails fare no better especially in light of the fact that the system is currently operating at 100% maximum capacity (Robinson A8), helping to make the conditions in which prisoners are forced to inhabit deplorable: "Two-thirds of all inmates in this country live in cells or dormitories that provide less than sixty square feet of living space per person—the minimum standard deemed acceptable by the American Public Health Association. Many live in cells measuring half that" (Hallinan 97). In addition to overcrowding, American prisons are filled with contagion and danger. Jeffrey Ian Ross posits that "four issues mitigate against an inmate's safety and health, and because of the outcome can make incarceration appear to be a death sentence: poor health-medical care, high levels of violence (especially proclivity to rape), unsanitary living conditions, and an increased number of people with chronic diseases living in close proximity" (311). If an inmate manages to survive the sordid living conditions and diseases such as AIDS and tuberculosis, violence is an omnipresent threat, even for those who would prefer to remain segregated from other prisoners and simply do their time. In the mid-twentieth century, when OSR was transitioning from a reformatory to a state penitentiary, the conditions were likewise often deplorable. As the increasing demand for additional space challenged the capacities of the facility, there was an instant doubling of cell occupation, from one to two inmates, and sometimes worse. A section of the prison was used for "overflow" when the cells were already full—a huge attic-like space with no windows and one small door that runs the length of the building and was lined with bunks. When the lights were out, it was pitch black. There were frequent acts of violence, sexual abuse, and even murders in this space since a guard was not present inside the room itself monitoring inmate activity, but instead was posted outside the single prison-barred door at the end of the long room. It was especially rough on the younger and more inexperienced inmates. Since the bunks situated in this "overflow attic" were located in an unventilated, cramped yet shared space, tuberculosis contamination, as well as other airborne diseases, flourished under these conditions.

PRISON TOURISM AND OSR

OSR began as an older juvenile facility, a place to give young adults a second or third chance in life; years later it became a maximum security penitentiary, part of the Ohio state penal system used to house adult felons; and now, no longer in service to the state, the structure has retired to become a tourist attraction drawing thousands of people each year, and a historical monument beloved by the citizenry of Mansfield and its surrounding areas. The architectural grandeur of Scofield's design helped facilitate the range of OSR's purposes over time, which parallel the evolutionary arc typically associated with "prison tourism"—from a once intimidating facility where men were either executed or warehoused for years in stone, to a backdrop for local wedding photographs, parties featuring fancy hors d'oeuvres with women wearing cocktail dresses and men in tuxedos, and the starting point for 7K summer racing events. These contemporary events appear strangely in keeping with OSR's history; even when the prison was in operation, the Mansfield citizenry used to visit its bucolic outside grounds for picnics.

As such, the continuance of OSR and other institutions similar to it invoke a complex set of responses that bring together interconnecting and sometimes contradictory debates about definitions of recreation, historical preservation, and the public's vicarious fascination with the punishment and suffering of fellow citizens. The concept of prison tourism carries with it a bifurcated response. On the one hand, preservationists—such as the Mansfield Reformatory Preservation Society and, later, the Mansfield Convention and Visitors Bureau—are advocates for saving dilapidated stone penitentiaries no longer in use because of their historical value and insights into past incarceration practices; others, such as Michelle Brown, view the concept of prison tourism as an insult to the memory and suffering of the people who were once forced to reside inside as captives. This latter position argues that there is something unseemly about using former prisons as places where visitors are paying to spend the night in a former cell, transforming the role of inmates serving hard time into a kind of role-playing game where a prurient tourist gets the cheap sensation of what it was like to be incarcerated, albeit with the doors unlocked and the opportunity to walk out at any time. The rise of prison tourism feeds into Brown's troubling assertion that "in most prison [tourism] contexts, all human life with any direct connection to the practice of punishment is omitted." In its wake, the tourist assumes the role of curious spectator, with audio tour guides in their ears as they walk through cellblocks, mess halls, and hospitals, alerted to flashpoints of sensationalism wherein the dramatic elements of the inmate experience are often emphasized over the daily horror of sitting alone in silence. Some prison museums, for example, proudly display cells where infamous criminals once resided, and the electric chair is typically one of the most popular sites on a tour. "Stops are made along the way at various points where stabbings, assaults, rapes, and murders occurred. These are some of the most descriptive and prolonged moments of the guided tours where … complex narrative constructions, much like a good ghost story, emphasize at the conclusion that all of this took place 'right where we are standing'" (Brown 106). On one of the several blogs devoted to exploring and exposing the American prison industrial complex, one writer argues, "prison tourism turns people into voyeurs of the incarceration experience rather than potential allies for transforming the current system" ("What Should").

The surrounding Ohio communities share a history with OSR, and the reasons for their commitment to this building, which was saved from scheduled demolition because of dedicated work from preservationists and historians as well as local fans of *Shawshank*, are as diverse and complex as the communities the reformatory continues to serve and inspire. Jacqueline Wilson's study of prison architecture posits that after a Gothic façade prison is decommissioned and it establishes a transition from a "venue of proximate suffering and menace to site of social memory, visual perceptions also begin to undergo a transition. The 'romantic' potential of the structure, so long latent, begins to influence the ordering of aesthetic priorities" (42). The grim evidence of failed penal reform has undermined a faith in the meliorated advance of penal conditions since the Victorian era, and its failure further suggests the perpetuation of a close affinity between the gothic horrors symbolized by the external façades of prisons and penitentiaries built in the nineteenth century and the very real horrors of contemporary prison life. Despite the naïveté present in Fiddler's effort to view penal reform as a linear, evolutionary process, his counter-discourse does manage to complicate a reductive perspective on prison culture and its architecture, setting up a dialectical tension "between real and imaginary, or real and reel" (195) that advocates the importance of distinguishing prison myth from reality. As such, Fiddler supplies an interesting context for studying the many accomplishments that took place inside the OSR especially during its early years. The OSR's history is reflective, at least at its best moments, of Fiddler's thesis: the successes of the reformatory stand in direct contrast to the prison's severe gothic architecture.

Scofield designed OSR based on his travels in Europe, using a unique combination of architectural styles: Victorian Gothic, Richardsonian Romanesque, and Queen Anne. Shannon Lusk, who at the time of our 2013 interview served as the official archivist for OSR, elaborated on the penitentiary's interior design: "There's a lot of Masonic symbols through-out the building. The pyramidal shapes, the pillars, the checkered floors. [Scofield] was going for the concept of 'uplifting' [for the] reformatory and so he chose German Romanesque with Gothic touches. If you look around Mansfield, you don't see anything that looks like our building" (Lusk). The Masonic totems noted by Lusk probably reflect both the pride the Freemasons felt in their elaborate construction work on OSR (indeed, a number of OSR inmates also worked on the facility's construction) as well as their belief in the power of God (who is referred by the Masons as the "Great Architect of the Universe") to abet the rehabilitation progress of prisoners housed in the reformatory. Since the foundational motto for the Masons is "Make Good Men Better," faith in the restorative design of a reformatory is in keeping with general Masonic code. As for the "pyra-midal shapes" located throughout the building, the pyramid traditionally signifies a state of harmony between the individual and his environment. More relevant to the original precepts of OSR, pyramid building requires a certain sequence of events: a solid foundation must be established in order to support layers heading skyward. This translates symbolically into establishing the foundational steps in human development, ostensibly the core purpose of a reformatory, beginning with the recognition that growth occurs in stages and is marked sequentially. Although extremely stable once it is established, a pyramid requires a solid base and consistent attention to subsequent layers in order to endure the stress that accrues the higher the pyramid rises. Less relevant to the role of OSR as a prison and more in keeping with its vision as a reformatory, the proliferation of pyramids and pillars at the prison may also reflect a yearning beyond the secular and towards an ethereal realm where stone walls and cell bars no longer were necessary, perhaps most resembling what Andy Dufresne meant when he describes the spiritual essence of music as emanating from "places not made of stone. Places that they can't touch."

Many of those who work extensively in and with the building hold that the prison, though made of stone, has a sentient will of its own. McKinnell relates: "Some of the ghost hunters ... the old time ghost hunters, the ones who've been here for years and years and years (me included) feel like the building itself has a soul. That the building itself is a presence. It's not just what's within the walls—it's the walls themselves. And if you study paranormal, this building is full of limestone and they'll say the limestone tends to hold energy" (Interview). The sense of those who work there seems to be that the building, often referred to as an older lady who needs to be taken care of, is a benevolent presence. OSR volunteer Chris "Zippy" Vance recalls that during a recent special event, a pair of young boys were running around the building, roughhousing playfully, "it was one of those moments where I just got that warm feeling like she [OSR] didn't mind that they were up there running around. She enjoyed the sound of the kids running around the hall" (Vance). Many volunteers attribute the benevolence of the building to the work done by architect Scofield. For them, the grandeur of the building is what remains its most indelible quality and not the corruption of Scofield's vision when the building was misused as a maximum-security facility in its later years. This is a somewhat sensitive subject for many locals—three new prison facilities are located just behind Scofield's majestic stone fortress and those incarcerated there may not necessarily feel that the community is as invested in their rehabilitation as it is in the old prison building that current inmates are forced to look at every time they are allowed out in the yard.

As we have seen, OSR was originally built to reform young adult offenders, a forced opportunity for them to reflect on their crimes and life in general, and turn away from their sinful pasts to rejoin society as spiritually rehabilitated men with job training sufficient to earn an honest living. Valuable civilian skills were available through the work inmates performed and courses they attended at the reformatory that could help some achieve a comfortable post-release middle-class existence. McKinnell notes that one of the best jobs available was in the boiler house: "The guards would actually drive [these workers] to Columbus to take their test and they would come out with a boiler's license. And up until just a few years ago, you had a boiler's license that was like gold. You could find a job anywhere. Because every major building, every school was powered with a boiler. You didn't have big gas furnaces, you had boilers and you had to have a licensed boiler to maintain that. They came out with a very tangible skill." This sort of training—and that of some of the other less rigorous jobs—helped maintain OSR's high success rate at rehabilitating inmates for civilian life. But, as McKinnell admits, most of the inmates willing to share their experiences are those who perhaps had a better shot of success to begin with: "Very, very few that I've spoken to spent all their time on East [cellblock], which meant they were better, more model inmates because they weren't problems. They had the better jobs" (Interview).

In the film, we see inmates working in the woodshop, the laundry, at the film projectionist's booth.[16] We are told there is a plate shop, metal and wood shops and are led to believe there are other jobs to keep all these inmates occupied. Yet, there is never any suggestion in *Shawshank* that any of these inmates will be released soon, nor is it evident that if they were to be released they would work in the trades they have learned. Despite many years as a model prisoner with experience in the woodshop (as well as a tax preparation assistant), Red is provided a job as a grocery store bagger and not as a skilled carpenter. This reinforces the idea that Darabont is primarily interested in highlighting the exploitation of prisoners rather than their rehabilitation and reestablishing a place in society. In contrast, those convicts who obtained the "better job" training at OSR generally succeeded post-release.

Many of the inmates at OSR created beautiful things as they learned their trades. The objects they built with their hands—clocks, beautiful furniture, clothing, and other artifacts that brought them a sense of pride—are still appreciated over a century later as prized articles residing in the OSR museum. Hundreds of other objects made by hand still occupy places in state colleges, universities, high schools, and other institutions around Ohio. "If you went to school in Ohio, [it is likely] the teacher had a big wooden teacher's desk. It was probably made here" (McKinnell, Interview). Shoes and clothing were made at OSR for children and adults in state institutions, such as mental hospitals, orphanages, and other prisons. Most recipients of the objects would never know where they came from—it was a rare desk or chair that still retained the paper label stating its place of origin as OSR. The financial viability of the reformatory was assured by the state requirement that particular items had to be ordered through the reformatory (Darbey).

We asked if McKinnell (and others) felt that the building appreciates the degree of renovation work taking place at OSR, and she responded that many believe this to be the case. In her interview, McKinnell speculated that

[The building feels] taken care of. Yeah. I mean, honestly, for a 501(3)(c), we're actually able to pay for renovations, which is almost unheard of, especially for Mansfield which is such [an economically] depressed area.

People come to this building. I said this in the interview with National Irish Radio. People come here because Shawshank was filmed. Or they come here because of the paranormal. They come here because maybe a grandfather worked here or something. Everyone walks away totally impressed by the *building*. The building is the star. The building is the gem ... Everyone walks away impressed as hell with the building.

The draw of the building itself is corroborated in the tour history associated with OSR. In an email interview with Mary Kennard, program director at OSR, she informed us that prior to the popular success of *Shawshank*, and still serving as a primary reason to visit the site afterwards, "many folks come to OSR purely because they are interested in the architecture or history." Of course there is much more than just the romantic lure of a gothic façade stimulating affection for OSR; in this particular instance, the connection is also rooted in the blurring of movie myth and reality. Kennard speculated that, "for a great many [fan tourists] this really is the Shawshank State Prison. *Shawshank* fans come from all over the world and speak many languages and yet are still able to understand and appreciate the symbolism in the film. The message is universal and transcends language and cultural barriers. Because this film is dear to so many, we at the reformatory feel a responsibility to deliver a meaningful experience for our guests." The universal, worldwide acclaim of *Shawshank*'s filmic quality and popularity forges a special bond between the place where this important movie was made and those fans that come, in turn, to connect with that place. This is generally true for anyone already a fan of the movie, but for those who actually live in the immediate vicinity of OSR, a bit more is at work. To some degree, seeing Shawshank State Prison on the big screen stimulated the community's collective imagination towards revisiting the significance of the OSR itself, especially since the enormous popular and critical success of the film brought a deep sense of civic pride to a town reeling from forty years of economic bad news. Suddenly, the whole world, or at least that portion of it intrigued by the movie, began to look at Mansfield as a place of interest, perhaps a place worth visiting, and certainly something more than just another nondescript town inside the great American rustbelt.

Mansfield's most enlightened citizenry also recognize that thousands of lives suffered while incarcerated in the OSR, and this suffering, in turn, produced hallowed ground that deserves to be remembered as well as respected. On the Shawshank Trail, current tours of the OSR do not permit tourists to visit the prison graveyard still located outside one of the walls of the former prison. While we might like to believe that this is out of respect for the families and the remains of the inmates who are buried there, memorialized by their OSR prisoner numbers instead of their names, it is in fact the location's proximity to the current state-owned prison complex (Mansfield Correctional Institution, or ManCI) that keeps curious visitors from exploring the gravesites.[17] Although OSR closed in 1990, there are families currently residing in Mansfield and its surrounding communities who were impacted directly by OSR—serving the facility as staff, guards, and as prisoners—making OSR a core part of central Ohio's history, and for multiple decades, its economy. Many of Mansfield's population grew up with the OSR as a constant presence in their lives, if not on a daily basis as an employer or place of residence, then as a physical structure that continues to dominate a slice of the landscape, an anomalous gothic castle that looms in a corner of the eye as well as the imagination. In interviews we asked tourists the question: What made you interested in touring OSR? A plethora of respondents (almost certainly local Ohio residents) commented that the prison was part of "our his-tory." The Mansfield Reformatory Preservation Society, the organization presently in charge of the OSR building, defines its mission in terms that place the former prison at a locus point where past and future intersect; more specifically, its mission statement also brings together the economic and communal potential available in a refurbished OSR: "To restore the reformatory and bring back to the Mansfield community, through adaptive reuse, a similar economic contribution that was Ohio State Reformatory's in 1896. A restored reformatory will provide a civic meeting location and many historical and educational opportunities as well as an increase in the current number of visiting tourists" ("Restoring").

We began this chapter with a discussion of OSR's convoluted and some-times contradictory history. The building itself possesses its own impen-etrability. It likewise bears an air of mystery, both in its looming limestone castle exterior as well as in the literal smell of its interior space—the latter, an Usher-like atmosphere of leaden timelessness that has held its breath for too long without benefit of fresh breezes or sufficient light, a stagnant pond of air you just know can't be healthy to breathe. Left unattended between 1990 and 1993, the OSR's interior weathered badly. Ohio's tem-perature extremes in winter and summer have taken their toll throughout the structure, and these untempered effects are strikingly visible within the core cellblock, the various connecting hallways, and the individual cells

Fig. 2.4   The Ohio State Reformatory, ca. 1950

inmates once occupied. Dangling from all the brick and concrete walls and ceilings are cracked flecks and strips of peeled or peeling white paint, a kind of leprosy that time has dulled an unattractive gray. But most of all, the contemporary visitor is confronted with the vastness of empty space. There may be others touring the site at the same time, but they are lost in their own thoughts, as you are in yours, and you thus remain barely noticed by each other, swallowed in the belly of the beast. Looking up from the ground floor at the base of OSR's cellblock, taking in tier after tier of deserted cells built in rows on top of one another, the strange symmetry of so many rusting orange iron bars create a feeling like the unnaturalness of standing alone in an empty sports stadium surrounded by the sights and sounds of human crowds that exist only in your head.

Yet, to demolish such a building, as was the plan in 1990, despite its periods of dark suffering, would have been a disservice to both the architectural aesthetics of the place and the cultural history of Mansfield, like destroying a medieval cathedral because of priestly sins. Although the historic reformatory is certainly an ominous structure, it is at the same time hauntingly beautiful. There is grandeur to the chateau-esque structure itself, with its imposing vista that can be seen at the flat horizon from miles away and that continues to grow in stature as one approaches it. In black and white photographs of the building and its grounds dating back to the mid-twentieth century, the sense of the prison as an anomalous collection of images from lost eras, including that of a large industrial factory—replete with sooty brick utilitarian structures, working chimneys, and a pair of railroad tracks paralleling the open farmland running along the outside wall to the left, all secreted directly behind the rambling white stone edifice of its tall fortress walls replete with turrets, gables, and window dormers—is impossible to avoid. OSR remains alive in the imagination, like a magnificent *Schloss* inspired by the romantic vision of a German aristocrat or Walt Disney himself, at the same time that it is creepily reminiscent of haunted dwellings from *Frankenstein* and *Dracula* to Auschwitz (Fig. 2.4).

THE AMERICAN PENAL SYSTEM AND *SHAWSHANK*

While Americans are respectful of individual expressions of freedom and generally are a forgiving people, their legislatures, acting largely upon what they perceive to be the will of their constituents, have established legal codes and penal systems that are relentless and punitive. American federal statutes contain more than 4500 crimes, and there are thousands more in the federal regulatory code ("What Were" 24). Although justly proud and protective of a constitution that guarantees an unassailable variety of personal rights and liberties, America is a culture obsessed with laws and punishment. While producing scholars and scholarship that rank among the best in the world in the fields of criminology and sociology, the American justice system and its reliance on incarceration often appears no more enlightened nor humane than those found in politically-repressed societies headed by ruthless dictators and religious oligarchies. Perhaps these contradictions reflect the inheritance of our collective Puritan past with its lingering fixation on sin and discipline, the ironic consequence of a free society saddled with too many rules, or an overly litigious culture composed of too many judges, prosecuting attorneys, and legislatures that operate in concert with an excessively zealous police force, each believing that jail time is the most effective—or at least the most expeditious—solution to solving the problem of crime.

Most criminal cases are resolved through plea bargains, where prosecutors, not judges, negotiate whether and how long a defendant goes to jail; after the police arrest someone, the prosecuting attorney is the most powerful figure in the criminal justice system, holding the keys to the jailhouse door. And state attorneys make these judgments almost entirely outside the realm of public scrutiny, as there are few rules to constrain or guide the exercise of their discretion (Toobin 24). The *New York Times* reported in 2015 that "a culture of violence" infests the New York State prison system, "where guards batter inmates for sport knowing that their union will protect their jobs and that district attorneys in small towns dominated by prisons will not prosecute them" ("Horror Stories" A34). Moreover, since many district attorneys use their job as a stepping stone to higher political office—judgeships, governorships, state and federal appointments—their record becomes their platform, and the higher the conviction rates and the winning of high profile cases with big sentences the stronger their argument for effectiveness in office. As a consequence, more Americans per capita currently reside behind bars than anywhere else in the world, rising from three hundred thousand in the 1970s to over two million by the year 2000. Although the United States has only five percent of the world's total population, its current two and a half million inmates represent twenty percent of the world's prison population, dwarfing the rates of every developed country and even surpassing those in highly repressive regimes such as China, North Korea, and Iran; we have created a nation imprisoned within a nation ("Real Time").

"The degree of civilization in a society," the Russian novelist Dostoyevsky reportedly said, "can be judged by entering its prisons." According to a 2014 Amnesty International report, more than forty states operate supermax prisons—i.e., where the entire prison is essentially a solitary confinement unit. The supermax has become the most expedient method of controlling an overcrowded and increasingly psychologically volatile inmate population. On any given day, there are eighty thousand U.S. prisoners in solitary confinement (Binelli 39). While politicians on both sides of the American political spectrum preach the rhetoric of human rights to less tolerant countries around the globe, 734 out of every 100,000 people—or, roughly, 1 out of every 100 Americans—calls jail home; 1 out of 31 is in some way entangled in the penal system: in jail, on parole, probation, court ordered surveillance, or under the periodic jurisdiction of Human Service Boards ("Prisoners"). Anyone who has ever been unfortunate enough to find themselves enmeshed in the elaborate labyrinth of the

American legal monolith—whether on the local or federal level—discovers quickly that the system, in which jail represents merely a terminal point in a deliberately drawn-out process, is a money-making big business, and while it is easy to fall into the system's machinations, it is extraordinarily difficult to get out. Once arrested, one's chances of ever being truly free of the system of control are slim, often to the vanishing point (Alexander 84). Since the recession of 2007, when state and local municipalities witnessed decreases in tax revenues and federal appropriations, the police and the legal process have helped to supplement these lost dollars through civil fines, protracted court costs, and more frequent jail time for minor offenses or whenever those charged with crimes ran out of money. The slogan "We Are All Ferguson" works in more ways than most Americans care to acknowledge. As a consequence, penal demographics that have always been slanted against the poor and the underrepresented, have become more exacerbated; we tend to incarcerate overwhelmingly along racial—a million black men are currently in jails and prisons (Alexander 179) and they are more than six times as likely as white men to be incarcerated— and class lines, and a vast percentage of the American prison population is there because of their involvement with illegal drugs ("Incarceration"). As the book *The New Jim Crow* argues persuasively, there are more people in prisons and jails today just for drug offenses than were incarcerated for *all* reasons in 1980, black people make up close to forty percent of the inmate population serving time for drug offenses, and most of them have no history of violence or significant selling activity. In the United States, a life sentence is deemed "perfectly appropriate for a first-time drug offender" (Alexander 60, 90). Mandatory sentencing laws have been championed by "law and order" conservatives and the U.S. Supreme Court, even as the price of sending people to jail has proven to be neither cost-effective nor a deterrent to crime. While it costs $7.50 per Diem in taxpayer monies to supervise a parolee, incarceration rates are $80 per day per inmate nationwide (*"Runaway"*). Jail has become America's version of the welfare state, increasingly maintained, ironically, by private, for-profit corporations. What Beaumont and Tocqueville wrote nearly two hundred years ago unfortunately still rings true today: "While society in the United States gives the example of the most extended liberty, the prisons of the same country offer the spectacle of the most complete despotism" (38).

Following the lawsuit filed by its inmates, the Ohio State Reformatory closed its doors in 1990 for "inhumane living conditions," three years before Darabont began the filming of *Shawshank*. "It was a very bleak place," Margaret Heidenry cites the director as commenting in her *Vanity Fair* retrospective essay on the movie's twenty-year anniversary. Actor Tim Robbins, who played the character of Andy Dufresne, added, "You could feel the pain. It was the pain of thousands of people." The production employed several former inmates of the OSR who shared personal histories similar to those found in *Shawshank*'s script, including, as Roger Deakins, the film's cinematographer, recalls, "the violence of the guards and throwing people off the top of cellblocks" (qtd. in Heidenry, par. 28). Nevertheless, many of the sociologists and criminologists that have since written about *Shawshank* frequently cite the film's Hollywood liabilities: its willingness to sacrifice prison reality in favor of indulging escape fantasies, its "bromance" that is obsessed with male friendship, its idealization of Andy Dufresne's character, and its excessive attention to issues of personal transcendence. How appropriate and fair is their critique? Which of these two oppositional positions does the movie tend to represent? In other words, how well does *Shawshank* capture the essence of penitentiary life—its daily routines and culture, the actual prisoner experience—as it might have existed in America during the second half of the twentieth century, and, to a greater or lesser degree, continues into the twenty-first?

The prison is just one example of an institution in Stephen King's universe. But it remains the dominant image that is likewise linked to and encompasses other institutions throughout his fictions and the film adaptations that have been inspired by them. Nearly every institution that appears in his canon—high school, organized religion, corporations, the military, the small-town community, governmental agencies, the workplace, the criminal justice system, even many marriages and the nuclear family itself—typically operates as a prison without walls. There are precious few instances where King treats any of these cultural and societal establishments favorably. And the majority of his narratives feature protagonists saddled with the problem of how to get out of the respective jails that they have either entered innocently or have had imposed upon them by an outside force. In almost every case, the reader recognizes that these are struggles featuring individuals pitted against inhumane, frequently violent cultural institutions, and that King is overwhelmingly sympathetic to the fates of the struggling individual. In *Shawshank*, the corruption of the legal system is first revealed at Andy's trial, where he is convicted on circumstantial evidence and forced to serve two life sentences for murders he did not commit. During the sentencing, the presiding judge's personal condemnation of Andy as "a particularly cold and remorseless man" is proven highly inaccurate in the course of the film. The judge's moral misjudgment extends beyond the court system and into the prison itself as Warden Norton runs an unchecked corrupt fiefdom of work schemes that profit illegally off the slave labor of inmates. Even worse, his guards are sanctioned to commit murder in order to maintain the warden's dominant control over the facility. Darabont's film adaptation of *Shawshank* is a relentless portrait of institutional corruption from Andy's trial to the moment when the authorities storm the warden's office to indict him based on the criminal evidence Andy provides. Only then, after Andy has already escaped, do we witness the system finally pursue some level of self-correction. But just as important, there is no verification offered in the film that the suicide of Warden Norton and the arrest of Captain Hadley have inspired any kind of systemic reevaluation of either the legal process or penal codes responsible for convicting an innocent man, sending him to place where levels of malevolence flourish unchecked, and making it impossible for a convict given new evidence in support of his innocence to reopen his case or even to discuss it in the absence of lawyers. His help in exposing Shawshank's corruption notwithstanding, at the end of the movie Andy is still considered an escaped felon wanted by the law; his legal standing has not been ameliorated as a result of blowing the whistle on Norton and Hadley, and Elmo Blatch, the man who actually murdered Glenn Quentin and Linda Dufresne, continues to avoid punishment for his crimes.

When Warden Norton is introduced in the film, he addresses the fresh fish with a throwaway line assuring them that they will learn "discipline" and the rules that govern Shawshank "as you go along." Actually, it is clear from the very moment the fresh fish are transported through the gates of Shawshank that the "rules" are already being applied and their bodies and psyches are undergoing the process of being disciplined. The erosion of prisoner individuality and dignity begins when Andy and the other fish first set their feet on Shawshank's ground. The fourteen convicted men who exit the bus with Andy are all linked together by a single padlocked chain that connects the waists of each prisoner to the man in front and also to the man standing directly behind, essentially forging the men into a tight single-file line separated from one another by about two feet of space. Each is further shackled with handcuffs at his ankles and wrists, the latter connected to the chain around his waist. Prisoner shuffling rather than walking advances the movement of the line. Because the men are so intimately connected to one another, in addition to creating a humiliating bondage redundancy, their place in the line also instills a perverse degree of uniformity among members of the group. This is their first taste of enforced penal confinement and conformity.

The new prisoners are transported into an exclusively masculine world divided into guards wearing dark blue uniforms and bearing guns, and prisoners dressed in gray uniforms. Walls, fences, barbed wire, and of course the imposing stone penitentiary itself demarcate the territorial divide between Shawshank and the rest of the world. This early scene does its job of announcing effectively the gap between "convicted felons" and those who are paid by the state to regulate and manage their lives. Additionally, the entire prisoner transition—from bus to the yard and eventually into the building itself—is accompanied by jeering in-house prisoners who spew gruff commentary, like "fresh fish" and "Come on in," along with physical gestures such as rattling aggressively the cyclone fence that separates them, pointing fingers, shaking fists, making motions to pantomime the reeling in of fish, and taking bets, "smokes or coin," on which new fish will crack during the night. This frenzied salutation is less a welcoming than an assault, as the veteran convicts inside Shawshank exhibit a particularly masculine style of taunting that is an admixture of catcalling and schoolyard bullying, a mean blend of fury and derision. One can only imagine how this additional human tsunami of unbridled testosterone affects new prisoners already lost in the traumatic sea of being securely bound and transported together, introduced to a hostile place surrounded by an elaborate system of containment fences, and scrutinized in a version of Bentham's panopticism (where prisoners are aware of being under constant surveillance in a structure of "invisible omniscience") beneath a phalanx of armed guards posted on the ground and on a tier directly above. Perhaps the closest comparison to the fresh fish experience exhibited in *Shawshank* is found in the assault women must sometimes undergo (alone or in the company of a small group of other women) when they appear—walking down the street or doing anything that in some way calls attention to their gender—in the presence of large, exclusively male audiences when the latter rises to raucous behavior either fueled by alcohol or emboldened by collective masculine bravado. Since the audience is to witness soon Andy's first two years at Shawshank, male rape culture is also announced within this initial prison montage, wherein the new convicts are purposefully objectified and feminized. While thus bound and displayed, the fresh fish are meant to feel a level of public vulnerability that women, the latter at least ostensibly protected by law and the police, experience when left exposed in dangerously compromised situations under an aggressive male gaze. At the same time, the very authorities that run Shawshank obviously sanction—and perhaps even encourage—the collective prisoner response by signaling that all untoward behavior towards the fresh fish will be treated as legitimate and without official consequences. Only the degree of separation distinguishes the frenzied mob reaction of this early scene from Bogs' chilling remark after his first awkward effort to seduce Andy in the shower, "Hard to get. I like that."

The job of any prison is to take men, who are typically incarcerated because of hyper-masculinized actions, and feminize them. The prison does this, ironically, by imposing an even greater level of masculine force to subdue these men—via the range of disciplinary power invested in the guards, the looming force of discipline, and the various levels of physical and psychological restraint that exists within the prison facility itself (e.g., cells, handcuffs, strait jackets, beatings, solitary confinement, sexual assault from fellow prisoners as well as guards, access to exercise and the exercise yard, lines to use showers, toilets, and to obtain food)—in order to dehumanize inmates and thereby make them more compliant to the state's patriarchal authority. This challenge to their masculinity occurs through the repetitive activities described above and on a multitude of levels, most notably via enforced submission to imposed prison rules and regulations.

Andy's introduction to Shawshank prepares the new inmates and the audience for the unqualified viciousness of the prison experience; it adds conviction to Red's comment that "prison is no fairy-tale world" (*RHSR*, 22). In Darabont's adaptation, inmates greet the new prisoners with a bizarre admixture of delight and fury; their arrival signals inclusion into the common misery that long-term convicts are only too happy to share. But there are also various levels of cruelty operating in this sequence, as Red and his crew, arguably the friendliest and most innocuous members of the prison population (compare them to Bogs and the sisters), make quiet bets at the prison yard's periphery on the fates of the new inmates. Instead of a communal empathy that the prison population might bestow on their newest inductees because of their own knowledge of suffering to come, human behavior is reduced to its basest level when the anguish of the fresh fish is turned into fodder for sport wagering and derisive mockery. Also, by helping to terrorize the new prisoners, the long-term convicts essentially reify the very design of Shawshank's hegemonic structure. At the same time, the frenzied state of the prisoners reveals the repressed level of frustration and anger that long-term Shawshank convicts feel towards the oppressive system under which they must live—and that they, in turn, redirect at the fresh fish. The scene ends with a close up of Andy's face staring with abject trepidation at the rising stone façade of Shawshank itself at the moment he is forced inside, swallowed whole into the belly of the beast. The only other time in the film when Andy looks more lost is after the warden kills Tommy and Andy has spent two months in solitary confinement.

Foucault describes the penitentiary experience as "the sum total existence of the delinquent, making of the prisoner a sort of artificial and coercive theatre in which his life will be examined from top to bottom" (251–2). This is an apt description of what the fresh fish undergo. Their "Welcome to Shawshank" is certainly turned into a "coercive theatre" and includes additional acts of humiliation that advance processing into the penal system. After the fresh fish pass through the prisoner gauntlet, the warden and Hadley outline the rigid hierarchy in place at Shawshank that will henceforth be imposed upon the new prisoners. The warden first introduces "Mr. Hadley, captain of the guards," then himself, and finally addresses the new prisoners as "convicted felons. That's why they've sent you to me." The diction of Norton's opening sentence signals a transference of identity—like the chain-linked bondage imposed when they first enter Shawshank—as individual men are again lumped together collectively as "convicted felons" who will henceforth bear prison tag numbers in place of names and whose lives now belong to the warden. The new prisoner who is impudent enough to ask, "When do we eat?" is silenced by the brutality of Hadley's nightstick and his summary explanation: "You eat when we say you eat. You shit when we say you shit. And you piss when we say you piss. You got that, you maggot-dick mother fucker?" There will be no grace period, no accommodations to ease the fresh fish in their transition from civilian life into the punitive system that will govern their every move. Even their most basic bodily functions are now under state control. Moreover, the penal hierarchy, like the gauntlet itself, is predicated not only upon a dynamic between those who have power and those who do not; as the fresh fish continue to discover, the Shawshank hegemony is reinforced by systematic rituals of humiliation: separated forever from their civilian clothes, hosed down with cold water, deloused with a white burning powder, and "naked as the day you were born," the prisoners walk to their individual cells carrying their folded gray uniforms and Bibles, once again paraded out under the collective gaze of the entire prison population—guards and fellow prisoners alike. It is interesting that the fresh fish are forced to walk naked to their individual cells as the culminating phase of their processing into the penal system. Their nudity is of course deliberately sanctioned as much as it is unnecessary, occurring outwardly as another act of humiliation and a reminder to all the inmates—fish and old-timers as well—that they have forfeited their rights to privacy and decency. The purpose of the nude walk is linked to the disciplinary gaze Foucault describes whereby the psychology of exploitation and surveillance replaced physical punishment as a means for controlling bodies in modern prison state. There is an insidiousness associated with the fact that the fish are publically displayed without clothes; they are again on display under the male gaze of the guards and especially the other convicts—fresh meat to arouse those, like Bogs and the sisters, by stimulating predatory male sexual behavior—at the same time that their nakedness reveals prisoner vulnerability and thus reinforces the power dynamic in place at Shawshank. The institution is extending the visual spectrum of oppression and shame that began the moment the fresh fish exited the prison bus. In fact, the fresh fish nudity is essentially just another form of bondage, as the prisoners are all pictured fleeing to their cells, humiliated and frightened. Each of the other humiliating events that constitute their introduction to Shawshank (e.g., Hadley's command to "unhook 'em") is designed to facilitate prisoner compliance and restraint. The final installment via the naked walk becomes a kind of "death walk" symbolizing the end of the prisoners' old lives, as Red says, "blown away in the blink of an eye," while highlighting their "birth" into the collective identity of the inmate population whose uniform they must now adopt.

Ironically, this highly affective sequence in the film also anticipates a complication that will take place later between prison reality and Hollywood's intrusion into the film. At OSR, prisoners existed *only* as their prison numbers, even the graves in the prison cemetery were distinguished solely by inmate numbers, never names. This policy resulted in many lost and compromised records of past prisoners who served time at OSR. In the film, by contrast, Andy is always referred to as "Dufresne," and never by his number. This is a purposeful lapse in protocol that serves to distinguish and humanize Andy's character for the audience. Darabont wanted the collective loss of personal identity to extend only so far in order that Andy's individuality might be preserved in a way that does not include the rest of the fresh fish. And it's not just the fresh fish: later in the movie after Andy escapes from Shawshank, Dufresne's name is continually uttered by guards and the warden alike; when Red is selected and questioned about Andy's disappearance, however, the warden refers contemptuously to the black man only as "*him*."

Its obvious cinematic effectiveness notwithstanding, Darabont is likely exaggerating the dehumanization of the fresh fish in this early scene out of an effort to cast Shawshank in the worst possible light. It is, after all, Andy's as well as the audience's first view of the institution, and it is a sequence that is not included in King's novella. Moreover, we were unable to uncover evidence that prisoner processing (referenced earlier in the chapter) into OSR included similar levels of inmate degradation depicted in the film and that culminates in the vicious beating and murder of Fat Ass. Because its cruelty is thoroughly established from the start, the screenplay creates a bond between the audience and the movie's characters: the latter must find a way to survive the institution's brutality, while the audience hopes they will manage to do so. On the other hand, it remains hard to imagine guards at a maximum-security state penitentiary, especially with the current emphasis on maintaining an always orderly—and often sedated—prison population, standing by idly while unrestrained felons are allowed en masse to work themselves into a frenzied state of aggressiveness as bound and then naked men are paraded in front of them. What happens to the prison inmates out in the yard, now aroused to the point of physical violence, once the fresh fish disappear inside Shawshank? How do the guards get them under control again? So, while the scene is highly effective in creating an empathic response from the audience, most never having seen the inside of a maximum-security facility, as it dramatizes the terror that is abruptly imposed on Andy and the other fresh fish, it also bears a degree of exaggeration in terms of what trained prison authorities would likely be willing to sanction.

Elsewhere in the film there are other moments where prison reality is stretched: when the four corners of Andy's poster of Raquel Welch adhere flush to the cellblock wall after his escape through the tunnel behind the poster; when inmates appear to wander the halls unimpeded and without passes; receive elaborate shipments of contraband, including Andy's rock hammer; are permitted to collect and store boxes of rocks obtained while out on work details; and move freely in and out of the prison yard without much guard supervision. When Brooks Hatlen threatens Heywood with a knife after receiving word of his parole, Andy, Red, and Floyd come to the rescue by engaging Hatlen in a persuasive dialogue that appeals to Brooks' sense of reason, eventually convincing him not to harm their friend. There is not a prison guard to be found anywhere in this prolonged scene. Both OSR inmates and guards confirm that prisoner movement was nowhere near as free as depicted in the film, nor was there the opportunity to form long-lasting friendships and to engage in intimate and nuanced conversations. Most inmates just hoped to avoid trouble during their time inside. In fact, time in "the yard" was highly structured. The film's depiction of relatively free movement and unsupervised activity in the yard is not historically accurate to OSR. McKinnell elaborates in her interview:

> From what these guys have told me—and mind you I'm dealing with, the oldest one is maybe from the '50s—they had *some* time out in the yard but it was primarily weekends. They were working or in school during the week. Yard time was basically weekends and actually here the area where they were playing ball [in the film] wasn't where they played ball. There was another area that they played [at designated times] ... Any yard time was strictly weekends, it was limited ... it was very regimented and I'm guessing it was even more so in the '40s. One guy [OSR Guard Ike Webb] who was here in the '50s told me you didn't go anywhere without a pass.

The effectiveness of *Shawshank* as a film is its ability to counterpoise a portrait of prison life that is at once brutal and inhumane against a romanticized portrait of affectionate male bonding with which the viewer identifies and empathizes. Indeed, the respective skill sets that Red and Andy bring to prison endear them even to the Shawshank authorities, leaving Warden Norton to admit, sentimentally and without any sense of ironic guilt, that "the place wasn't the same without you" while Andy was forced to serve two months in solitary confinement. Red and his inmate group form a kind of men's club at Shawshank where the former, because he is a man "who can get things," is able to secure special privileges for himself and his friends from the guards, such as the opportunity to tar the license-plate-factory roof. Red's reputation is only enhanced when he adds Andy to his group, especially after Andy's business acumen curries favor with the warden and the guards. Yet despite the fact that Andy is "a nice pet to have," who "works cheap" dispensing "sound financial advice," it is probably a stretch of verisimilitude when Captain Hadley, "the hardest screw that ever walked a turn at Shawshank State Prison," supplies Andy and his fellow inmates cold bottles of beer that they are permitted to drink leisurely in the sun. Like the soprano aria from Mozart, the scene on the factory roof creates an important bonding moment between Red and Andy and Andy and the audience. Hadley's intelligence is exclusively predatory: he sees the possibilities inherent in exploiting Andy's business acumen and then lets the warden in on it. Thus, it is hard to imagine Hadley accepting any deal (tax help securing his brother's inheritance in exchange for "three beers apiece for [Andy's] co-workers") brokered by a "smart wife-killing banker" that surely risks Hadley's unambiguous reputation, if not his career, and poses the additional danger that the captain "could end up in here with [Andy]." The two murders that the audience sees Hadley commit, brutally beating Fat Ass to death and shooting Tommy in the back, are far more in keeping with the captain's ethics and the reigning hegemony in place at Shawshank than supplying convicts with cold beer. Some accounts by OSR prisoners detail the existence of more sympathetic relationships between guards and inmates, such as the one Andy shares with the guard he locks in the bathroom and those who wish Brooks and Red well when they leave the prison to begin their paroles. But Hadley, like the warden, was cast without any redeeming features. After Andy supplies the authorities with incriminating evidence about both men, they reveal their true cowardly natures: for a moment the warden considers using his pistol to defend himself, but then elects to commit suicide, while Hadley responds to his arrest by "sobbing like a little girl." Clancy Brown, who played the role of Captain Hadley in the film, has confirmed in post-production interviews that his character was meant to represent the archetypical "worst of the worst" (qtd. in *Shawshank: The Redeeming Feature*). Thus, the glamorized ideal of male camaraderie that exists among the men in Red's crew—particularly between Red and Andy—and on those occasions when guards treat the inmates humanely stands out as all the more striking when counterpointed by the sadistic cruelty and cowardliness of Captain Hadley and the warden.

Shawshank represents an unstable blend of prison reality and Hollywood, the real and the "reel." Maintaining the secret existence of nearly a two-decade-old tunnel located behind the paper posters in his cell and inside a prison that features frequent surprise inspections is more plausible than some of the events that take place after Andy crawls through it. The film would have us believe in several highly unlikely occurrences necessary to complete Dufresne's underground escape. OSR has retained and displays the actual sewage pipe prop in its bullpen that was used in the film when Andy initially glances down its length before his descent into "five hundred yards of shit-smelling foulness." According to Rebecca McKinnell, the prop was made out of cement in order to "make it look rough," an accurate representation of the "cast or galvanized iron interior sewage pipe" used in the construction of OSR before the advent of PVC ("Sewer Pipes"), cut to about eight feet in length, and at least three or four inches in diameter thickness. Andy has already chosen a night when there just happens to be a convenient thunderstorm; the latter is necessary to disguise the clanging made by the concrete rock he uses as a tool to break through the pipe. While the pipe in King's novella is made out of ceramic tile, and therefore easier to break, regardless of the size and sharpness of the piece of concrete presumably extracted from his cell block that Andy finds alongside the pipe, it "would take a man six hundred years," the length of time Red muses that would be required to tunnel out beneath Shawshank, to create a hole in either the prop's concrete or OSR's use of cast iron sewage pipes (even with the aid of the sewage's mysterious fluid pressure that inexplicably dissipates immediately after Andy breaks through) large enough to accommodate Andy's entire body. Hollywood would have us believe that he accomplishes this feat with just *three* well-placed and well-timed swings of that concrete boulder (the screenplay originally called for him to employ the puny rock hammer to break through the pipe) (Fig. 2.5).

Fig. 2.5 Prop used for Andy's escape into the Shawshank sewer system, on permanent display at OSR. Note the thickness of its concrete opening

We likewise learn via Red's flashback narration and visualization that Andy steals the warden's shoes, white shirt, and tie prior to his escape (the warden's suit coat, which Andy also takes, on the other hand, is never actually revealed hidden beneath Dufresne's prison garb). He will need all these articles of clothing to present himself as the businessman, Randall Stevens, to the managers of the "nearly a dozen" Portland banks he visits prior to leaving town with the warden's money. Yet the film offers no plausible explanation for how Andy manages to get all these clothes out with him through the sewage pipe. The clear plastic bag attached to Andy's ankle with the length of rope Heywood provides contains his carved chess figures inside a cigar box, a bar of soap, identification documents to prove he is Randall Stephens, and the financial ledgers from Norton's safe, but neither the warden's shoes, shirt, pants, nor his suit coat are ever pictured being packed or folded inside that bag. And if Andy is still wearing the warden's clothes underneath his prison uniform, as he is when Red pictures him sitting in his cell, why isn't he still dressed in them when he emerges from the sewage pipe and drops down into the drainage ditch located outside of Shawshank? Viewers are so thoroughly preoccupied with Andy's glorious escape and rebirth that we fail to notice the absence of the warden's dress clothes when Andy strips off his prison uniform and t-shirt to go topless in the rain. And as a corollary, we also overlook the fact that in the scene that takes place the next morning when Andy is shown entering the Maine National, the first of the banks to make a withdrawal, he enters wearing the warden's suit—sharply pressed with spotless white shirt, tie, and "polished to a high mirror shine" shoes. As Red asks in the beginning of this flashback sequence, "How often do you really look at a man's shoes?" Red is not the only one who fails to pay enough attention to Andy's footwear. In the flashback, the audience watches Andy substitute his own worn brown prison boots in the box that is supposed to contain the warden's black dress shoes, and we watch Dufresne walk back to his cell wearing the warden's polished shoes. But this sequence also begs the follow-up question: What footwear is Andy wearing during his escape through the sewer pipe and into the creek? It's a nice touch of ironic payback—that Andy appears dressed in Norton's clothes at the very moment when he is stealing his money—but another kind of thievery occurs in this montage as well, and it is cinematic as well as sartorial: it belongs to Red, and, by extension, to Frank Darabont himself, in what they both managed to slip by *Shawshank*'s distracted audience.

One final point about the financial arrangement that Andy Dufresne shares with Warden Norton. The money that Andy has invested for the warden in Randall Stevens' name was obtained illegally, through kickbacks and schemes run by Norton and his minions. Andy refuses to see himself as culpable in any of this. As he tells Red, "I don't run the scams; I just process the profits," but he's still engaging in fraudulent actions and creating false identities—felonies that would put him in Shawshank Prison were he not already serving two life-term sentences. Andy claims to have lived an honest life as a banker on the outside; it was only in prison that he felt compelled to help Norton for purposes of self-preservation and to cajole certain favors. Nevertheless, Andy is the one who launders the money and increases its value exponentially, and after his escape from Shawshank, Dufresne does not hesitate to abscond with all the ill-gotten gains held in Randall Stevens' name. Furthermore, in the novella *Apt Pupil,* one of the companion narratives published alongside *Rita Hayworth and the Shawshank Redemption* in the collection *Different Seasons,* Stephen King deliberately complicates the young banker's moral transparency when we learn that Dufresne and the Nazi war criminal Kurt Dussander also have a financial relationship. Dussander informs his young American protégée Todd Bowden that he has been able to remain at large because of "Stocks I picked up after the war under yet another name ... Through a bank in the State of Maine ... The banker who bought them for me went to jail for murdering his wife a year after I bought them ... Dufresne, his name was—I remember because it sounds a little like mine" (*AP*, 122–3). By advising Dussander on his stock portfolio and enabling him to live off its dividends, the reputation of the hero of *The Shawshank Redemption* is further muddled. It is likely that Andy viewed Dussander as just another client, that he did not know about his Nazi past—and certainly Andy does not possess the same insights into the former concentration camp commandant that he does after years of working for Warden Norton—but this seemingly minor intertextual overlap in *Apt Pupil* still casts a shadow over Dufresne's self-commentary that "On the outside I was an honest man, straight as an arrow. I had to come to prison to be a crook."

Michelle Brown emphasizes *Shawshank*'s failure to communicate "any fundamental aspect of incarceration (the 'real') [in] the staging of an existential framework for the spectator through a model friendship" (61). She further laments that because the film and novella focus entirely on Red and his friends, the audience takes "no journeys with the imprisoned who remain locked in. We know them only from a distance and less so than their celluloid counterparts" (63). Brown's frustration is never more justi-fied than when Andy returns to his friends after completing "two weeks in the hole" as punishment for his Mozart "stunt," looking slightly dishev-eled but preternaturally cheerful, announcing flippantly, "Easiest time I ever did." His response manages to present to the audience a simplistic view of solitary confinement that is super-human and heroic, encouraging Brown to conclude that "the film's desire to rebuild hope and redemp-tion, at a moment in which retribution and incapacitation were to achieve unparalleled privilege in the American prison system, culminates in a mes-sage so abstract, so fantastic, and so centered within traditional conven-tions that the audience is seductively encouraged to walk away from the theater deep in metaphors about their own lives and romanticized assump-tions about the production of justice" (63).

More accurate representation of the penal experience in the film is perhaps found in Andy's response to his first night at Shawshank; Red informs us that Andy "cost me two packs of cigarettes. He never made a sound." *Shawshank* is perhaps at its most realistic in conveying the silence and loneliness of the prison experience, those nights when, after the lights go out and each prisoner is left alone in the darkness of his cell, as Red notes, "time can draw out like a blade," or when Andy scuttles away from sudden intrusions of light during the terrible weeks he is forced to endure alone in solitary confinement. In a sense, several scenes resemble Jeremy Bentham's concept of the "panopticon"; Andy and Red always appear alone in their cells, never in control of surprise inspections or who might look at them. Both inmates' cells are located on the second tier of a three-floor stacked cellblock, a structure that is similar to OSR (although there were two additional floors in the reformatory's central cellblock), with open bars on their sliding doors all along the front wall of their cells. While Andy and Red never had to share their cells with another prisoner, prompting the warden to refer to Andy's accommodations at Shawshank as a "one bunk Hilton," their isolation, paradoxically, meant never having any real privacy. Scenes of silence and isolation in the film confront the spectator with the contradiction arc of institutionalized punishment: men who have behaved badly when provided the opportunity to interact with others are denied access to social interaction for long periods of time, purportedly to make them fit for a return to society. As we discuss in detail in the next chapter, these moments of silent reflection help to bring Andy to an understanding of his role in his wife and her lover's deaths, but they occur at the price of two life sentences without the possibility of parole. Years of a curtailed social life have also produced degrees of institutionalization that drive Brooks Hatlen to suicide and Red to a crippling fear of something as big as the Pacific Ocean. Just as Andy's wife sought a new, radical outlet to counter the silences of her "closed book" husband and marriage, Andy finds alternative outlets to express his own reaction to the long silences of life inside Shawshank. Andy's personal transformation consists, at least in part, of confronting his civilian failings and by expressing in Shawshank what he was unable to demonstrate while living on the outside. As a successful banker, Andy was purportedly "locked" inside a conservative self; in Shawshank, he transforms into a teacher and a good friend, which serve as vehicles for him to connect to a side of humanity—and himself—ignored during his earlier life. Andy confesses to Red that on the outside when he was a banker, he "was an honest man, straight as an arrow" and that he "had to come to prison to be a crook." One might extend this argument to conclude that Andy also had to come to prison to become a human being. But let us be clear here: Andy's "rehabilitation" comes in spite of what he experiences as an inmate; it should be read as another way in which he defies the system and its efforts to break his humanity. This personal renovation is in keeping with the film's desire to present Andy as an existential rebel who distinguishes himself from the experience of the other prisoners. In researching this book we came across similar narratives of personal reclamation occurring to prisoners at OSR as well; in the end, prison rehabilitation seems to occur less as a result of the conscious efforts enforced by a penal institution than the willingness of individual men to use their hours of introspection as an opportunity for personal change.

We are made privy to other scenes in the film that portray a similarly accurate presentation of prison life. Andy's assaults by Bogs and the sisters are both vicious and realistic. Bogs is never shown "getting to" Andy by himself; he always relies on the help of two or three of the sisters to subdue his prey. Gang assaults, like those Andy is forced to endure, are typical occurrences in American prisons. Moreover, the breakfast that Andy is served his first morning at Shawshank consists of a repulsive oatmeal slop containing a living maggot that Andy decides not to eat, instead passing it over to Brooks Hatlen who, in turn, feeds it to Jake, the baby raven he is nursing back to health. The quality of the cuisine proffered at Shawshank is apparently still a problem in most American prisons. For years a misshapen block of baking staples, shredded carrots, and unskinned potatoes called Disciplinary Loaf has been served to prisoners in solitary confinement. The taste is so unappetizing that one prisoner confessed he "would taste it and just throw it away. You'd rather be without food than eat that." The brick loaf was only recently banned in all New York State prisons, but a version of it is still on the menu in Pennsylvania and Illinois (McKinley A32).

In a final analysis, *Shawshank* is a work of fictional art, not a prison documentary, and to critique its liabilities solely on terms that adhere to realism is to do the film a disservice. Although the movie owes a certain allegiance to rendering as true and accurate a portrait of prison life as it can, or at least enough truth in order to convince the audience of its potential veracity, this representation must ultimately serve the purpose of the story and the storyteller's art. This is a nuanced and ultimately impossible balance to maintain, as we have seen in our preceding discussion of that mix of scenes when Hollywood renders a faithful representation of penal life and those occasions where it configures the prison experience unrealistically. To legitimize Andy and Red's quest for freedom, the audience must be convinced of the injustice of their incarceration. After all, the movie is asking us to side with these individuals against the authority of the state, that their right to live together in Mexico for the rest of their lives supersedes the state's right to determine how much prison time satisfies two albeit wrongly convicted life sentences and what constitutes the parameters of parole. How we justify the illegalities that Andy and Red indulge, however, is dependent on the personal ideology of the viewer, our attitudes towards incarceration, and the degree to which we concur with Andy's self-judgment that "Whatever mistakes I made, I paid for them and then some ... that hotel, that boat, I don't think that's too much to ask."

Part of what shapes the audience's sympathy towards these two men, in addition to Andy's fundamental innocence, is the amount and degree of suffering that they experience as inmates at Shawshank. The brutality of the sisters and Captain Hadley, the corruption of the warden, Andy's terrible weeks in solitary confinement, and the amount of personal time Red and Andy have wasted behind bars raise issues that remain pertinent to any larger discussion "about the production of justice" and the philosophical rationale underlying long-term incarceration. Like *The Green Mile*, Darabont's next adaptation of a King novel, *Shawshank* renders a critical view of the American justice system, thereby complicating Brown's critique of the film's "romanticized assumptions." And since both films are also concerned with exploring unusual male friendships, with the quest for personal liberation, and with the "desire to rebuild hope and redemption," the inclusion of the "deep metaphors" to which Brown objects (63) must be allowed their rightful place. Of the two adaptations, *Shawshank* is less reliant than *Green Mile* on supernatural events and hyperbolized, idealized relationships between guards and inmates, but if it were solely dedicated to providing a wholly accurate portrait of penitentiary life, *Shawshank* would be a study in corruption and perhaps another compelling plea for prison reform, but it would not be art. Those moments where Michelle Brown correctly notes that the film's message is most "abstract and fantastic" in melodramatic assertions of human dignity, rebellion from oppressive rules and regulations, and the romantic endurance of friendship—in other words, the most unrealistic portrayals of prisoner behavior—are also responsible for creating the aura that allows audiences to connect and empathize so profoundly with its characters. Without such inclusions, the forces of institutionalization would overwhelm both the film's characters, and, most certainly its audience, the same way that institutionalization has affected the majority of the prison population currently residing in American penitentiaries (Fig. 2.6).

Fig. 2.6 The central cellblock at OSR. Solitary confinement cells are located on bottom floor; one of these was refurbished and then used to imprison Andy during his time in the hole in *The Shawshank Redemption*

Notes

1. "The Field" was an informal name sometimes used for the Ohio State Reformatory by inmates. The name was likely taken from the euphemistically named "Fields High School" located onsite for inmates' educational needs. A brief overview of the history of education at OSR can be found at http://www.drc.ohio.gov/ocss/ocss_history.htm

2. The inmate likely had in mind James Cagney's roles as hardened gangsters Tom Powers (*The Public Enemy*, 1931), Rocky Sullivan (*Angels with Dirty Faces*, 1938) or Cody Jarrett (*White Heat*, 1949), and Humphrey Bogart's tough PIs Sam Spade (*The Maltese Falcon*, 1941) or Philip Marlowe (*The Big Sleep*, 1946).

3. OSR's atmosphere is perhaps even more akin to an early avant-garde silent adaptation of Poe's work, *The Fall of the House of Usher* (1928). Using trick camera work to create an Expressionist effect, the film features jagged moving fractal patterns of stones colliding with one another until the images are rent apart revealing a *Caligari-esque* set of angular and distorted walls and windows in a claustrophobic space. The effect is dizzying and disorienting.

4. *Dante's Inferno* recycled footage from an earlier, silent adaptation (1924).

5. Paranormal activity has been reported at the following *Shawshank* locations: OSR, the Haunted Bissman Building, Malabar Farm State Park, and Renaissance Performing Arts Theatre (hauntedmansfield.com).

6. Events in 2015 included: Home and Garden Shows, numerous Ghost Hunts and Ghost Walks, car shows, Civil War Weekend with evening Lantern Tour and Reenactments, "Ink in the Clink" tattoo and music festival, Shawshank Hustle 7K race, Vintage Base Ball, and Halloween's Haunted Prison Experience.

7. http://ncarchitects.lib.ncsu.edu/people/P000138

8. After his war service, he married Elizabeth Clark, an active philanthropist, and had two sons who later joined his architectural firm. He was a member of the American Institute of Architects and is buried in Lakeview Cemetery in Cleveland, Ohio. Scofield also designed five of Cleveland public school buildings between 1869 and 1883 (Bishir) and commercial buildings.

9. OSR's historian Rebecca McKinnell was unable to confirm accounts that stated the inmates built the wall surrounding the prison (McKinnell, Interview).

10. Contract labor in the Northern states generally involved private businesses or industries paying to use inmate labor. The inmates would be supervised and provided the raw materials by the businesses.

11. http://www.correctionhistory.org/html/chronicl/docs2day/elmira.html

12. Inmates were paid a daily stipend of 2 to 5 cents, depending on number of dependent children.

13. The Ohio State Penitentiary Fire gained notoriety quickly and was memorialized in music and literature. The 1934 *Esquire* short story based on the fire "To What Red Hell" was written by African-American author Chester Himes, then an inmate. The songs "Columbus Prison Fire" (Carson Jay Robison) and "Ohio Prison Fire" (Charlotte and Bob Miller) were written within days of the event.

14. The Boys' Industrial School was the juvenile facility for offenders aged 8–18 in Lancaster (Fairfield County), Ohio, from 1884–1964.

15. http://time.com/3052468/what-28-years-of-solitary-confinement-does-to-the-mind/

16. Film projectionists were widely unionized until the 1950s, long after safety concerns prompted by the use of nitrate films in cinema's early years abated. Due to the danger of handling nitrate prints, projectionists were required to obtain specialized training in safe handling of the prints, as well as training in proper operation of the equipment.

17. Ohio cemeteries are generally open to the public when located on state or county land, but this is not always the case. Access to some cemeteries is restricted, even those of historic significance, and permission must be obtained before visiting. In the case of the OSR/Shawshank cemetery, its proximity to a maximum-security prison facility necessitates restricted access.

CHAPTER 3

Interpreting *Shawshank*

Only where the state ends, there begins the human being.

Friedrich Nietzsche

The Shawshank Redemption was the second film Frank Darabont directed based on a Stephen King text, following *The Woman in the Room* (1983). Although the film adaptation of *Shawshank* did not initially perform well at the box office, it was nominated for seven Academy Awards, but failed to win any, as *Forrest Gump* swept most of the hardware that year, including Best Picture category.[1] Mark Kermode notes in his book on *Shawshank* that during its initial release period the movie recouped only $18 million of its $35 million investment, this at a time when blockbusters such as *Speed*, *Pulp Fiction*, *Dumb & Dumber*, and *Forrest Gump*, the major Hollywood competitors *Shawshank* faced in 1994, were regularly taking upward of $100 million (Kermode 11); *Gump* grossed more than $109 million in its first nineteen days. It was only when *Shawshank* was resurrected on video that it broke all marketing trends and expectations to become one of the worldwide top-rented videocassettes in 1995. The movie owed its initial popularity to word of mouth recommendations and the rewards attendant to watching the film in the privacy of individual living rooms. If anything, the film's popularity has only increased since 1995, as another generation has now discovered *Shawshank* in part because of its frequent appearance on cable television. Channel surfers often remark on the difficulty of turning

© The Author(s) 2016
M. Grady, T. Magistrale, *The Shawshank Experience*,
DOI 10.1057/978-1-137-53165-0_3

away from the movie when they find it on television, however far along in its plot. According to the Internet Movie Data Base subscribers' poll, the film has toppled *The Godfather* as the most popular movie of all time for at least the past four years. And as its popularity has grown, so, too, has *Shawshank*'s critical reputation. Scholarship on the movie (critical attention on King's novella has remained centered on its role as the movie's source text) has proliferated since the late 1990s and into the new millennium. It is interesting that much of this critical work, just as likely to be authored by criminologists and sociologists as cinema and cultural studies scholars, tends to employ the film as a reference point for larger agendas, such as prison tourism, racial relationships, and critical examinations into the American justice system itself. Perhaps the most surprising area of research *Shawshank* has so far inspired, however, is in the film's use of music—in particular, opera; articles and book chapters on this subject, including articles by Allanbrook, Hunter, Nero, and Chua, are typically written by musicologists who bring their specializations to the realm of film studies.

Forrest Gump and *Shawshank* happen to share inimitable parallels in addition to their coincidental year of release: both films rely on a persuasive voiceover narration that moves seamlessly between comedy and tragedy; their main characters are beset by forces that are often beyond their comprehension and ability to control, caught as they are in what Andy Dufresne calls "the path of the tornado"; in the face of extremely trying circumstances, the two films emphasize the power of hope and the enduring value of male friendships; the close relationship that Gump and Bubba enjoy is, like Andy's and Red's, an interracial bond that never calls attention to race; the movies follow the lives of their respective protagonists over extended periods of time and during the same overlapping American historical epoch; and both films have gone on to establish their own vibrant fan-based communities, websites, and even business ventures, such as the Bubba Gump Shrimp Company with stores in Florida, California, Hawaii, and Japan.

Gump offers several scenes that expand the magic of moviemaking (e.g., those moments where Forrest finds himself sharing the same frame with historical figures such as Presidents Kennedy, Johnson, and Nixon) while also stretching the perimeters of the romance-comedy genre, as Gump and Jenny technically spend more time running away from each other than they do together. Although *Shawshank* is also a love story, arguably even more so than *Gump*, it likewise defies rigid categorization in its ability to complicate and subvert traditional filmic genres and audience expectations. Both films sometimes descend into the realm of sentimentality because they are paeans to eternal friendship and hope. Probably the two pictures are best aligned with melodrama, a genre associated with heightened emotional situations focused on, to paraphrase director Todd Haynes, stories where the characters' opportunities to make heroic choices are extremely limited. The genre has been part of the movies since the beginning, and though critics often deride the form as being too sentimental, audiences have embraced *Shawshank*'s and *Gump*'s reliance on strong male-to-male love relationships that remain asexual.

Gump and *Shawshank* are "feel-good" narratives about the resiliency of the human spirit—its ability not only to survive tornado damage but to triumph over it. The optimism of these movies strikes a similar cord in their audiences. We all want to believe that in the end things will work out—that in spite of whatever personal suffering and tragedy we undergo, we will look back on our lives, as Forrest and Red and Andy do, with a quiet satisfaction that the journey was worth the struggle after all. Whether this faith proves to be well-founded or not is almost irrelevant to fans of the films. It is the hope that stirs us, that endears us to these works of spirit and transcendence, for they are clarion calls to live life with greater determination. As portraits of light amidst deep sadness, each film is heartbreaking at the same time that it is inspiring. Mark Edmundson argues that the American public loves both movies because their messages of hope and idealism stole the heart of the heartland, serving "as a vacation, a few hours away from more pressing gothic fears" (76). Beneath their surface popularity, however, the two films are quiet ruminations that debate and confront the issue of how much control each of us has in a seemingly deterministic universe; to what degree is it possible for human beings to exert influence over the destiny that Forrest's mother believes is firmly in place? Reflecting her faith in the benevolence of this destiny, *Gump* trusts in the human spirit's buoyancy to accept and endure whatever adversity it encounters. Each time Jenny breaks his heart and leaves him bereft, for example, Forrest simply allows her to go with neither pursuit nor complaint. Contrastingly, *Shawshank* advocates a more proactive stance. While it is also a paean to endurance, the movie argues for the active involvement of human agency in responding and ultimately altering the bad news that fate oftentimes delivers. Dufresne's signature line, "Get busy living or get busy dying," underscores the difference between exerting human will and a passive acceptance of fate's decree.

Shawshank ends up confirming the core tenet of Christian existentialism: that man is more than a terminal product of conditioning, environment, or the past; he has the potential to transcend these things and find redemption. If there is a level of transcendence at work in *Gump*, and we believe that there is, it centers rather on the simple maxim of Christian suffering, a loyal faith in the resiliency of goodness and a commitment to slow and steady wins the race. Indeed, the act of long-distance running evolves into the operative metaphor for Gump's character—a good-natured man-child with a fixed code of simple values—employed as a kind of meditation exercise to help him sustain his balance and identity against the volcanic forces of chaos and change that seem less to involve Gump personally than to go on around him. In *Shawshank*, on the other hand, to remain similarly oblivious becomes equivalent to a living death; men must consciously assert themselves against the deadening forces of institutionalization wherever they encounter them. We witness two actual suicides take place in *Shawshank*, while other threatening descents into madness and self-destruction haunt the film's perimeters. Andy offers the only viable alternative to institutional despair. But whereas Gump maintains a capacity to accept stoically the traumas that never appear to affect him deeply, Andy and Red are required to confront and overcome theirs directly, employing acts of defiance and embracing change as alternatives to escapism or passivity.

In a final analysis, *Shawshank* bears more nuance and resonance than *Gump* because so much of its revelatory power relies on the hard-earned interwoven redemptions in which Andy and Red participate during and after their incarcerations. By the end of the film, they truly become "changed men"—ironically echoing the cant phrase Red employs unsuccessfully in his first two parole board interviews. Red and Andy embrace radical personal transformation during their incarcerations in a static place that fosters deadening routine, "old life blown away in the blink of an eye, nothing left but all the time in the world to think about it." Forrest, in contrast, remains a consistent—some might say, static—presence in a world that spins its historical upheavals around him (consider, by way of difference, the tortured adulthood that his girlfriend, Jenny, experiences). As Edmundson notes, "She's like the picture of Dorian Gray, recording the ravages of the 60s and beyond, while Forrest, with his drooler's grin, stays clean" (75). In several ways, *Gump* is a reactionary motion picture especially compared to *Shawshank*; its attitude towards liberated women and the sixties, for example, is extremely negative, suggesting that Jenny's brand of feminism is a catastrophic blend of drugs, promiscuity, and irre-sponsibility. Indeed, Jenny only rises above shrew status at the end, when she returns home to Alabama and settles in with Gump, chastened by motherhood and an incurable disease, most likely AIDS. As we will argue elsewhere in this chapter, *Shawshank* has a much more positive perspec-tive—both in its references to women and on the era of the sixties. *Gump*'s attitude towards race never rises above the simplistic, most blatantly in its unflattering portrait of the Black Panthers. Additionally, Bubba (his name alone is often used outside the South as a pejorative to mean a per-son of low economic status and limited intelligence) never transcends the stereotype of a Magical Negro, enabling the movie's white protagonist to achieve success in the shrimping business after Bubba dies and Gump appropriates his business plan. While *Shawshank* also steers clear of con-fronting racism directly, it nonetheless offers a more nuanced treatment of the subject, notably in empowering its only black character by putting him in control of the narrative.

Gothic *Shawshank*

Stephen King has been telling stories that focus on superannuated cars, pets, cell phones, hotels, cemeteries, towns, houses, and human beings for the past half-century. His narratives often center on places and things possessed of a history of malfeasance that radiate evil in an effort to pull outsiders into their realm. While it is possible to argue that King has spent his career animating the inanimate, it is his attention to haunted places—human dwellings, in particular—that links him most directly to the gothic tradition in literature and film. John Sears has traced this trope in early works by Stephen King, arguing that "place effectively indicates the inter-penetration in gothic modes of inside and outside, of concealed psycho-logical depths in human minds and their unfolding, their manifestation outside themselves in the worlds they perceive and create" (161).

Throughout his fiction, from the Marsten House in *'Salem's Lot* to the metastasizing mansion in *Rose Red*, King's major work revolves around what he calls in *Danse Macabre* the "Bad Place," "psychic batteries, absorbing the emotions that had been spent there, absorbing them as much as a car battery will store an electrical charge" (*DM*, 253). King goes on to acknowledge that this association was an initial impetus for the plotline of *The Shining*: "with my rigorous Methodist upbringing, I began to wonder if the haunted house could not be turned into a kind of symbol of unexpiated sin … an idea which turned out to be pivotal in the novel *The Shining*" (*DM*, 253). While this is certainly true, the "Bad Place" archetype haunted King's literary imagination even before *The Shining*; in fact, as early as *'Salem's Lot* the Marsten House sends out a psychic call to Ben Mears, a writer who is also the novel's main protagonist and chief vampire slayer, compelling him to return to the house and town because he is haunted by unresolved childhood terrors associated with the Marsten history. Indeed, the house is always within sight, looming, visible from nearly every place in the town, as if it is keeping watch over the inhabitants while at the same time also demanding that the townspeople maintain a constant awareness of its presence. "There may be some truth in the idea that houses absorb the emotions that are spent in them," Mears speculates about the supernaturalism of the Marsten House. "Perhaps the right personality [could] cause it to produce an active manifestation … of a monster" (*SL*, 48). When Mears arrives back in the Lot, he's not certain why he feels such a strong need to be there, much less what his new novel will be about, but "he had asked Eva Miller specifically for this room after looking at several, because it faced the Marsten House directly" (*SL*, 51). And it is thus no accident that when Barlow, the paternal vampire, arrives and begins to implement his design to turn the town into a rural wasteland of the undead, he chooses the Marsten House as his central command.

Sears reminds us of the "affinity between and functions of the two fictional places" (160), that the Marsten House's dark history is a prelude to what the Torrances find when they move into the Overlook hotel. Hubert Marsten's suicide serves as merely the culminating moment in the house's history that includes a variety of felonious offenses, including child abuse and murder, "which meant it stood on unhallowed ground" (*SL*, 338). In their study of the connection that Edgar Allan Poe's "The Fall of the House of Usher" shares with King's novel, Perry and Sederholm suggest that "Like the sentient House of Usher, whose sentience was inexplicably characterized by its very structure, fungi, and reduplication in the tarn, the Overlook seemed to be powered by the collective mind of its former inhabitants, who channel invisible forces into … all manner of supernatural effects" (172). The Overlook's past in *The Shining* is most potently archived in the scrapbook that Jack discovers in chapter 18. As a record of the hotel's secret and public past—the unpleasant memories of its history—the scrapbook represents a critical component in establishing a collusion between Jack and the Overlook. Between its covers, Torrance finds a mélange of newspapers, letters, photographs, diary entries, and seemingly random notations that chronicle events from the hotel's sordid past. It is as if the Overlook is revealing its most intimate relationships and experiences as well as its most mundane, filling the darkest chambers of the writer's mind with details of its dark history while he sits alone in the dark corner of its basement musing on this past. Jack, in turn, connects with the place, dimly aware of some unconscious bond he shares—perhaps it is the hotel's failure to live up to its expectations as a business venture; perhaps it is the sad vulnerability revealed in its flaws; perhaps it is simply that Jack feels privileged in gaining private insight into the hotel's secreted moments of spectacular decadence. Whatever the reason, from this point on Jack never views the Overlook with any degree of objectivity; his destiny is forever aligned with that of the hotel. One might argue that after his introduction to the scrapbook, Jack belongs more to the Overlook than he does to his own wife and child.[2]

The ability of gothic places to seduce and corrupt King protagonists is restated time and again throughout the writer's canon. In *Pet Sematary*, Louis Creed is seduced by the power of a Native American burial site, initially dormant, but reanimated by the power of human grief that Creed experiences in first the loss of his daughter's cat, but even more poignantly in the death of his son. In the course of the narrative, Louis' inability to resist the temptation to return to the unholy ground weakens in inverse proportion to the growing power of the place itself, which seems to ramp up its range and potency with each introduction of fresh human carnage. The supernatural forces at work in *'Salem's Lot*, *The Shining*, *Pet Sematary*, and *1408*, the psychologically tortured short story about a haunted hotel room and its powerful film adaptation, are all vampiric in nature; in fact, King's evil avatars always embody, to a greater or lesser degree, vampiric qualities—either literally, as with Barlow in search of human blood and revenant converts, or through a psychic vampirism, as is the case with the cosmopolitan ghosts that reside at the Overlook and in room *1408* as well as the primitive spirit of the Wendigo that animates the polluted pull of the graveyard in *Pet Sematary*.

The connections between these various "Bad Places" and Shawshank Prison are, on the surface, perhaps less obvious than, say, the haunted gothic mansion in *Rose Red*, which was written as a homage to Shirley Jackson's *The Haunting of Hill House* and its protagonist, Eleanor Vance, who King calls "the finest character to come out of [the] new American gothic tradition" (*DM*, 268). What we find in King's prison is an unbroken line of corruption and perverse violence that is essentially a variant on the Marsten House, the Overlook Hotel, Hill House, or any of the other centers of evil in the King fictional universe. Warden Norton, the only Shawshank warden during Andy Dufresne's nineteen-year incarceration in the film, is an amalgamation of the three wardens King introduces in the novella: "The man was the foulest hypocrite that I ever saw in a high position. The rackets I told you about earlier continued to flourish, but Sam Norton added his own new wrinkles" (*RHSR*, 47). Moreover, King unconsciously links Norton's tenure to a religious zealotry that is reminiscent of OSR's days as a reformatory; inmate discipline is presented within a strict religious code of ethics; Norton introduces himself in the film via his verbal commitment to the Bible and pious self-discipline. Unlike OSR's commitment to moral reformation, however, Norton's intentions are always self-serving and hypocritical: "He had a Bible quote for every occasion, did Mr. Sam Norton ... [he] must have subscribed to the old Puritan notion that the best way to figure out which folks God favors is by checking their bank account" (*RHSR*, 47–8). King has always surrounded his gothic "Bad Places" with a secret past of evil and sin that becomes reanimated when innocent (and not so innocent) men stumble upon them. When Montague Summers suggests that the architecture itself is the central protagonist in gothic fiction—often more important than the gothic villain, maiden, and hero, but also typically aligned with the villain—he underscores the importance of the past as exerting a dramatic influence over the present. The dark corridors and secret places create a physical hold over characters that translate into psychological bondage as well (Summers 78). King acknowledged his own awareness of this genre trope during an interview several years ago: "A lot of the fiction I write follows the gothic tradition wherein the past has this unbreakable hold on the present. This obsession with the past throughout gothic literature, up to and including my own work, is an unpleasant thing. It is a twisted influence that restricts and even changes the present" (Magistrale, *Second Decade* 10). Behind the walls of Shawshank exists an alternate universe— where justice is meted out according to the will and whim of guards and penal administrators, where the very definitions of right and wrong are reconfigured and distorted to satisfy particular circumstances, where a man is likely to lose his very identity in the struggle against institutionalization.

It is clear from the novella that King had in mind a cavernous stone building that closely resembled OSR in his writer's imagination, "a place of graded limestone, when they cut this place out of the side of a hill" (*RHSR*, 18), but it took Darabont's location crew to track down an actual structure commensurate to King's vision. While King may not have been referencing the OSR specifically when he fictionalized Shawshank State Prison, Frank Darabont quickly recognized the power of OSR to evoke the same gothic sensibilities that animate the Overlook Hotel and Rose Red. It's no surprise that the Shawshank Trail's crown jewel—the Ohio State Reformatory—which features guided tours of the OSR throughout the year, virtually shuts down public tours of the prison during the months of September and October, as the building is prepared for its consummate festival: Halloween.

Regardless of one's attitude towards incarceration, reformation, and the American penal system, OSR/Shawshank is a facility that, like a vampire, often drained the life and spirit out of those unfortunate enough to serve as its victims. Although probably a necessary evil in human society, the prison system embodied in both OSR and Shawshank's histories remains testaments to man's inhumanity to his fellow man. In this way, Shawshank Prison resembles Poe's Usher mansion and any number of the haunted houses from countless horror films where the negative forces residing in the structure exert a terrible presence or pull over its human inhabitants that eventually either destroys them or drives them mad. In this context, the zombie-like condition of institutionalization, which plays such an important role in *Shawshank*'s film adaptation, appears as the most benign affect the prisoner experience imposes after prolonged exposure to these houses of horrors. While the penal universe prides itself on the efficacy of its regimentation and outward adherence to law and Christianity—the gold cross and patriot pins that Norton is pictured wearing on his suit lapels—in reality, Shawshank is more of a gothic dungeon, replete with sexual violation and violence, than it is a state-sponsored facility subject to American laws and the Geneva accord insuring human rights for prisoners. Although neither King nor Darabont's narratives detail the prison's history to the degree to which King elaborates the history of Rose Red or the Overlook's past in the novel's scrapbook chapter, we know enough of Shawshank through its successive penal administrations depicted in the novella during Red's tenure or in the film's portrait of Warden Norton and the guards to recognize that it also shares a similar level of corruption, violence, and moral equivocation. And, too, a prison, with its successive collective histories of sin, social violation, and exculpation doesn't require as much historical background to serve gothic purposes as does a hotel or a house, the latter carrying its own particular and personalized charge. Such levels of malfeasance are apparently not only limited to prison officials and guards, as Andy confesses to Red that he was an honest businessman on the outside, "straight as an arrow ... I had to come to prison to learn how to be a crook."

The Shawshank Redemption owes as much to the history and various permutations of the gothic narrative as it does to prison narratives that precede it; in *Shawshank*, as well as in other novels, films, and television dramas, the two genres often share points of intersection. Thomas Doherty has remarked upon this connection, positing "prison movies are more apt to construct the world behind bars as a fantastical horror landscape ... as a social institution, the prison is perverse and punitive not just because it cages its inhabitants but because it segregates them by sex" (192). We would do well to remind ourselves at this point that elements of the gothic permeate the whole of the American literary canon—from Poe and Hawthorne in the nineteenth century to Stephen King in our own. Additionally, from its cinematic inception America was drawn to horror celluloid with its reliance on icons popularized from the literary gothic a century earlier; the Frankenstein creature, Dracula, Mr. Hyde, and their infernal children and brethren were staples of Universal's monster menagerie during the 1930s. As the screenwriter for the remake of *The Blob*, the sequel to *The Fly*, and the director-screenwriter for *The Mist*, Frank Darabont is not only acutely aware of the literary and cinematic traditions of horror in America, he also understands that these traditions employ the classic gothic themes of entrapment, forced incarceration, and violence.[3]

Indeed, some of the earliest examples of American literature revolve around the theme of the Indian Captivity Narrative, wherein an individual—often a woman, as was the case with the first example authored by Mary Rowlandson—is kidnapped by native Americans and held as a prisoner against her will. Such tales of attack, capture, and escape were extraordinarily popular because they told stories of bravery and guile amidst strange places and pagan customs. The primary theme of the captivity narrative, continuing as it does from forms indigenous to the New World to black slave narratives in the nineteenth century, forms a major component of the gothic romance. And not surprisingly, these narratives typically intersect with many of the motifs found later in the prison film genre, such as prolonged incarceration, cruel and violent treatment, degrees of sadomasochism and bondage, the threat of sexual assault, and forcible cultural and identity change wherein the victim finds herself trapped within a foreign culture and is forced to adjust expectations and behavior accordingly in order to survive.

Incarcerated in a gray, stone, castle-like fortress that Kermode point-edly describes as "one part cathedral, two parts Castle Frankenstein" (18), OSR/Shawshank is heavily invested in gothic iconography: the prison's imposing and intimidating stone edifice makes it appear as a vast fortress or castle; the labyrinth of corridors, tunnels, turrets, and rooms filmed both within OSR and on the specifically built set in a Mansfield, Ohio, warehouse nearby; the subterranean terror and clamminess of the soli-tary confinement cells that are claustrophobic and dark, emitting light through only a single food opening in the sliding metal door; the aware-ness of being trapped within the airless and lightless heft of stone walls and steel, even during filming of outdoor shots; and the gray omnipres-ence of the building's internal atmosphere and the washed-out color of the prisoners' uniforms that contrasts with their pasty white faces. The film gives these locations and environments oppressiveness as though they were projected through an anguished dream. An antecedent to OSR/ Shawshank is Giovanni Battista Piranesi's pen and ink prison drawings produced in the middle of the eighteenth century. These were important influences on subsequent gothic writers and the construction of their mas-sive physical structures. Piranesi's endless, vast interior spaces are intimi-dating to the mind's eye and threaten to extend beyond reason and into infinity. Contemplating these images that create a contradictory admix-ture of containment and looming space, like OSR/Shawshank itself, is a challenge to rationality as the viewer identifies more with punishment within this entombed arena than any hope for redemption. In the film, it is finally impossible to separate the prisoners and particularly Warden Norton—the latter appears twice addressing the public and convicts in the yard while framed by OSR's stone edifice—from the extraordinary and imposing effect of the building itself. Perhaps this is why the film's Tommy is so surprised when the warden elects to interview him outside the fence at the perimeter of the prison yard ("Out here?" he asks the guard incredulously); while he certainly doesn't recognize the location as part of the warden's trap to murder him for a manufactured escape attempt, Tommy's confusion may also be attributed to the constant asso-ciation the film makes between Norton and core areas of the prison itself.

Darabont and King Americanize the European gothic castle in *Shawshank* by refashioning certain props and locales that had served their literary (and filmic) predecessors. Horace Walpole, Ann Radcliffe, Matthew Lewis, Charles Maturin, Edgar Allan Poe, and Bram Stoker had interred their protagonists within the walls of castles, mansions, and monasteries since the end of the eighteenth century. In their capable hands, the literal haunted castle, monastery, and house were transformed into what Benjamin Fisher describes as a "natural setting conducive to unrest and fears, or, in yet another kind of development, to a haunted mind … the corridors of the psyche sufficing to engender such a frisson" (75). King and Darabont revived these traditional enclosures to create a similar sense of claustrophobic space in *Shawshank*. Just as earlier gothic heroes and heroines had to grope their way through darkened dungeons and passageways in an effort to discover a way out of haunted abbeys and castles, Andy Dufresne escapes from the gothic's destructive, vertical dynamic captured in the tiers of cells present at Shawshank, and literally crawls his way horizontally to a bodily escape through its sewage system. Like Poe's hero in the novel *The Narrative of Arthur Gordon Pym of Nantucket*, Dufresne's gothic quest takes him from a world of black, suffocating enclosures and into the whiteness of a limitless world of imagination and escape, as we view him via Red's cinematic vision in a red convertible, wind blowing through his hair, driving along an open stretch of roadway that borders an immense ocean vista. In many gothic novels, the protagonists are delivered from their symbolic deaths and burials inside the castle or haunted house and reenter society after enduring their subterranean entrapments.

As we have seen in Chap. 2, modern arguments for prison incarceration were often inspired by religious principles; prolonged solitary punishment ideally translated into introspection which in turn led to personal reform. Accordingly, Kermode mentions the "oddly positive parallels between release and death which haunt *The Shawshank Redemption*" (53), while in *Discipline and Punish* Michel Foucault likewise relies on spiritual metaphors that link the prison cell to a crypt: "In this closed cell, this temporary sepulcher, the myths of resurrection arise easily enough. After night and silence, the regenerated life" (239). But it is criminologist Michael Fiddler who applies the death-to-rebirth argument directly to the symbolic dualism of Andy's prison cell serving as both tomb and womb: "A womblike space implies the possibility of being reborn. The capitalized word MOTHER is positioned just above each of the three posters of iconic womanhood that cover the hole in Andy's cell. The word MOTHER literally labels this as an intra-uterine space. The film clearly sets up the space of Andy's cell as a vehicle for his rebirth, his *change*" (199). In a facility rife with corruption and murder, as the *Portland Bugle* eventually splashes across its front page, Andy ironically actualizes the intention of modern penal reform Foucault identifies, attaining a level of self-awareness and moral activity that is the result of his years of incarceration at Shawshank—even as this self-realization also motivates his decision to escape and take with him the warden's illegal cachet.

Much more than King's narrative, Darabont's screenplay is a kind of cinematic *bildungsroman*, or narrative of education that occurs to a man who himself becomes an educator of men. The film reveals that Andy's most serious crime was his inability to express love for his wife. "My wife used to say used to say I'm a hard man hard to know. Like a closed book," he confesses to Red. "I didn't pull the trigger, but I drove her away. And that's why she died, because of me, the way I am." Although falsely imprisoned, Andy's punishment at Shawshank nonetheless consists of nineteen years of hard reflection on his own culpability in the failure of his marriage, and his rehabilitation—and perhaps even his redemption—is found in the reformation he puts himself through by learning how to express such emotions to Red (for example, he is able to admit to Red that he loved his wife) and the other men who become his friends and students at Shawshank. During his long prison term, forced to undergo a sentence of constant introspection and acceptance of his indirect role in his wife's violent death, Andy is caught inside a cerebral maze of guilt confined as he is to the dungeon of the self, certainly the blackest of all gothic spaces. Too often guilt leads only to self-pity and impotence, but this is not how it affects Andy. His descent into the gothic bowels of Shawshank puts him in touch with himself to the point where he learns to see himself more clearly and to balance the moral polarities of his situation (perhaps this self-clarity is the reason he gives up drinking alcohol in the film, if not the novella).

While he accepts his failings as a husband that precipitated the murder of his wife, Dufresne also measures this against the fact that he "didn't pull the trigger" that legally convicted him to Shawshank and that "whatever mistakes I made, I've paid for them, and then some." By the time of his escape, Andy is capable of balancing his culpability with what he has undergone as punishment. In the course of his incarceration, Andy evolves from a man whose initial distrust of women is echoed in his first words to Captain Hadley—"Do you trust your wife? Do you think she'd go behind your back and try to hamstring you?"—to a man who acknowledges his own role in the suffering of women and empathizes with their oppression, even, as we will see, identifying personally with their rebellion against it. The trajectory of his moral development is similar to a kind of geological breakdown perhaps best represented on a continuum that takes Andy from the film's opening montage as a jealous and potentially violent husband to Andy as the calm negotiator who reasonably convinces Brooks Hatlen to put down the knife he holds against Heywood's throat in favor of expressing his emotions verbally. The film's theatrical poster art, featuring Andy, arms outstretched and standing knee-deep in a creek during a rainstorm as he strips away the vestiges of his prison clothing, underscores the binary images of crucifixion and rebirth that accompany Andy's emergence from his entombment within Shawshank. Although he begins his term at Shawshank as "a closed book" in a state of self-imposed isolation and under sexual siege at the hands of Bogs and the sisters, Andy leaves Shawshank with a legacy of being a great teacher and as a member of a cadre of close friends who have come to immortalize his actions as if he were a god or hero. His suffering and consequent redemption are more convoluted and interconnected than most film scholars and fans of the film have heretofore acknowledged.

In addition to the literal gothic structure that represents Shawshank prison, Andy's combination of innocence—the only innocent man in Shawshank—and refined demeanor, a cultured bank vice-president incarcerated among hardened felons, link him to the persecuted yet intrepid gothic maiden in eighteenth- and nineteenth-century literature who is besieged by various hypermasculine monsters that are an omnipresent psychological and sexual threat. The course of Andy's feminization is both psychological and physical, and it further connects him to the various female figures with which he aligns himself at central points throughout the film. Rita Hayworth, Marilyn Monroe, Raquel Welch, (and even Linda Ronstadt who serves as an additional celebrity poster King includes in his novella) represent the choices of Andy's wall art that disguise the tunnel he is excavating inside his prison wall. As will be discussed in greater detail later in this chapter, these are all strong women who, in either their personal lives or in the context of the specific movie role depicted in their respective posters, employ femininity as a means for asserting themselves against the entrenched male power dynamic each encounters. From the fierce sexual independence evinced by Linda Dufresne, to the scheming sopranos from *The Marriage of Figaro*, to the movie and recording starlets staring down from his wall, these self-confident women model for Andy the "doubleness of space" that Eve Sedgwick suggests is a major convention of the gothic established by the deconstruction of gender boundaries and the blurring of traditional behavior norms (20). Andy both embodies the subversive behavior associated with these various women at the same time as he finds himself identified with them as a sexualized object of male desire. Dufresne stands apart from the other inmates at Shawshank because he integrates a full range of feminine behavior traits into his personality. One of the most satisfying aspects of *Shawshank* is watching a man evolve through his increasing identification and contact with the feminine; Andy becomes a better man as a result of acknowledging his feminine anima. Ironically, the plotline of *Shawshank* comes full circle when Andy Dufresne follows the seditious example set by his own wife: he likewise abandons an unsatisfying relationship in an oppressive institution to "get busy living" on the shores of Zihuatanejo, the Mexican town on the Pacific Ocean whose native name in Nahuatl Cihuatlan means "the place of women."

Within the prison culture itself, Andy serves as a teacher, friend, and nurturing presence to a degree that would have been gendered "feminine" during the 1950s and beyond. He designs and maintains the Shawshank library and tutors a dozen other convicts, enabling them to obtain high school equivalency diplomas. In effect, Andy becomes the surrogate "mother" (also the very word carved into his wall that, at least according to Red's flashback, provides Andy with the initial inspiration to breach his concrete cell) all these inmates are sorely missing in their misguided lives. He refuses to be intimidated by male authority figures in the penal system or by the fury and violence that is directed at him sexually. Throughout the first quarter of film and novel, Bogs and the sisters continually pursue Andy in a way that is similar to how undesirable men often pursue women, using their masculinity as a tool to overpower them. His sexual violation is as integral to the first quarter of both film and novel as Isabella's in Walpole's *The Castle of Otranto* or Clarissa's in Richardson's early eighteenth-century gothic novel.[4] Andy's gender affiliation is further blurred when King makes a point of feminizing male rape by connecting it to menstruation: "The bleeding really is like a menstrual flow; it keeps up for two, maybe three days, a slow trickle. Then it stops" (*RHSR*, 22). Even Red feminizes and sexualizes Andy in the film, calling him "a tall drink of water with a silver spoon up his ass" when he first views him entering Shawshank. In fact, all the new fish are subjected to the male gaze of the veteran inmates and the guards in the sequence that films their arrival at Shawshank. Being raped cannot, of course, turn a man into a woman, but it does symbolically align Andy with gothic heroines who live in perpetual fear of this fate. Moreover, in a heteronormative Hollywood context, the subject of the male gaze is nearly always gendered female. As Laura Mulvey notes, the camera tends to see the "woman as image [and] man as bearer of the look." Further, Mulvey argues that "the determining male gaze projects its fantasy on to the female figure" whose appearance is "coded for strong visual and erotic impact so they can be said to connote *to-be-looked-at-ness*" (Mulvey 719). At the end of the scene when Andy and Red first meet, Andy walks away, bends down, and picks up a rock. He chooses to bend with his back, bottom up, in a manner that reveals the creases on his tight-fitting uniform. He also bends in a way that enables him to look back at Red and smile at him coquettishly. Red's observations of Andy extend in this same scene to include further references to his anus, the site of Andy's sexuality while inside the prison, when he questions if Andy thinks his "shit smells sweeter than most."

As is the case with many historical gothic heroines in the genre, Andy's identity is aligned with several core images that appear throughout *Shawshank*: the tunnel he crawls through located literally behind the posters of his Hollywood actresses operates as a symbolic vagina/birth canal that provides him entrance into a new life (Fiddler says that Andy "figuratively crawls between Raquel Welch's legs to be reborn. It is as simple and crude as that" [199]), while the sewage pipe he navigates immediately afterwards is a journey through the male bowels of Shawshank where he is eventually evacuated. Just as these two contrasting images of the feminine and masculine abject are joined during Andy's escape, his sexuality and gender are ambiguous throughout the film, and serve to underscore the obtuseness of Mark Browning's claim that "matters of gender are almost irrelevant" in *The Shawshank Redemption* (153). Dufresne's gender and sexuality may remain fluid and unstable, but their significance is always relevant to the meaning of the film. He is definitely feminized in a way that we do not see associated with any of the other prisoners; Andy draws the entire prison population to him—out of a desire to befriend him, or to exploit his intellect, or because of his attractiveness to possess him sexually. Like the traditional gothic heroine in literature and film, Andy is always under personal siege and must constantly protect himself against masculine intrusions that either endanger his sexuality or personal code of conduct. Bogs and the sisters are obsessed with penetrating Andy orally and rectally, in spite of his strenuous efforts to defend himself: "There was a little hiatus, and then it began again, although not so hard or so often. Jackals like easy prey, and there were easier pickings around than Andy Dufresne" (*RHSR*, 25). Although King suggests that there may have been "easier prey" than Andy at Shawshank, Bogs and the sisters prefer him, and this in spite of the repeated beatings and time in solitary that Bogs receives as a consequence of indulging this predilection. Darabont's film provides neither references to nor examples of "easier" sexual alternatives: Andy is the *exclusive* target of the sisters' violent sexual lust. Indeed, Andy remains the only prisoner whom we see assaulted sexually; Red and the other members of his crew never discuss, much less are visualized, incurring such trauma.

In addition, once Bogs exits the movie confined to a wheelchair and the sisters decide to leave Andy alone, he becomes the warden's "bitch," helping with his illegal schemes in exchange for "certain exceptions," such as his private cell, his collection of female poster art, and the opportunity to build the prison library. In a 2014 conversation shared with Bob Gunton at the twentieth anniversary of *Shawshank*'s theatrical release in Mansfield, he told us he came to perceive his character's relationship to Andy as a "seduction dance, the two of us circling around each other, feeling each other out. The warden knows Andy is different from the other men at Shawshank, and that difference intrigues him. We first see this in the scene where we challenge each other with dueling scripture passages, and, later in the movie, I ask him, 'How do I look?' while pirouetting in front of him" (Gunton). The warden goes on to make his own, more explicit allusion to Andy's sexuality and intimations of homosexual rape late in the film when he threatens to "pull [Andy] out of that one bunk Hilton and cast you down with the Sodomites. You'll do the hardest time there is. You'll think you were fucked by a train." Homosexual violation may not mean for the warden what it does for Bogs, but this remark indicates that the warden likewise views Andy's sexuality as negotiable in the context of the prison's violent power dynamic; Andy's rape—especially in the intimidating and graphic terms the warden employs—is an immediate option for Norton in his quest to insure Andy's loyalty and submission, even if the warden prefers to have the act performed through sublimation proxy. Also clear is that while the warden may repress his own homosexual interest in Andy, it nonetheless remains an impulse never far from his mind. Indeed, when Norton introduces himself to Andy and the other fresh fish in the film adaptation, his final comment to the inmates is to "put your faith in the Lord, your ass belongs to me." Such a statement takes on added weight in light of the warden's homoerotic-encoded relationship with Andy and the looming threat to "cast [Andy] down with the Sodomites." Norton's greeting therefore contains a double meaning: while the new inmates' faith in God will remain sacrosanct, the fate of their bodies—and particularly their sexualities—now belongs to the warden.

If Andy serves as a version of the gothicized female in the film, because his gender ambiguity is much less explicit in King's novella, the warden plays the role of the classic gothic villain, replete with an obsession with Andy's sexuality, a wholly compromised moral code, and a contradictory God-Satan complex. All through the film, Norton self-referentially aligns himself with the Divine, from his opening statement where he informs the inmates they are a shared possession, owned both by the Lord and the warden, to Norton's preferred choice of biblical quotes when he first meets Andy, "I am the light of the world." Despite his early insistence that "I'll tolerate no blasphemy," Norton reveals this dictum to be yet another of his hypocritical lics, as it excludes his own blasphemous self-comparison to God the Father. The film actually presents the warden in mise-en-scènes that noticeably align Norton with Satan, rather than any kind of Godhead, a more traditional orientation appropriate to the gothic villain, although a common hubris unites all the religious allusions connected with Norton. Like archetypical gothic villains from Matthew Lewis' Ambrosio to Melville's Captain Ahab, the warden is often associated with darkness and all that symbolically implies, literally emerging from out of it or slipping back into it. His introduction to the fresh fish and his duplicitous meeting (betrayal) with Tommy are two prime illustrations where the movie's employment of lighting allows the warden to reveal his true gothic affinities. As Kermode concludes, "in apparently identifying himself as 'the light of the world,' Norton also invokes the specter of Lucifer, the bearer of light, with whom he seems rather more closely acquainted" (48). In addition, the warden is linked to modern and postmodern non-fictionalized versions of the gothic villain: first, bearing a close physical resemblance to Richard Nixon, the disgraced American president; and, later, Adolf Hitler and other fascist dictators. After Tommy's murder, when Andy refuses to continue running Norton's illegal schemes, the warden threatens in retaliation to shut down the prison library—"sealed off, brick by brick"—followed by a massive burning reminiscent of Joseph Goebbels' infamous book burning in the Berlin Opernplatz during the Nazi era: "We'll have us a little book barbecue in the yard. They'll see the flames for miles." In light of the warden's threat, it seems appropriate that Tim Robbins, the outspoken liberal activist actor who plays Andy in the film adaptation of *Shawshank*, twenty years later would chose to narrate an audio version of Ray Bradbury's *Fahrenheit 451*, a parable about state censorship, fascistic oppression, and book burning.

INSTITUTIONAL MEN

Frank Darabont has been generous in his praise of the source text upon which the movie was adapted. In a 2007 interview with Hans-Ake Lilja, for example, he credits King for producing a novella with "tremendous humanity to it that makes for the best kind of storytelling ... [King] writes deep, and with that story he was writing deeper than usual. All I had to do was translate it to the screen and not screw it up" (qtd. in Beahm 492). The degree of humility underscoring this statement belies the significance of Darabont's contributions, not merely in the act of producing a cinematic work of art but also to deepening the humanity in its "storytelling." One major reason the film version of *Shawshank* has garnered such universal critical acclaim is because of Frank Darabont's decisions, as both its director and screenwriter, regarding when and how to edit— and especially to embellish to a degree that goes beyond the merely cosmetic—King's source work. Darabont's adaptation is an excellent example of the transformative potential of art, a theme of deep importance to the film that is often overlooked by *Shawshank*'s fan base and acknowledged only in fragments by the movie's critical interpreters. Darabont chose to borrow heavily from King's effective use of dialogue in the novella, sometimes taking long verbatim excerpts directly from the text. He also pursued the novella's core plotline and its structure, "rendering that narrative into a linear piece of screenwriting" (Katz 13), by holding back the details of Andy's escape and building suspense as the audience shares with Red a concern over Andy's fate. On the other hand, Darabont produced "a linear piece of screenwriting" much less frenetic than King's novella, as the latter has a tendency to employ a scattershot chronology reflecting Red's piecemeal efforts at assembling the narrative over long gaps in time. Perhaps most important of all, because King's book is barely a hundred-pages in length, Darabont provided inclusions of supplementary material in order to enlarge the scope and depth of the narrative. This fact alone is quite unusual, especially when adapting a Stephen King book, as Hollywood screenwriters are typically forced to do the opposite: to condense and often eliminate subplots and characters of large novels to accommodate a two-hour movie (see, for example, David Cronenberg's cinematic adaptation of *The Dead Zone*). Although Darabont has said he "always tries to keep in mind what the author intended in terms of character, in terms of theme, before I invent something" (Katz 13), his "inventions" proved to be far more than ornamental, and include the choice to rely on one warden, Samuel Norton, as a much more developed character than the multiple, superficial administrators who enter and depart throughout Red's lengthy incarceration in King's book; enriching Andy's humanity by making him a reading and writing teacher in addition to King's "valuable commodity, a murderer who did tax returns better than H & R Block" (*RHSR*, 89); and the prescience to include the *Marriage of Figaro* opera scene, a triumphant addition that has become an audience favorite and is completely absent from King's novella.

King introduces the concept of "institutionalization" into his text, but this largely occurs in two brief installments. When Andy wonders if Red might wish to join him someday in Mexico, Red shares his misgivings in sentiments that likewise find their way into the Darabont screenplay: "I couldn't do it. I couldn't get along on the outside. I'm what they call an institutional man now" (*RHSR*, 71). A second reference to institutionalization is provided by the example of Brooks Hatlen, a secondary character in King's novella, who "died in a home for indigent old folks up Freeport way in 1953, and at that lasted about six months longer than I thought he would" (*RHSR*, 39). After his parole in the film, a distraught Hatlen hangs himself alone in his boarding house apartment. In King's text, Hatlen is described as a "tough old con who killed his wife and daughter" (*RHSR*, 39), whereas in Darabont's screenplay he is a kindly, grandfather-type played by the soft-spoken James Whitmore who, like the Birdman of Alcatraz, nurses a baby raven to adulthood. Since Darabont's script tends to adhere tightly to King's source work, his cinematic changes, whenever they do occur, are always noteworthy and raise important questions, as in this particular instance: why did the screenwriter-director feel compelled to enlarge and soften Brooks' character, and why does the film posit a much more gruesome conclusion to Brooks' life than that which occurs in King's novella?

Darabont's screenplay is far more concerned with exploring the concept of institutionalization as central to the movie's meaning than it is in King's book. To begin, Brooks Hatlen's history is reduced to a single page in King's text, while his purpose in the film operates as both a parallel figure for Red and a pessimistic counterpoint to Andy's embodiment of hope and redemption. Darabont has referred to the enlargement of this theme as "the thematic spine for the entire movie," and it required an expansion of Hatlen's character (Katz 13). In the film adaptation, Brooks and Andy represent two polarities of a dialectic in which Red mediates; at first he maintains an empathetic relationship with Hatlen's institutionalization

as an inevitable consequence of too much time in prison, like contract-
ing cancer because of a lifetime of working around asbestos, but gradually Red modifies that deterministic stance as he comes to identify and
embody Andy's resilient spirit of defiance and hope. Red understands
Brooks' condition on an intellectual level, garnered through years of careful observation and Red's own institutional ossification; Andy's alternative side of the dialectic, however, is presented to Red as a more emotive,
instinctual example, and unfolds through dramatically charged moments
that force Red to challenge his conviction about the inevitability of institutionalization. After fifty years of living in the universe of Shawshank, the
cinematic version of Brooks Hatlen is that of a broken man, frightened
and alone outside the stonewalls that provided him with personal security
in exchange for his independence and self-confidence. "These walls are
funny," Red posits in the film in an effort to explain why Brooks commits
suicide. "First you hate them. Then you get used to them. Enough time
passes, you get so you depend on them. They send you here for life and
that's exactly what they take." During the yard scene where Red attempts
to explain Brooks' plight to his fellow inmates, many of them disagree
strongly with his interpretation; one convict, Floyd, even tells Red, "I do
believe you are talking out of your ass." Of all the prisoners in this film,
Red is the only one selected to interpret and articulate what happened to
Brooks, and this is because Red has been incarcerated in Shawshank long
enough that he has gained insight into the effects of institutionalization
on himself. In addition, Red has likewise bought into the philosophy that
the only way to survive prison is to submit passively to it. His own, as well
as the parole rejections of others—"same old shit, different day"—have
taught him that in prison "hope is a dangerous thing"; indeed, that the
only way he's ever getting out of Shawshank alive is after the institution
has reduced him to an old man with a "long gray beard and two or three
marbles rolling around upstairs." Correspondingly, Darabont also wishes
to emphasize that Red is the convict most likely to pattern himself after
Hatlen's fated example, as Red acknowledges alongside the prison wall
during his last talk with Andy and the audience witnesses directly once
Red is paroled.

It is worth noting here that Hatlen's fear of the outside world—and his
miserable, death-in-life status after he serves his term and is set free—corresponds well with the citizens in King's various fictional towns who have
fallen prey to evil's design. Throughout the King universe, there is a possibility for anything and everything to become a prison. In an interview that

King gave to *Time Magazine*'s Gilbert Cruz, he responded to Darabont's assertion that in *The Mist* he finally broke out of the mold of only directing prison movies written by Stephen King. King disagreed, and supplied a wry correction: "It's still a story about people in prison. They're just in prison in a supermarket." Similar to the institutionalization theme in *Shawshank*, the trapped customers in *The Mist* are divided into those who try to escape and those who enfold their convictions within a single passive mindset. In King's canon, various evil incarnations share a similar mode of operation: the demand that citizens of small towns collectively relinquish moral choices, surrender independent thought, and abandon individual conscience. This is equivalent to the form institutionalization takes in *Shawshank*, posited as social paranoia "as terrible to Brooks as the Western Seas had been to superstitious fifteenth-century sailors" (*RHSR*, 39). Castle Rock, the town that is at the center of many of King's earliest novels and short stories, is nothing short of a prison, and one in which Chris Chambers desperately seeks to escape in *The Body* and its film adaptation, *Stand By Me*. The train that nearly kills the boys in this narrative as they journey to view the dead body of another child is a metaphor for the mechanical, hard-heartedness of a town that seeks to destroy its own progeny. The train never makes any effort to slow down even when the engineer sees the trapped boys on the track in front of his train. And the tracks that carry these trains (the latter always coming from the direction of the town itself) also represent the future social roles that Castle Rock has tracked for the boys who walk them. Gordie and Chris manage to escape their destinies for a while, but Vern and Teddy are doomed, succumbing to the town's deadening force of institutionalization.

From Flagg's Las Vegas empire in *The Stand*, to the Little Tall Island community in *Storm of the Century*, to the nomadic True Knot tribe that is sustained by human suffering in *Doctor Sleep*, to the adults who inhabit Derry in *IT*, or Haven in *The Tommyknockers*, King's monsters—human and supernatural—frequently manifest themselves as a monological presence, thriving in a controlled and highly ordered microcosm where individual men and women live in constant fear, and eventually surrender their independence and conscience to a collective groupthink. Institutionalization is the standardizing by-product that comes from the "discipline" Warden Norton promises to instill in Andy and his fellow fresh fish while incarcerated at Shawshank; it is a variation on the conformity that tolerates and perpetrates various societal pathologies throughout King's fictional canon. A societal-wide version of institutionalization explains why for generations

Pennywise continues to haunt freely the sewers and barrens of Derry in *IT*: the town's adult citizens live in fear of the clown's oppressive will and have intuited that their silence and capitulation is a prelude to group survival. It is this same conformist and motivated by fear mindset that freezes the collective moral will of the adults living in Little Tall Island and dooms the Anderson child and his family in *Storm of the Century*. Instead of supporting Mike Anderson and standing up for the welfare of his child, embracing the civil disobedience advocated by another New Englander, Henry David Thoreau, and his enlightened "majority of one" (21), the town sacrifices one child for the benefit of the whole in an effort to appease the diabolical Andre Linoge. Looking for a way to survive in a world dominated by complexity and change, the citizens of King's Maine towns avoid difficult and challenging decisions, surrendering their individualities for expediency. Linoge understands this human weakness and preys on it with his mantra: "Just give me what I want, and then I'll go away."

Concepts of institutionalization in King's fictional universe are frequently aligned with the corruption that attends adulthood, and this is particularly evident in his earliest novels; in *'Salem's Lot*, for example, Henry Petrie recognizes that "the eventual ossification of the imaginary faculties ... is called adulthood" (373). By relinquishing these imaginative faculties, the population of the Lot becomes a metaphor for the larger, numbed population of post-Viet Nam, post-Watergate America. The adults who inhabit the Lot embody many of the same traits identifiable with institutionalization as it is defined in *Shawshank*: they capitulate easily to fear, are rendered immobile, and are incapable of exerting individual moral agency. As they unwittingly collude with the revenants that take over their town, King makes an elaborate point in each of the four subsections entitled "The Lot" to show the reader that the town was already (spiritually) undead even before vampires arrived to provide its denizens with the additional burden of nocturnal hunger. In Stoker's novel, Dracula chooses young beautiful women as prey because he knows the potency of their vampiric sexuality is an effective tool to corrupt men in Victorian culture; in *'Salem's Lot*, on the other hand, the chief vampire Barlow is not interested in claiming beautiful women or even women at all. Nor is he interested in heightening the sexualities of his victims; his focus is on completing the process of turning the entire town into a collective society of mindless zombies that will serve his will, regardless if they are men, women, ugly, sexual or not. Thus, the Lot suffers from a group malaise similar to what produces institutionalization in *Shawshank*, and Barlow chooses the place because it embodies his design. As he acknowledges in a rare moment of candor while reflecting on the reasons for coming to the Lot: "I am from many lands; but to me this country ... this town ... seems full of foreigners. The folk here are still rich and full-blooded, folk who are stuffed with the aggression and darkness so necessary ..." (*SL*, 245–6).

Less than two years after the publication of *Lot*, King makes an even more direct allusion to institutionalization in *The Shining* that anticipates the more specific use of the concept in *Shawshank*. The main protagonist from an early short story that Jack Torrance published, Paul "Monkey" DeLong, a child molester on the verge of committing suicide, is incarcerated in a psychiatric hospital. In this tale-within-a-tale, Monkey recognizes the danger inherent in institutionalization: "the longer a man is in an institution the more he comes to need that closed environment, like a junkie with his smack" (*Shining*, 260). This reference is relevant not only to Monkey DeLong's condition; it speaks as well to Jack Torrance himself who is also trapped within a "closed environment" at the Overlook Hotel. Although Torrance fails to appreciate the metatextual connection he shares with DeLong, Jack's deepening involvement with the ghosts at the Overlook produces a corresponding madness in him that crosses over into self-destruction, implying that over time institutionalization engenders a form of madness by narrowing the individual's range of physical and psychic freedom and independence.

The deadening consequences of institutionalization that Brooks exhibits are paralleled in the nonfictional misery of convicted felons who have served their term and seek to rejoin society. Institutionalization is not only dangerous because it reifies a detrimental groupthink but also because the longer the individual remains incarcerated, the harder it is for him to rejoin the outside society. To gain social reintegration, if we can even make use of such a misleading term, requires American ex-convicts to overcome the stigma of felonious conviction: the difficulty of finding housing, much less a job; the inability to collect food stamps; to attain licenses for a variety of professions; access to education and health benefits; and the forfeiture of their ability to vote or serve on a jury. As Michelle Alexander points out, "Once a person is labeled a felon, he or she is ushered into a parallel universe in which discrimination, stigma, and exclusion are perfectly legal ... People who have been convicted of felonies almost never truly reenter the society they inhabited prior to their conviction" (94, 186). King demonstrates his awareness of this perfectly legal prejudicial status when he posits that if Brooks, the former Shawshank librarian, "went to the Kittery library and asked for a job, they wouldn't even give him a library card" (*RHSR*, 39). As a citizen of this American undercaste, i.e., the felony record, even Andy, a highly educated bank vice-president, would have difficulty finding employment—and certainly never again as a banker—were he ever paroled from Shawshank.

For Brooks, the outside world is scary and unpredictable; the inside world of the prison, although brutal and oppressive, is at least familiar and comprehensible, a place where, as Red points out, Brooks was "an educated man," a "someone." Outside of Shawshank, Brooks describes being overwhelmed by the social changes that have occurred during his incarceration. The film sympathetically details Brooks' frightening new world where automobiles chase him back to the sidewalk; the grocery manager for whom he works treats him with condescending scorn; a woman customer at the store criticizes him in third person, as if he were not present. Brooks is an old man, in his late seventies at least, yet he is forced to work a menial job as a grocery checkout bagger, a job typically handled by adolescent boys. Instead of retiring to a family that includes grandchildren and a pension, Brooks is a figure of total isolation and alienation. Lost in a vast hinterland of apathy, a listless limbo in which even his landlady looks gruffly inconvenienced when she introduces Brooks to his squalid little apartment, Hatlen performs an empty routine where his daytime fantasies about killing the manager of the market where he works are complemented by restive nightmares and acrophobia. Trapped in a spiritual wilderness where he is profoundly self-aware of being out of place and out of time, Hatlen's outlook in every sense is undeniably doleful, when it is not actively baleful. It is clear that Brooks has merely exchanged one prison for another, and his social prison is the worst of the two. His plaintive carving "Brooks was here" on the wooden banister that eventually supports his weight within a hangman's noose is a desperate plea for identity recognition—evidence that a man actually lived in the Brewster boarding house, and not just a ghost. At least while incarcerated in Shawshank, Brooks was friends with some of the other convicts and was never treated condescendingly. Upon his release, even his pet bird, Jake, abandons Brooks; the ubiquitous pigeons that crowd around the old man sitting alone on the park bench only deepen his despair and loss. What is perhaps most relevant about Brooks' tragedy is the truth inherent in Red's summary comment: "He should have died in here [Shawshank]," because an old, institutionalized man living outside the walls of a prison facility is as vulnerable as a newborn child.

Darabont provides us with this detailed portrait of Brooks Hatlen in an effort to show that Red's fate was destined to parallel Brooks' had the black man not become another of Andy's students, even though Red never competes for a high school equivalency diploma. The fact that Red is paroled into Brooks' job at the grocery store and into his very apartment may appear a little heavy-handed, but it is meant to underscore the doomed parallels between the two men. After his parole, when Red gazes into a pawnshop window, the camera lingers over a row of pistols before it sweeps to reveal a row of compasses on the level above, a subtle indication that at this junction in his life Red is "lost" spatially and spiritually, in desperate need of alternative bearings to counter Hatlen's journey towards self-destruction, and that "only the promise I made to Andy" keeps Red from choosing a gun instead of a compass as a means for expressing his own institutionalized despair. In two filmed sequences that Darabont eventually deleted from the movie's final cut ("*Shawshank Redemption Rare Deleted*"), Red is featured after his parole, disheveled and wandering alone, out of place in the same park where Hatlen feeds pigeons on a bench. His sense of estrangement is even greater than that of Brooks', however, highlighted as it is by Red's inability to bear the presence of actual women walking along the sidewalk beside him. Although he was denied access to women while incarcerated at Shawshank, Red's experience among them as a free man makes him feel even worse; as an inmate, women were only a recollection, fantasy, or representation from a movie. On the streets and in the park, it is their living reality that tortures him in the immediateness of their unavailability and otherness. "I forgot they were half the human race ... I find myself semi-hard most of the time," he confesses. He is also surrounded by young people, all of them white, in the park smoking pot and playing rock music during the "summer of love" (circa 1969), although Red feels so alienated from them he prefers to call it the "summer of lunacy."

In an even more graphic deleted sequence, Red undergoes a full-fledged panic attack inside the grocery store where he works. Unaccustomed to being around children, one white child shoots him repeatedly with his toy gun while his parents stare aggressively at Red as he hustles to bag their groceries. The scene is shot to emphasize Red being inundated by customers and their groceries, as a checkout conveyor belt keeps throwing items at him to bag, and the sounds of frenetic activity overwhelm him. Finally, out of breath and in obvious distress, Red flees into the protective isolation of the store's bathroom, accompanied by the soundtrack of his accelerated heartbeat and a distant, reverberating interior command to return to his cellblock issued surrealistically from the Shawshank PA system. The scene is extraordinarily effective as Red finds himself again surrounded by whiteness (in both the faces of all the grocery store customers as well as the walls and toilet inside the bathroom stall) and confined within a space (the bathroom) that resembles closely, as it is filmed from above, a solitary confinement cell. Both these scenes were constructed to dramatize Red's degree of institutionalization and his proximity to a nervous breakdown; his own post-parole estrangement proves to be even more dysfunctional than Hatlen's because it emphasizes Red's sexual and racial separation from the white cultural mainstream. While Darabont made a difficult (especially true for the powerful breakdown sequence inside the grocery store) but judicious decision to expunge both scenes from *Shawshank*, it is clear he wished to illustrate the profundity of Red's disaffection, and that his fate was destined either to result in suicide, like Brooks', or a criminal action that would have put him back in prison. Darabont's own justification for deleting them is the result of an understandable desire to maintain the audience's focus on Red and Andy's reunion, but it still must have presented a hard editorial choice because these scenes are almost too powerful to lose.

Darabont's screenplay forges a bond between Andy's love of music and the integrity of his personal identity that is not present in King's text. His appreciation of Mozart's opera is meant to contrast with the deadening silence that typically characterizes the atmospheres of Brooks' apartment, the prison exercise yard, and the interior of the Shawshank cellblock. In the film, we view Heywood listening contentedly to a Hank Williams record in the prison library, an indication that Andy has brought more than just books into "the best prison library in New England." Andy is frequently associated with music during his time at Shawshank: Red links him to the "exotic birds" of *The Marriage of Figaro* scene and, later, continues the metaphor by linking Andy to "some birds aren't meant to be caged, their feathers are just too bright." As we will consider later in this chapter, Dufresne is also linked to Rita Hayworth in the scene from *Gilda* where her husband compares her to a singing canary; lastly, Andy purchases a harmonica for Red as a reminder that music can take us to "places not made of stone. Places that they can't touch. That's yours."

Shawshank's close correlation among birds and music and images of freedom is strongly reminiscent of Emily Dickinson's poem 613, "They shut me up in Prose," which describes her rejection of those who would have her write prose instead of poetry; in the nineteenth century, the writing of poetry would have been considered a genre more worthy of serious male writers than women. Dickinson's poem is full of images of imprisonment associated with producing prose, like being shut up in closet when a girl so that the poet would be kept "still." The effort to silence the poet in the speaker is underscored by the startling comparison where Dickinson mocks the attempt to silence her as if trying to impound a bird in prison. Like Andy, Dickinson refuses to stay "shut up" in a silent closet of convention imposed by others. The true singer breaks out of jail, as does the poet/bird by an effort of will that abolishes her prosaic captivity and sets her free to sing. Furthermore, the prose versus poetry theme in Dickinson possesses larger and more general implications associated with being a woman struggling within the restrictions of a masculine world, just as Andy's love of music and his association with birds includes deeper, more resonate implications, which are likewise relevant to a rebellion against traditional gender roles. Andy recognizes music is more than just beautiful sound, an expression of human emotion and communication, and a stimulus to the imagination. Like all the arts, it can also be a subversive expression of personal individuality, something inside "they can't take away from you." As Dickinson's "treasonous" bird refuses to remain "lodged … in the Pound" (a *Shawshank* viewer might also be reminded here of Hatlen's bird, Jake), music cannot be confined behind walls or pushed into cages; the quest for human liberation is neither easily regulated nor suppressed. In *Shawshank*, the reason Red associates Andy with "exotic birds" is because they are as unrestrained as music, traveling beyond the walls of Shawshank and back out into the world. Even the red convertible Red envisions Andy driving into Mexico after the latter's escape from Shawshank in 1967 is a Pontiac GTO *Phoenix*. A small image of another "exotic bird" with its wings outstretched, the phoenix that this particular model was named after in 1967—mythological symbol of rebirth and resurrection—can be seen riding along with Andy, stenciled in silver leaf on the back of the car's trunk. There is even a moment near the end of this imaginary sequence where the camera appears to launch out over car and road, providing the audience with a glorious bird's eye view of the Pacific. That Red's speculation puts Andy riding in a red Phoenix immediately following Dufresne's emergence from his symbolic burial within and beneath the prison and subsequent rebirth when he drops down into the redemptive waters of a creek and rainstorm is yet another example of the degree of detailing and rich thematic resonance on display in this film.

In choosing the *"Canzonetta sull' aria? Che soave zeffiretto"* ("The Letter Duet") from Act 3 of Mozart's *The Marriage of Figaro* (1786) to play to the population at Shawshank Prison, Dufresne knows exactly what he is doing. He knows what the duet is about, and he selects it deliberately from all the other recordings available in the shipment box. Like the work songs sung by black slaves in the antebellum South, the aria is an example of Andy's identification with music as a means of expressing disobedience towards the oppressive, only Andy's empathetic response crosses gender lines instead of race. The Mozart duet concerns the troubles women share in a world dominated by men—and it is on this level that Andy, an inmate in a male institution, establishes a metatextual connection with women struggling against male authority. The sopranos featured in the aria are a chambermaid (Susanna) and her mistress (Countess Almaviva). They are plotting a scheme to chasten as well as win back the amorous attention of Count Almaviva, the countess' wayward husband who has lost sexual interest in his wife and is currently bent on seducing the younger and more comely Susanna. Just prior to her duet with Susanna in Act 3, the countess laments her husband's duplicitous behavior: "To what a humiliating state I am reduced / by a cruel husband who, after marrying me, / with an unheard mixture / of infidelity, jealousy and scorn, / first loved, then offended, / and at last betrayed me / now makes me turn to one of my servants for help" (*Marriage*, 3.8).

The duet between the Countess Almaviva and her servant creates an obvious self-referential narrative that mirrors Andy's own situation: a spouse's sexual betrayal. But the language of the aria goes on further to outline a plan of action that empowers the women by altering a condition that is frustrating to them both. In this way, their scheming is an act of defiance against the patriarchal authority of the count and the ancient privileged custom of *le droit du seigneur*, whereby a lord possesses the right to sleep with any of his domestics. The rebellious plot that the two women hatch in song must be viewed as paralleling and possibly even inspiring Dufresne's decision to subvert the warden's power by first refusing to "turn it [the music] off," and then increasing the volume of the recording while smiling and staring directly into the warden's face with a gleam of defiance and delight in his eyes. It is not enough that Andy has challenged the prison's hegemony by commandeering the warden's office and public address system and by locking one of the Shawshank guards in the men's room as well as the door to the warden's outer office; he also betrays the trust the prison authorities have placed in him by granting him special access to all these things. He essentially usurps complete control, albeit briefly, over the entire prison facility—the warden's office, the men's room, the woodshop, the infirmary, and the yard itself. Although the warden and everyone else in the prison are oblivious to its meaning, the choice of playing this particular Mozart aria emboldens Andy to the point where he is able to pronounce his two weeks in the hole "the easiest time I've ever done." In response to the taunting his fellow convicts provide this statement, Andy's assertion that he had "Mr. Mozart to keep me company" is as much a comment about savoring his defiance in the face of the warden—as Susanna and the countess exemplify in their duet at odds with the will of the count—as it is recollecting the emotive beauty of Mozart's music. There are several elements that have made this one of the most memorable scenes in the movie. There is, of course, the sheer beauty of the sound itself that manages to shock the audience nearly as much as it does the inmates and guards. But as we've noted above, it is also that Act 3 of *Figaro* is about undermining patriarchal authority; the subtext beneath the lilting sweetness these sopranos create in song contains a serious message, perhaps even a desperate one, that tends to undercut the sweetness of the duet and to which Andy can relate. It's difficult to ascertain whether Andy's great joy in this moment is more inspired by the beauty he has unleashed into the prison and shared with men who are out of touch with both beauty and acts of sharing or his own awareness that he, Andy, finds himself in a position where he is able to join with the countess and Susanna in extending the subversive collusion they initiated.

Unlimited access to music, literature, and cinema are some of the cultural privileges missing from the lives of the incarcerated in Shawshank. The prisoners are incapable of appreciating their importance because none of them, other than Andy, has been trained and encouraged to recognize their value. When Red informs us in voiceover narration that he is a "man who can get things" past the guards and into Shawshank, "a bottle of whiskey … chewing gum, reefer—if that's your thing," none of his customers apparently ever asks for a record player, much less a boxed set of Mozart operas. After Andy plays the aria from *The Marriage of Figaro* and does his time in the hole, Heywood teases him with the remark, "You couldn't play something good, like Hank Williams," certainly intended as a comic throwaway line, but it also serves as an indication of the limits of Heywood's own musical appreciation. The fact that no one in Shawshank has any idea "what those two Italian ladies were singing about," and nor do they ever seek to find out, signals the collective level of institutionalization that has numbed the Shawshank population. Even the guards reflect this insensitivity insofar as they appear to believe the inmates do not "deserve" art; when Andy receives the donated books and records that are delivered to the warden's office, Captain Hadley tells Andy to "get all this cleared out of here before the warden gets back," and makes a dour face that projects to the audience his personal attitude towards music and literature: mere clutter. Meanwhile, the other guard in the warden's office, while clearly impressed by Andy's accomplishment, admires more the latter's perseverance at extracting monies from a parsimonious state bureaucracy rather than the actual music and books his determination accrues, as the guard then retreats to the men's room stall to read not one of the new books just delivered, but a *Jughead* comic book. In the only scene in which Andy and Red argue in the film, Red reveals his own unconscious degree of capitulation to institutionalization in the remark that he gave up playing the harmonica when he went to prison because he "lost interest in it. Didn't make much sense in here." Andy counters that in jail is where music "makes the most sense" because it represents freedom. The most important legacy that Andy imparts to Red is the hope stimulated and revivified in acts of defiance—in art as well as in daily life—that ultimately affirms individual human agency in the face of deadening forces, such as institutionalization. As Daniel Chua affirms: "Freedom hibernates in the eternal guise of beauty; it is hope in a pod, the promise of freedom, the very song of the self ... Once inside, the music is indestructible, because its beauty articulates the timeless dimension of the self, which is our ineradicable identity" (348). Darabont puts enormous faith in the power of art to rescue us from the mind-numbing monotony of life, and especially life in prison. In *Shawshank*, this is a faith more audibly and visually represented than verbalized, more mysterious and mystical than expressive. Beauty has the potential to save the world, or at least the soul of the individual who keeps himself open to it (Fig. 3.1).

When Andy plays the Mozart over the prison yard, it is projected over an old and corroded PA system that earlier in the film (when Andy and the other fresh fish enter the prison building for the first time) delivers background processing orders about the movement of prisoners from the exercise yard back to their cells. This is the primary function of the loudspeakers mounted outside in the yard: a tool for managing the movement of male bodies. As such, the orders that are issued from the megaphone become, for prisoners and guards alike, part of the background drone of daily life in the yard. But when the convicts hear the Mozart played over

Fig. 3.1   Under the spell of Mozart via the Shawshank PA system

this same speaker system, they are unable to move. Red would have us believe that their collective silence and suspension of bodily motion are visual representations of their response to beauty and a reminder of freedom. His explanation implies that institutionalization takes such things away from us; the loss of beauty, whether highbrow or lowbrow, is in itself a kind of punishment. But another reason the inmates appear stunned is also the same reason why Warden Norton is so infuriated by Andy's bold musical interlude: Andy has subverted a major tool used to facilitate the operation of Shawshank's stultifying bureaucracy. He has brazenly dared to introduce song into the prison's drab and silent processing; he has replaced the deadening bureaucratic monotone of middle-aged male voices issuing robotic institutional commands with the glorious lilt of feminine singing beautiful enough to inspire even a poetical response from Red: "Those voices soared, higher and farther than anybody in a great place dares to dream. For the briefest of moments every man at Shawshank felt free." Mirroring the introduction of the feminine into the realm of the prison yard that is clearly identified as masculine space, this violation also originates within the inner sanctum of the warden's office and therefore becomes all the more egregious since Andy is a feminine representation cut loose and undermining an exclusively masculine domain. It is a moment that concludes in Hadley breaking through the glass portion of Norton's door, employing the phallic baton that has already been used to murder "Fat Ass" to reassert patriarchal compliance through force. As he taps the baton on the glass door window, the guard's line uttered with pathological glee, "You're mine now, Dufresne," becomes yet another veiled homosexual threat imposed on Andy to punish his waywardness. At the same time, the conclusion of this scene subtly foreshadows the warden's exit from the film when the police, once more because of Norton's inability to control Andy, will breach another of his locked office doors. "Truth lives on in the illusion of art," Schiller predicted, "preparing the shape of things to come" (57).

Because cinema requires the visualization of events and personalities, Andy and Red share the film version of Shawshank equally, while King's novel, because it is a first-person narrative conceived and composed by Red alone, belongs more to Red, "it's all about me, every damned word of it" (*RHSR*, 100). Moreover, the film, although voiceover narrated by Red throughout, is divided between these two characters; roughly, the first half is Andy's story, while Red's tale assumes prominence after Andy's escape from the prison. But in both film and novella, Andy's influence on Red is impossible to overestimate, and it grows even more powerful after the two men are separated. As Red acknowledges in the novella: "Andy was ... that part of me that will rejoice no matter how old and broken and scared the rest of me is. I guess it's just that Andy had more of that part of me, and used it better" (*RHSR*, 100). Perhaps the most important asset that Dufresne brings to Red is the enduring power of hope; Andy refuses to sacrifice his dignity or the dignities of other prisoners in the face of a penal system that demeans and dehumanizes the incarcerated, turning men into numbers who must "ask permission before taking a piss."

A brief but powerful moment in *Shawshank* occurs late in the film, sometime after Andy has tunneled out of the prison. Red is pictured alone in OSR's pauper's cemetery located in the back of the prison on his hands and knees tending the graves. It is one of the only times in the movie when Red is viewed alone outside the confines of his cell, and as he works his hands into the soil above the graves, he reveals in a voiceover the personal loneliness that has filled the void since his friend's abrupt departure. While Red acknowledges that "some birds aren't meant to be caged," by way of justifying the honest "rejoicing" he feels over Andy's successful bid for freedom, Red also recognizes his own loss, summed up in the heartfelt admission, "I guess I just miss my friend." One gets the sense that Red has experienced such private sentiments on more than just this one occasion. This moment of tender vulnerability, however, is more than just an indulgence of self-pity, especially given the fact that Red is thinking them while in a graveyard. The scene becomes a *momento mori*, a reminder to both Red and the audience that life is fleeting, transient, and that we all must, like Andy, confront choices that allow us to make the most of what time is left. Red's musings also occur in a pauper's graveyard filled with anonymous graves of anonymous men, literally demarcated by OSR prisoner numbers without names, as discussed elsewhere in this book. Although most likely unaware of the symbolic import that he inspires, Red is, in a way, tending the specter of his own grave in this somber soliloquy; like Hamlet, addressing pensively the skull of his deceased friend, Yorick, Red also mourns the metaphoric "death" of Andy in the wake of his departure. At this point, there is no certainty that Red will ever get paroled, that Andy is alive and still living in Mexico, or that the two friends will ever see each other again. This brief scene actually initiates a sequence that permits the audience insight into Red's suffering—certainly over the "passing" of his best friend, but, even more important, the cumulative impact that Andy's memory creates in reshaping Red's personality and challenging his defeatist tenet that "hope is a dangerous thing" capable of producing only disappointment. The pauper's graveyard scene is yet another reminder where the viewer—if not yet Red himself—visualizes a core concept in the film that human agency carries with it the burden of choice: Red can choose to become, like Hatlen, another corpse without a name; or he can choose to transcend his own history of institutionalization by identifying himself as a beautiful bird, that, like Dufresne, refuses to be defined by the cage in which he resides (Fig. 3.2).

It takes Red years to comprehend the full ramifications of his own phrase "some birds aren't meant to be caged": the inherent dignity of the individual, the transformative potential of transgressive art as an inspiration to human action, the implication of civil disobedience and its relationship to freedom, and Andy's attitude as a model of defiance worthy of emulation. But the fact that Red emits this phrase and that it belongs to his verbal lexicon implies at least his own subconscious identification with cageless birds. Red's "education" at Shawshank remains incomplete until after Andy escapes and the black man has the opportunity to muse—as he does so poignantly in the paupers' graveyard and at the supper table listening to other convicts reminiscence about Andy—on what his friend has left behind as a legacy. Just as Andy experiences a kind of rehabilitation in his willingness to accept blame for his wife's death and to open his

Fig. 3.2 Nameless graves in the shadows of OSR's prison graveyard

personality emotionally, Red also incurs his own degree of change via his capacity to learn from Andy's behavior and embrace it as a model for his own. The first two times Red faces the respective state parole boards considering his case, he tries to impress them with his appearance as a submissive product of institutionalization: humbly holding his inmate cap in his hands, averting his eyes downward, addressing the two all-white, all-male boards with self-depreciating politeness, and assuring its members that he is "no longer a danger to society," that he's a "changed man—no threat to society here." In the film, his simpering posture is racially encoded; it confronts the unspoken historical politics of race and incarceration as Red seeks to convince each of the two white boards that his time in prison has rehabilitated him into a "docile Negro," displacing the violent black man who was sent to Shawshank as a murderer. Over the years and for reasons the movie and novel do not explain (probably because the board senses Red's lack of authenticity), this cant posturing has netted him only rejections.

His meeting with the third parole board, however, occurs in the scene that immediately follows Red's musings in the pauper's graveyard. This is significant because it implies that Andy's spirit is hovering over Red as he confronts this last board. For in this scene, Red transforms into himself into a version of Andy, perhaps recalling the soprano duet from *Figaro* as well: defiant in answering the board's officious questions, calling one of its members "sonny," mocking their pseudo-empathetic understanding of rehabilitation as just "a made-up word—a politician's word" that matters only because it insures board members will continue to have jobs. Indeed, to whatever extent the filmgoer recognizes the "rehabilitation" Red and Andy undergo individually, it has nothing to do with Shawshank as an institution; the two men change because of each other and in spite of the system in which they are incarcerated. Red is shown clearly unafraid of another processed rejection; he even tells the board to "stamp your form … I don't give a shit," linking the form to Shawshank's PA system: just another example of the petty penal bureaucracy that remains disconnected from Red's real self or worth as a human being (Darabont 109–10).

The Red we see face the last parole board is for the first time in the film truly "a changed man" who experiences his own moment of heartfelt introspection paralleling Andy's earlier acceptance of his role in the death of his wife. Red confesses that he wishes he could reencounter his younger self, the "young, stupid kid who committed that terrible crime," in order to "talk some sense into him," supply him with aged counsel and suggestions for alternative behavior. Red didn't acquire these values sitting alone in his Shawshank cell; he learned them from his exposure to Andy. And now Red admits he wishes he had the opportunity to follow in Andy's footsteps as a teacher—by educating a less consciously aware younger self that is now, unfortunately, "long gone." This is not the perspective of an institutionalized man who would be more likely to emphasize only the despair of time's tragic waste, "this old man is all that's left." What Red imparts here, contrastingly, is a revivification of Andy's "hope"—that an older, wiser version of Red understands more about life than he did earlier—and that, if it were only possible, would go back and change the history that resulted in so many wasted years at Shawshank. Just as important, it signals that Red is now ready to view himself differently from the man who faced his two earlier parole boards by spending what remains of his life engaged in meaningful, and, as this scene illustrates, honest action. That this action is not ideally representative of the kind of behavior that a typical parole board is looking to uncover in a repentant murderer is one of the ironies of Red finally being granted parole. Perhaps the fact that the scene takes place in the late 1960s—with a woman finally present on the five-person board—is meant to signal the emergence of penal reform more reflective of the changes that were taking place at the time in American society, more responsive to inmate honesty and introspective reckoning. As one of the few blacks residing in Maine's Shawshank Prison, that final parole board decision may also be reflective of white guilt, a consequence of the tumultuous racial conflict that emerged in the early sixties and forced America into a thorough reconsideration of its racial politics. The board's affirmation may likely reflect both these societal influences operating simultaneously.

One of the most quietly satisfying, but seldom commented upon aspects of the film adaptation of *Shawshank* is that Andy's influence on Red assumes its place gradually and in stages over time, as best illustrated in the montage of scenes just examined. Another of these small, personally transformative moments occurs once Red is finally paroled: he does not immediately travel to Buxton to dig up the mysterious "something" Andy has left for him buried in the meadow. Instead, he struggles, like Brooks, sleeping alone in the same dreary boarding house and working the same mindless grocery store job, spending enough time out of jail to recognize that he's "living in fear" and "no way [he's] going to make it on the outside." Until he is "guilty a second time in [his] life of committing another crime: parole violation," embracing his status as an outlaw "border crosser" in breaking out of the United States, only then does he complete his identification with Andy. Charles Nero interprets this final act of rebellion as the culmination their friendship because Red has joined Andy as an escaped felon wanted by the authorities: "Neither Red nor Andy can exist in the 'real world.' *The Shawshank Redemption*'s ending represents a utopian world where the bonding of Andy and Red is possible" (55). As we have seen, all through the film Andy conceives of himself as a boundary crosser, a man who willfully violates rules and takes risks. For Andy stands in opposition to whatever forces submit, constrain, mortify, and deny. His alienation from Shawshank is because he recognizes it as an institution that under the ruse of rehabilitation actually seeks to limit man's potential and creativity by accentuating restraint in the name of a moral code, which is in itself evil for it distorts man's true potential. Despite spending vast amounts of time in solitary confinement as a consequence of his deliberately flagrant rejections of authority, Andy is a man who exists beyond the realm of discipline and punishment, making him a dangerous adversary, as the warden fails to appreciate until it is too late. But fulfilling Andy's request for Red to visit an oak tree in Buxton is one thing, continuing all the way across the border as a "free man" into Mexico is quite another.

Throughout the film, there are maps of the United States pictured in the backgrounds of several mise-en-scènes. There is a large, tan and green geographical relief map hanging on a wall of the prison library that is partially visible in the scene when Red and Andy are stacking books together and Andy reveals the existence of Randall Stevens, and it is again pictured in a complete frontal view directly behind Tommy just before he walks away frustrated after his GED examination. Later, Red uses a map of Texas to find where Fort Hancock is located, the place where Andy crossed the border over into Mexico. And painted on the right window of the Trailways Bus station where Red purchases his own ticket to Fort Hancock is an outline of the United States painted in black with red lettering. Each of these maps pictures only the United States. The country of Mexico is not identified on any of them because Zihutanejo is meant to suggest a place that resides in the imagination, "a pipe dream ... way down there," and therefore must be rendered invisible until Red and Andy finally reconnect on Mexican beachfront. Seemingly inspired by a passage in King's text where Red is haunted and taunted by "cruel" images of "blue water and white beaches" (*RHSR*, 83), Red informs us in the film that one of his last hopes is that the Pacific is "as blue as it has been *in my dreams.*" But what is perhaps most important about the presence of these various maps is that they form nascent reference points for illustrating Red's expanding scope of spatial consciousness, an evolving break from institutionalization in his willingness to follow Andy's metaphorical and literal path. Bureaucratic institutions such as Shawshank Prison are dedicated to the perpetuation of habit. Habit is what leads Brooks Hatlen to be terrified of change, Red to fear hope as a dangerous thing. But the chief means of defeating or circumventing habit is the imagination, the development of consciousness. Over time, without cultivation of imagination or consciousness, it is too easy for the senses, for all their merits, to become dulled, beguiled into mere habit. Something else is needed: a sixth sense, critical and subversive, to rise above the numbed five. The sixth sense is the imagination.

Red admires Andy and he respects him. Their prison friendship blossoms into such a unique relationship that causes even the warden to acknowledge (with the same degree of disdain that he reserves for Andy's Hollywood poster women and the Mozart aria played inside his office) that the two men are "thick as thieves." But the question that drives the final third of *Shawshank* is how much does Red actually *love* Andy? Perhaps the reason Red is sent to the same rock wall in Buxton that holds so much meaning for Andy's marriage is that it is a test for both men. In bringing Red to this sacred place where Andy made love to his wife and asked her to marry him, Andy demonstrates that he is again willing to trust, to open himself to Red in a way that he never could to his wife, and to risk failure once again. Although his marriage may have ended tragically, Dufresne hopes that his relationship with Red will not; although he failed to appreciate love when he had it before, Andy hopes he has now learned how to communicate its value to Red. In Darabont's film, after receiving parole and his subsequent awareness that "no way I'm going to make it on the outside," Red's future depends on his continued effort to break free from the habits which have defined his life both in and out of Shawshank, and to identify with Andy. That's why when he arrives at the Buxton meadow a harmonica begins to play softly in the background. These non-diegetic notes are important because they signal the ultimate triumph of music and Andy's imaginative worldview over Red and Brooks' suicidal impulses. When Andy first gifts Red with a harmonica as a "parole-rejection present," Red refuses to use it; later, he plays it only once, and then it is only a single note that he whispers into it sitting alone in the darkness of his cell. At this point in his life, Red is not yet ready to appreciate fully the symbolism of what Andy offers him; Red is still operating under the belief that "hope is a dangerous thing" and "has no place on the inside" of Shawshank. He lives under the sign of slavery that William Blake laments in his poem "London": Red's "mind-forg'd manacles" (112) deafen him to the power of music and, more importantly, to all that it symbolizes in this film, threatening to make him "like Brooks," as Andy warns at the conclusion of their argument in the mess hall scene. Once he follows Andy to the Buxton meadow, however, Red's decision "to get busy living" (the last word he speaks in both the film and novella is "*hope*")—and his rejection of Brooks' despair—is accompanied with a steady harmonica score as Red crosses the meadow and makes his way to Andy's oak tree. Mary Hunter has noted "accompanying his decision to look for the buried money that will enable him to join Andy in Mexico, the background score accompanies this revival of hope with a snatch of harmonica music" (105). It is, however, more than just a "snatch" of harmonica music that fills this scene, and Hunter fails to develop the connections between this score and Red's earlier unwillingness to acknowledge the value of music/ hope. The background harmonica music is deliberately pensive and soft, like the summertime ambiance of the meadow itself (which, significantly, is also filled with constant birdsong), inspiring a quiet self-reflection and determination that occasions the final stage in propelling Red out from under Brooks' gray shadow and southward towards the spectacular blues of the Pacific, and Andy himself.

Some first-time viewers of the film share the initial speculation that Andy's intentionally vague insistence about the "something" buried in the Buxton hayfield might be leading Red to the gun that was never fired and has been missing since the beginning of the movie. But this of course proves to be a red herring that ignores the trajectory of the film and the development of the Andy-Red friendship bond. Instead of the gun that is suggestive of his destructive past, Andy leaves Red the materials necessary to inspire a different future: a box with a boat on its cover located beneath a black "piece of volcanic rock that has no earthly business being in a Maine hayfield," enough cash to reach Mexico, and a short letter that is the first communication Red has received from Andy since his postcard from Fort Hancock. The boat on the box anticipates the charter fishing that Andy envisions providing for his guests in Mexico, so it is appropriate that he is pictured "fixing up" just such a boat when Red arrives in the final scene of *Shawshank*. The audience is now fully alerted, in his deliberate selection from *The Marriage of Figaro* and the symbolism inherent in the starlet posters on his wall, that Andy is a master of semiotics—and also of geology. The black, volcanic rock, in a film that identifies Andy as a "rock hound" (his surname "Dufresne" is a French derivation of the word "mineralogist"), suggests the protean potential that Andy recognizes in Red, as when he cautions him not to "underestimate" himself after the black man reveals that the Pacific, a place, by the way, filled with active volcanoes, "about scares me to death something that big."

While most critics writing about *Shawshank* tend to appreciate the movie's overall quality, there is likewise a nearly uniform resentment about the film's conclusion that reunites Andy and Red on the shores of Zihuatanejo. The beach sequence was originally Castle Rock's suggestion, but the decision on whether or not to include it was left to Darabont to make; as he explains in his screenplay notes, "I was skeptical about this suggestion [but] I wasn't convinced Castle Rock was wrong" (Darabont 167). However, Kermode is convinced that it was: "That final image leaves me frustrated and irritated" (88) because it renders visibly a "picture-postcard depiction of a place which should remain both invisible and unimaginable" (86). Browning concurs, calling the "Hollywood Ending" on the beach "overly sentimental" (154), Michelle Brown feels it "resolves all the film's ambiguities and contradictions in one swoop" (62), while Kenneth

Turan likens it to "a big glob of cotton candy" (qtd. in Heidenry, par. 36). Despite the fact that the Mexican beach scene is beloved by millions of *Shawshank* fans, these critics prefer the ending of King's novella and Darabont's original screenplay: Red heading out at the start of a "long journey whose conclusion is uncertain" (*RHSR*, 101).

What each of these critics fails to consider, however, is the organic connection the beach scene maintains with the rest of the film. *Shawshank*'s conclusion is much more than just a tacked-on sentimental overindulgence. In truth, it ties together for a finishing moment many of the major tropes and symbols presented throughout the course of the film. Even more than in the novella, the film version of *Shawshank* constantly alludes to rocks and geology. Andy shapes chess pieces and other figurines out of soapstone and the other minerals Red and his friends bring to him, he is the owner of a rock hammer that he uses to tunnel he way out of prison, and Red explains Andy's urge to escape in distinct geological terms: "Oh, Andy loved Geology. I imagine it appealed to his meticulous nature ... Geology is the study of pressure and time. That's all it takes, really. Pressure and time. That, and a big goddamn poster." In a film that is obsessed with rocks, that is set primarily inside a limestone monolith, and that ends by taking one of its main characters to a stone wall where a piece of volcanic rock resides alongside it, the white sands of Zihuatanejo epitomize the ultimate breakdown of rock into its most minute form: sand crystals. Given its symbolic context throughout the film, beach sand turns out to be the final distillation of Andy's efforts to "tote his wall out into the exercise yard, a handful at a time," to crumble the physical stonewall that has entombed him for nineteen years, and to set himself free. The satisfactory sense of narrative completion embodied in the beach reunion also signals Red's journey out of institutionalized fear; his arrival there fulfills his acceptance of Andy's written challenge to "go a little further," to take a leap of faith, to trust his imagination, and to overcome his fear of freedom. If a serviceable definition of institutionalization can be said to be the condition of being "walled off," restricted in a universe defined by hardened bureaucratic rules and unable to adjust to life in society among people who are not criminals, the ending's wide-open stretch of ocean and beach rimmed with bright green grass invokes a final break from Brooks' narrowly deterministic path, continuing Red's movement back into the natural world that began with his trip to the Buxton hayfield.[5]

Andy's beach stands in ultimate contrast to years of incarceration in stone. In contrast to the suffocating, colorless gothic dungeon of

Shawshank, the final scene presents a vision of limitless boundaries: sea, sky, horizon, and dazzling color—particularly liberating shades of blue and aquamarine. "By ending with that final image," Darabont notes, "we've brought the viewer on a full journey that begins in tight claustrophobia defined by walls and concludes where the horizon is limitless … from colorlessness to a place where only color exists, from physical and spiritual imprisonment to total freedom" (Darabont 158). Their embrace on the Mexican shoreline also symbolizes the culmination of Red's and Andy's "border crossings"—the border they've crossed is as ethical as it is geographical. Mexico is more than just another country; it's another dimension, a heaven that remains as far away as possible from the warden's bifurcated distortions of Christianity. Their respective journeys reach a common conclusion: from a dark, enclosed, man-made stone-fortified place—to a natural environment of wind, light, water, and actual birds. Just before Red and Andy embrace on the beach to conclude the film, Red shares the mise-en-scène with a flying gull swooping down just above his head, a perhaps coincidental last reference to the association Red's narration makes elsewhere between Andy and birds. In addition to the select posters of the famous "fantasy girls" that adorn his cell, Andy's wall art also contains several photographs of beaches, ocean views, and boats sailing on water (the opposite of a landlocked prison). Upon reflection, at least after the initial viewing, the attentive viewer may indeed wonder if Andy's sustaining fantasies about spending the remainder of his life in "a warm place" are at least as well represented in the nature and boating photographs with which he surrounds himself as they are in what is literally secreted behind the posters of the Hollywood starlets.

During the last conversation Andy shares with Red in the film and novella, he supplies his friend with directions for finding "something I want you to have"; that "something" is located, as Andy instructs, "along the base of a rock wall, right out of a Robert Frost poem" (*RHSR*, 98). In an email exchange with Stephen King, we asked which specific Frost poem(s) Andy had in mind when formulating these directions. King's response alluded to only one: the 1914 poem "Mending Wall" (King, "Question"). In Frost's famous work, two neighbors "meet to walk the line" replacing the individual stones, "some are loaves and some so nearly balls," in a rock wall that demarcates the legal perimeters of their respective properties. Each year, winter frost breaks apart sections of the wall, and it must be repaired in the spring in order to "set the wall between us once again." As is often the case in Frost's poetry, which is why we wondered if King might have had additional poems in mind to enlarge Andy's reference, physical nature often inspires metaphorical ruminations on man's spiritual condition. "Birches" and "After Apple-Picking," for example, inspire meditations on human destiny, mortality, and the afterlife. As Marion Montgomery has noticed, "Whenever Frost talks directly of natural objects or creatures, we feel that he is really looking at man out of the corner of his eye and speaking to him out of the corner of his mouth" (141). "Mending Wall" likewise is a poem that is about more than two neighbors repairing winter's damage to their mutually shared rock wall; it is also about the walls people erect to separate themselves from others. The narrator of the poem understands that this is an opportunity for the two men to work with one another rebuilding and fortifying the wall after a long New England winter of separation—he is even the one who "lets [his] neighbor know beyond the hill" when it is time to reconstruct the wall. At the same time, the speaker cannot help but wish to tear down the metaphorical walls that isolate men from one another, duly symbolized in the rock wall. However, his line "Something there is that doesn't love a wall, / That wants it down" is met by the other man's firm counterpoint: "Good fences make good neighbors." The *why* of the wall is finally the sole province of the narrator, who plays with ideas in his own head because his neighbor has withdrawn too deeply into himself to risk questioning the habitual behavioral codes that have sustained him (and his father before him and presumably generations particular to a New England clannish regionalism before him).[6] Why do we share this compulsion to repair walls that only serve to separate us? What purpose do walls serve? Are barriers necessary to sustain social civility? Man occupies a precarious position in Frost's poetry. Certainly the majority of his poems argue that each individual must face his own "desert places" alone. But there is also a vital impulse towards the social in Frost—a need to recognize the common loneliness that we share with other selves that might then translate into a responsibility, even a love. As the poet acknowledges in "Birches," "Earth's the right place for love: / I don't know where it is likely to go better."

Shawshank is a novella and a film that is centered on another set of New England stonewalls and the psychological impact over time these barriers create inside the men who are condemned to live behind them. When Red posits his definition of institutionalization and its affect on Brooks Hatlen, he begins by referring to the walls of the prison directly: "These walls are funny … " Although neither of Frost's characters are convicted felons,

"Mending Wall" is essentially another discussion about how the affects of prolonged institutionalization contribute to the creation of psychological prisons. The neighbor is a man who will not question, much less "go behind his father's saying," that walls are important to preserve privacy and maintain a necessary barrier to strangers. Brooks Hatlen and Red find echoes of their institutionalized separation in Frost's neighbor's refusal to consider "What I was walling in or walling out, / And to whom I was like to give offense." Although Frost's neighbor makes a deliberate choice of his own free will, while institutional processes beyond their control trap Brooks and Red, what began for all three men as a self-protective reflex eventually becomes a self-destructive withdrawal from the world. Red arguably goes even further than either Hatlen or Frost's New England neighbor in his belief that the only way prison life can be made endurable is by resigning oneself to a hopelessness that only serves further to isolate men, turning them into "old-stone savage armed / ... mov[ing] in darkness." Andy's example of hope, on the other hand, finds resonance in Frost's narrator's "elves-like" proposition that perhaps "I could put a notion in his head": to imagine a world that deconstructs the various walls men elect to live behind inside their own self-constructed Shawshanks, laboring under the debilitating belief that they have no other choice than to mirror the quiet desperation of their own experience (or their father's) by living in isolation. Andy's wife accuses her husband of being a "closed book," but it is really Brooks and Red who close themselves off from deep emotion and other people. The "rehabilitation" Andy earns and eventually manages to communicate to Red offers proof that husbands can change, that "closed books" can break down internal walls and open up into libraries, that "hard men to know" can become teachers of hard men doing hard time, and that we don't necessarily need to remain trapped in the repetitive habits that demarcate our pasts. Andy's marriage constituted another example of institutionalization, but he learns from being "a bad husband" as the film tracks his progression into a man determined to express his emotions instead of walling them off. There may be a difference between walls that are imposed by the state on an individual versus walls that we construct of our own volition, as in Frost's poem, but the end result is the same: erected walls often prove to be insurmountable—and with each one that he builds, man hastens his total isolation. This is the common lesson about institutionalization that *Shawshank* and "Mending Wall" teach us. A life lived behind stone walls is a terrible place to reside, but even worse is to reside in a prison of the mind's own making.[7]

When Red crosses the border into Mexico, he is not merely "breaking parole" and thereby committing another crime against the state; he is also breaking free of oppressive conventions that likewise restrict the neighbor in Frost's poem, who, like Brooks Hatlen, is similarly trapped by the past and its conditioning reflex. Red frees himself from the literal walls that separate him from Andy at the same time that he breaks through the psychological wall that produces his fear and follows in Brooks' footsteps. Hatlen and Red's respective capitulations to institutionalization are the consequence of years of "walled-in" oppression, institutional rejection, and the evolving conviction born from despair that "hope has no place on the inside." Andy, in contrast, never loses hope; like the speaker in "Mending Wall," he is future-oriented, and constantly imagines fresh possibilities—building a new library, educating illiterate men, tunneling out from under an oppressive institution, communicating with others, residing in a place "that has no memory"—instead of adhering to the limitations that attend the conformity of obedience. As Fiddler posits, "He will become Randall Stephens, 'a phantom; an apparition; second cousin to Harvey the Rabbit' ... simultaneously emphasizing both the artificiality of [his] new identity and the fact that Andy will cease to be. He will change into a new identity and 'Andy' will be forgotten by the Pacific" (200). One of the first things Red notices about Andy while watching him stroll in the prison yard is that he appears to walk with "an invisible coat that would shield him from this place." This is the opposite of Hatlen's and Red's self-constructed "walls"; the confidence of Andy's attitude—even at the very start of the film—actually serves him as a personal barrier *against* institutionalization, as a "coat" or a "shield" that protects him from the deadening condition that happens over time cowed by the hegemony of Shawshank. Andy does more time in the hole than any of the other prisoners in either the novella or the film, yet his institutional punishments as well as the various physical violations he experiences against his personhood fail neither to erode his individual identity nor to destroy his fundamental optimism. As Red informs us early in King's novella, "I can tell you he was the most self-possessed man I've ever known ... If he ever had a dark night of the soul, as some writer or other has called it, you would never know" (*RHSR*, 9).

Often overlooked by readers and film audiences alike is the degree of risk implicit in Andy's resonating tagline: "Get busy living or get busy dying." His last night in Shawshank must have come as close to "a dark night of the soul" as any man is likely to experience. Consider the factors that would freeze most men into inaction: Andy cannot be certain of any-thing beyond the hole at the end of his tunnel. He doesn't know if he will be able to break through a thick metal sewage pipe using only a large piece of concrete, if he will suffocate on his "more than five football fields" crawl through that underground pipe, the location and direction where this sewage pipe ultimately exits and even if it does so in a place that will facili-tate his escape,[8] if he will then have enough time to collect the warden's Portland bank money and get out of town before the authorities track him down, and if he will ultimately make it all the way down to Mexico. What Andy does know is that if he is caught, he will either be killed or brought back to Shawshank to "do the hardest time there is" courtesy of the warden. If ever there was a moment where hope proved itself to be a dangerous thing, it is while Dufresne appears sitting on his cot, rope in hand, contemplating his next move. Yet Andy chooses to go; he takes a leap of faith based only on hope and his realization after Tommy's murder that the warden is never going to allow him to walk out of Shawshank alive. And as he waits for another bolt of lightning and its accompanying clap of thunder to time the sound of his rock against the sewage pipe, classic film aficionados may well recollect another birthing scene and the famous utterance, "It's alive!" that results during a similar lightning storm in James Whale's *Frankenstein*. The willingness to risk is what separates living from dying, individuation from institutionalization: death is the bar-gaining chip we must sometimes bet on to get another chance at living a real life on our own terms. If institutionalization is ultimately the corrup-tion of independence and self-confidence mired in a deathless "dark night of the soul," Andy's personal "shield" is a touchstone to sanity, a prophy-lactic that preserves his self-possession at the same time as it allows room for growth and change. The magic of *Shawshank* is that Andy's "shield" proves transferable—in the course of the narrative, it passes from Andy to Red, and then to the reader/viewer—and it probably best explains why so many people who have never spent a single night in jail still manage to identify so personally with this story. For we all share a need to believe that personal redemption is always possible even as we struggle within our own daily prisons of habit, bad marriages, the evolving awareness of our limited mortality, loneliness, drug and alcohol addictions, chronic illness, unsatisfying jobs, the legacies of mental or sexual abuse, and memories of lost or dead children and parents.

In the film version of *Shawshank*, Andy's message of hope contains a seldom-discussed political subtext, especially since it occurs within the historical context of the sixties time frame. Andy, and by extension, Red eventually as well, comes to embody the spirit of the age in many respects. The trajectory of Andy's personal development while incarcerated at Shawshank corresponds to the opening of American culture as it emerged from the conservative fifties to the more self-expressive and rebellious sixties. As will soon be detailed elsewhere in this chapter, Andy establishes bonds with subversive women artists who must be viewed as historical models for an emerging feminism's challenge to patriarchal authority.[9] Additionally, Dufresne becomes a man who gains profound self-knowledge, taking command over his own life by defying both the corrupt system that has misjudged him and the limits of his own stereotypical masculinity that we see symbolized at the start of the film when Andy responds to his wife's infidelity with clenched fists, an intimidating refusal ("I'll see you in hell before I'll see you in Reno") to grant her a divorce, the urge to resort to gun violence in response to her betrayal, and a descent into alcoholic self-pity. The Andy Dufresne that emerges from his "progressive rehabilitation" after nineteen years in Shawshank is defined not by a capitulation to institutionalization, but in terms of his connection to others: a broadening appreciation of his feminine side that allows him to identify with the women starlets on his cell wall and as a teacher of difficult men, a close and emotive friendship with Red, and a fierce commitment to expressions of personal liberation and acts of defiance. If Andy can be said to begin the film as a traditionally masculine representative of the late forties/early fifties (suit-wearing bank vice-president, "closed book," stone-faced inability to express himself emotionally), he exits as a star-child of the sixties—an outlaw who has forfeited all traces of his earlier identity and dropped out of the system, driving along open Mexican roads wearing cool sunglasses, his shirt unbuttoned, and savoring the ocean wind in his hair with no particular place to go. A phoenix rising (Fig. 3.3).

It is an interesting but also an unnerving coincidence that the commencement of arguably the darkest days in OSR's history—when the institution transitioned from a reformatory into a maximum-security penitentiary—roughly coincide with the time period when Andy and Red are incarcerated fictionally in Shawshank. As noted in the preceding chapter, beginning in 1958, OSR began the process of accepting serious felony career criminals into its already overcrowded general population; OSR's transformation into a maximum-security prison was fully completed in 1970 and retained this status until it closed in 1990. Red predates Andy's

Fig. 3.3   Andy cruising in his red Pontiac Phoenix

arrival in 1947 and remains in Shawshank for some time after the latter's escape in 1967, most likely, judging by the clothes and automobiles
that Red encounters post-parole and in the deleted scene from the movie
where Red walks through a park during "the summer of love" ("*Shawshank
Redemption* Rare Deleted"), obtaining parole in 1969.

And equally by accident, the histories of the OSR and *Shawshank* can
be seen to parallel one another as profound representations of the two-
sidedness of human nature. OSR fostered a long epoch of reform whose
emphasis on rehabilitation underscored a faith in the inherent goodness
of men; that any inmate—through a combination of education, religious
awakening, and prolonged periods of introspective accountability—might
actualize his potential for a personal renaissance and the ability to alter the
trajectory of his life. As a reformatory, OSR was founded on and inspired
by reasons for hope. Like Andy in *Shawshank*, the prison operated under
the belief that education had the potential to elevate a young man's vision,
and that an employable skill could provide a viable alternative to crime. As
the institution expanded in population size, joining the Ohio Department
of Corrections as a maximum-security facility, and type of prisoner, however, this vision was occluded by the need to stockpile bodies. Faith in
rehabilitation guided the facility for decades, at least until the reformatory transitioned into a repository for hardened felons, who—for whatever

other combination of reasons, including too many dangerous prisoners beyond the facility's capacity to control—came to inhabit a realm beyond the possibility of redemption. OSR began as an institution that was premised on the belief that the purpose of incarceration is to provide inmates with the opportunity to reflect constructively on past offenses while also providing the tools and talents necessary to lead socially responsible lives. It devolved into a prison that more closely resembled the rigid state facility pictured in *Shawshank*: an unequivocal force for discipline and punishment and a place for warehousing social undesirables. Although the film's narrative embodies the spirit that was born out of the American sixties, ending in hope and love, a reminder of what is noble in the human spirit—its potential for dignity, personal change, and survival—the cinematic adaptation, more than King's novella, likewise presents the film viewer with a sobering rejoinder. As if paralleling the historical trajectory of OSR itself, the film very clearly states that without a conscious mentoring of hope, whatever is best in the human spirit stands in danger of extinction. In his letter to Red near the end of Darabont's film, Andy assures his friend that "hope is a good thing, maybe the best of things, and no good thing ever dies." The mid-to-late twentieth-century history of the OSR, the corresponding punitive incarceration rates and time spent in prison for minor offenses that has characterized the criminal justice system of late twentieth- and early twenty-first-century America, the institutional values exposed at Shawshank, and the fate of Brooks Hatlen serve as sobering qualifiers to the spirit of Andy's optimism. These histories are both real and "reel," and are, unfortunately, as much a part of the Shawshank experience as Dufresne's example of human redemption.

RACE AND *SHAWSHANK*

Although *Shawshank* scrupulously avoids any direct references to the conflicts and changes which were occurring in the larger society beyond the prison walls, the influence of the sixties time context is also apparent in Darabont's subtle referencing of racial politics, most specifically in his choice to cast Red as a black man who possesses genuine agency and dramatic presence as the only African-American among a group of white friends at Shawshank. In King's novella, Red is presumed to be white; his nickname is "Red" because of his Irish heritage and his recollection of a younger self as "a kid with a big mop of carroty hair" (*RHSR*, 55). Initially, Rob Reiner and Castle Rock envisioned Harrison Ford playing the role of Red. But as a politically astute Hollywood director with left-ist sympathies, Darabont made a very deliberate decision to cast Morgan Freeman as Red, thereby reconfiguring King's source text within what Donald Ingram Ulin identifies as "the tradition of the biracial escape narrative, reaching back to *The Adventures of Huckleberry Finn*" (2). The unlikely friendship between an uneducated black man and a highly cultured white bank vice-president defies realistic social barriers of class and race. Jan Alber goes so far to insist that Dufresne's triumphs over prison bureaucrats and convicted rapists and murderers "glorifies restoration of the clever white working class" (173), although as a former vice-president of a bank, Andy hardly qualifies as a member of the "working class."

The novella's ending where Red is writing one last journal entry alone in his room at the Brewster boarding house "so excited [he] can hardly hold the pencil in [his] trembling hand" (*RHSR*, 101) as he anticipates his trip to join Andy is certainly a compelling moment in its own right, but its power is increased exponentially when visualized cinemagraphically in the racial context of Darabont's film. The director chose to picture Red actually riding in the back of a bus. Since this film moment is set chronologically during the late sixties, especially coming on the heels of the Montgomery bus boycott, Red's journey through the Deep South assumes an unstated racialized resonance that is missing in King's text. Indeed, that resonance deepens when Red acknowledges that the trip fills him with "the excitement only a free man can feel." While he is perhaps expressing his sense of freedom in escaping the American penal system, Red is also, even unconsciously, acknowledging the unspoken politics of race insofar as he still remains a prisoner of American racism (see the grocery store sequence in "*Shawshank Redemption* Rare Deleted"), so his sense of excitement and liberation take on added meaning as the black man anticipates leaving the United States to establish a new identity in a foreign country, a place where he will exist among other people of color and outside the influence of American prejudice. Red's anticipation in the film at least is stirred by more than just the thought of reconnecting with his best friend.

In the essay "Diva Traffic and Male Bonding in Film: Teaching Opera, Learning Gender, Race, and Nation," Charles Nero asserts that Andy is placed in a dominant position over Red in the film adaptation by virtue of his superior knowledge base and the ability to dictate a future agenda that Red passively follows: "Lest we forget, this bonding is possible only between social superior and inferior. Andy decides the location ... Red acts as his assistant … Andy controls the bonds of friendship" (55). The apparent obviousness of Nero's argument eventually reveals itself to be too reductive, imposing an implicit level of racial license that downplays Red's conscious choice to follow Andy as an independent exercise of his free will. Nero's one-sided construction of their racial hierarchy also overlooks that Red and Andy share the task of taking care of each other all through the film. It is, after all, ultimately Red's ability to procure the Hollywood posters and rock hammer that makes Andy's escape possible. In a departure from the novella, Red is the one responsible for getting Andy work on the outdoor detail tarring the license plate factory roof; in the novella, Red and Andy were randomly selected by lottery. So, in the film, Andy's progression out of the laundry and into the library is really triggered by Red and his in-house connections, including putting Andy on the work crew where the latter then reveals his financial acumen to Captain Hadley. Nero's argument privileges Andy racially as the consistently dominant figure in their relationship, but this interpretation fails to appreciate that the narrative is always under Red's control. Red is motivated by a "promise [he] made to Andy" that helps him to choose between a compass and a revolver, but in the end, Andy is down in Mexico when Red must confront this decision, and the black man is left to act alone. Finally, Nero is negligent in failing to recognize Andy's commitment to Red within a union that both inverts and subverts the racist paradigm of the "magical Negro" that has doggedly been associated with Stephen King's black characters throughout his literary career: John Coffey in *The Green Mile*, Dick Hallorann in *The Shining*, Mother Abigail in *The Stand*, Speedy Parker in *The Talisman*, and Sara Laughs in *Bag of Bones* have all been interpreted as racist stereotypes. Film scholar Sarah Nilsen defines the "magical Negro" trope as "special magical powers endowed by nature … necessarily linked to their [black] race, and also lead[ing] to their death. Rather than being able to use their powers to liberate themselves or their community, in fact, these characters are often sacrificed in order to sustain the white social order" (133–4). In essentially inverting the black trope by taking on the mantle himself, Andy risks exposure to the prison authorities that are still hunting for him, potential betrayal in telling Red about the existence of Zihuatanejo, and in brazenly mailing him a postcard from Fort Hancock, Texas. These turn out to be lifelines for Red, Andy's efforts to rescue him through the magic of imagination and friendship, in much the same way as "magical Negroes," such as Coffey and Halloran, exist to rescue white characters elsewhere in the King canon. Conversely, *Shawshank* features a white man using his prodigious powers and risking his own freedom to aid in the rescue of a black man.

Although Dufresne comes from privilege and Red does not, Andy's friendship with him is neither one-sided nor exploitative. When Red admits that he finds the game of chess "a total fucking mystery. I hate it," Andy offers to teach him how to play. And despite the fact that Andy works on carving his own chess set out of rocks, and clearly prefers chess ("a game of kings," he tells Red in an attempt to entice him), he is still willing to play checkers in order to accommodate the preference of his friend, as we see them so engaged on two separate occasions in the film.[10] More to the point, *Shawshank* offers a sentimental portrait of race relations; racial difference is never even mentioned, much less confronted. This is especially notable given that the film's theatrical release predates by only a few months the Sentencing Project's groundbreaking report that found one in three black American males lives under some form of criminal justice supervision (Brown 61). Although partly reflective of Maine's racial demographic, the guards, administrators, and other prisoners in Shawshank are overwhelmingly white. It's not just Andy and Red who subsume all matters of race under the lure of harmonious male companionship and mutual respect; the other white prisoners, both those who are friends with Red as well as the other members of the inmate population at Shawshank, also treat him without racial prejudice. Furthermore, none of the prison guards, Hadley included, ever participates in any overt linguistic or physical acts motivated by racism. Hunter underscores these points when she posits that the movie transcends the determining power of race, becoming "a 'sentimental prison buddy story' that promotes the values of democratic inclusivity and universal brotherhood" (93). Compare this with the overt and omnipresent racism present in *The Green Mile*, where John Coffey is a black Christ doomed despite his innocence as a result of being a black man associated with the murders of two white girls in the Deep South. Why is it that race proves to be a deterministic element in *The Green Mile*, but is seemingly irrelevant to *Shawshank*? Are audiences to believe that a blatant racism flourished in Louisiana during the 1930s but was nonexistent in Maine less than two decades later? Indeed, white and black interactions in *Shawshank* bear nothing in common with the volatile history of interracial contact among prison inmates as tracked by Robert Weiss: "Racial hostility and mutual paranoia are fueled by a flood of downwardly mobile casualties … in an era of reconsolidation of state power, social debris of all colors [are] seething with misplaced hatred" (175).

Donald Ingram Ulin was the first scholar to notice that *Shawshank* ends up sharing much in common with arguably the most important fictional narrative on race in American history: Mark Twain's *Adventures of Huckleberry Finn*. The fact that racism remains endemic in America—a legacy that dates back to the antebellum South—makes "the solutions suggested by both *Huck Finn* and *Shawshank*, founded as they are on the myth of the romantic individual, more reassuring than effective" (Ulin 3). Certainly neither text tries to proselytize in universal or nationalistic terms about racial issues or solutions; instead, they are narratives that rely on their compelling storylines and protagonists to cut against the racist stereotypes of their respective eras. Yet, all four of the texts' main characters survive because of their reliance on their racial counterparts. As we have discussed elsewhere in this chapter, Red helps Andy endure nineteen years at Shawshank by providing him with a reason to love and trust again; the same can be said about Andy's importance to Red. Just as Red is a pragmatic person "who can get things," Jim knows how to build a platform raft that doesn't leak and can navigate the customs of the river. These are respective skills much admired by both Andy and Huck. Twain's Jim ends up teaching Huck the value of humility and Huck repeatedly finds himself in circumstances where he acknowledges Jim's humanity. Conversely, Huck is probably the only white person Jim has ever loved; their bond serves as a substitute for the aborted father-son relationship that leaves Huck bereft of his biological father Pap, as the institution of slavery has cost Jim contact with his own family. Andy parallels Huck's intention to light out "ahead of the rest," but without the "promise I made to Andy" Red succumbs to the same institutionalized fallout that destroyed Brooks Hatlen. In short, *Huck Finn* and the film adaptation of *Shawshank* work the magic of racial reconciliation by relying on the power of friendship to construct color-blind microcosms, and they do so effectively because both novel and film refuse to call attention to themselves as referendums on race.

Like Twain's Huck and Jim, the mere existence of Andy and Red's bond could be read as subversive, as Lionel Trilling noted of *Huck Finn* as far back as 1948 (100) and Warden Norton similarly recognizes too late. However, *Shawshank*'s many interesting racial implications notwithstanding, race is simply not an issue that the audience pays much attention to in this film. Because Darabont has established such a compelling portrait of male friendship, the racial and class ramifications associated with it are neutralized and rendered invisible. This, in turn, helps to explain why

Darabont chose to eliminate the intense scene featuring a post-parole Red undergoing a panic attack in the all-white supermarket, eventually retreating alone into the bathroom ("*Shawshank Redemption* Rare Deleted Scenes"). To retain that sequence in the final cut of *Shawshank* would have opened up a racial divide that is simply not present elsewhere in the film, and thereby forced a discussion that, while definitely relevant to the time and place of the film's setting, might have also distracted from its harmonious portrait of male friendship. All these issues make it easy to overlook that the union Andy and Red fashion is sustainable only in the ahistorical confines of a prison, where class lines are erased in the equalizing homogeneity of the prisoner experience, or in a foreign country (Mexico) untainted by America's racist past.

The racial portrait of their friendship provides perhaps another, more subtle reason for the universal popularity of Darabont's adaptation. America wants desperately to believe in the dream of interracial harmony, despite the fact that this goal has been and still remains problematic on the streets and in the headlines. White people in particular want to control the utopian narrative in the belief that racial relationships continue to improve, indeed, that we have evolved into a "post-racial" society. This optimism, even if undercut by daily realities mainstream culture would prefer to ignore, ultimately helps to minimize our own complicity in the horrors of America's racial past. The reason why so many white people resist the slogan "Black Lives Matter" that followed the unrest in Ferguson is because they view it as drawing attention to the separation that continues to divide white and black in America best symbolized in the way the police and judicial system operate on two different racial planes. Interestingly, whenever a poll is taken about the status of racial relations in America, whites are always considerably more optimistic than blacks regarding the progress that has been made and the potential for future improvement. Thus, in exchange for sacrificing social realism, Darabont revivifies the political "pipe dream" that sparked the liberal white imagination in the sixties—and continues to do so today—in much the same way that Zihuatanejo inspires Red and Andy's hope for new lives together. *Shawshank*'s "dream" goes on to imply that the fates and fortunes of the races are so closely aligned that one cannot exist without the other.

The above argument proved to be once again problematic in the early 1990s when Frank Darabont was writing the script for *Shawshank* and working with Castle Rock to select its cast. Since race bears no relevance in King's 1982 novella, one has to assume that Darabont's decision to bring race into his 1994 adaptation was at least unconsciously influenced by heightened racial tensions in Los Angeles caused by police brutality against Rodney King in 1991 and the urban riots that followed the 1992 acquittals of the policemen who beat him. These racially explosive events were occurring in the same city, literally in Darabont's backyard, as he was composing the *Shawshank* screenplay and engaged in pre-production preparations (such as the selection of Morgan Freeman to play Red) to direct the film. A year later, in 1994, the world would once again find itself galvanized by the city's racial politics during the O.J. Simpson murder investigations and subsequent trial. In this context, then, Darabont's adaptation can be read as a positive answer to Rodney King's plaintive *cri de coeur*, "Can't we all get along." The film's ending offers the forceful implication that neither race's quest for wholeness or happiness will be realized until the two are united; moreover, the bond between Andy and Red is so deep they are both willing to risk their newly won freedoms in order to be together. Perhaps this helps to explain why the concluding embrace between a black man and a white man lingers as the most compelling moment in the movie: it is not only a personal reconnection between two old friends who have overcome so much to be together but the symbolic fulfillment of a dream America is still chasing.

We want to conclude this section with another controversial point about *Shawshank*'s controversial Mexican beach reunion. After two and a half hours of watching Red and especially Andy suffer degrees of humiliation and injustice, after nearly a third of the movie where the two best friends are separated from contact with one another for years, the actual visualization of their physical reunion on a pristine beach, accompanied by the soundtrack's stirring high-pitched orchestral string and kettle drum music, taps into a wellspring of emotion that cuts across gender lines; this is the point in the film where men as well as women find themselves confronting and often indulging the urge to cry. The tears flow mostly from happiness at *Shawshank*'s successful resolution of its emotive storyline, its closure, and the confirmation of our belief that it is possible to triumph over even the worst of adversities; it illustrates Robyn Warhol's thesis in her study of sentimentality and popular art, *Having a Good Cry*, that the tears of melodrama are much more evoked by scenes of triumph than by scenes of sadness (45).

Hollywood typically reserves such closing scenes for white heterosexual couples whose next move is the altar. Over the decades, how many romantic comedies, soap operas, commercials, televised melodramas, situation comedies, and love stories have finished in a similar place with a similar embrace as *Shawshank* does? Because of American culture's homophobia and its sexist reaction to labeling sentimentality as pejoratively effeminate, however, males are required to negotiate this territory carefully: our culture does not possess easy access to language necessary for understanding the depth of a friendship between two men that points the way to crying. Mainstream America can acknowledge with alacrity the strong bond that may flourish between two males who play sports together or engage in violent combat against a common enemy, but we are less comfortable when that masculine bond is removed from the arena of war or sport and turns its focus to the range of interpersonal emotions friendship inspires. Tim Robbins (Andy) has noted that men will sometimes approach him on the street in order to single out their affection for *Shawshank*. The film both visualizes and legitimizes the emotional component inherent in male friendship, an element not typically addressed in American culture and another explanation for the film's popularity, especially among men. According to Robbins, "As American males, we don't get that model in films, that there is a real chance to have an emotional bond with another man that is a significant and important part of your life" (qtd. in *Shawshank: The Redeeming Feature*).

Women have long been granted the freedom to cry over novels and especially films that have traditionally been "marketed at females, who received cathartic enjoyment out of watching someone else overcome tribulations" (Hinds D13). In most of the films where this occurs, males are conspicuously absent from the audience, or at least embarrassed if their own response turns out to be as emotive as their wife's or girlfriend's. As Warhol points out using the example of nineteenth-century American women's literature, feminist academics have worked hard to "rehabilitate sentimentality" (33), but male academics typically steer clear from encroaching on most discussions considering the topic of sentimentality, in literary criticism and otherwise, even when they are interested in nineteenth-century women's literature. Part of *Shawshank*'s achievement is that it represents a strange amalgamation of seemingly contradictory elements that manage to work in seamless harmony: bringing together a melodramatic love story between two men that appeals as much to males in the audience as it does to women. That Darabont reserves his movie's final shot for an interracial male bonding moment—the only time in *Shawshank* when these two best friends are pictured physically touching each other—is another subversive element in a film that quietly and relentlessly undercuts the perimeters of classic genre filmmaking and strains Hollywood's own heteronormative constraints for defining portrayals of love. For in what other film and in what existing film genre would a predominately heterosexual audience cheer the conclusion of an interracial love story between two males?

THE CINEMAS OF *SHAWSHANK*

The thesis of Mark Kermode's BFI volume, the first book-length analysis of the movie, posits that *Shawshank* is a deeply spiritual film. He traces the frequent biblical parallels and references in the work, noting that Darabont's adaptation climaxes in the moment of Andy's escape when he is "stripped to the waist, arms held out in crucified triumph ... an image of a man finally freed from the horrors of his earthly shackles, offering himself up to the heavens" (75). Critics and fans are often drawn to the religious elements that echo throughout *Shawshank*. They have argued convincingly that the film is a parable of Christian suffering, exculpation, forgiveness, and redemption. Mexico becomes a kind of heavenly reward where Andy and Red find themselves reborn in the warm waters of the Pacific. Additionally, the many parallels between Andy and Christ are impossible to ignore. After his "resurrection" out of Shawshank's stone crypt, Andy leaves behind a group of apostles who keep his memory and principles alive through frequent and reverent conversation. Red may serve as the "Peter" of this church, the man upon whom Andy has had the greatest impact. There exists a certain tranquility to the last quarter of the film following Andy's escape—a Christian certitude, if you will, that transcendence is available to those who possess enough hope and faith to believe that human suffering is never the final word. Taken in such light, the viewer is left to contemplate, along with the warden, Andy's biblical message to his tormentor, "Dear Warden, you were right. Salvation lay within." The Exodus reference alongside the shape of the rock hammer carved into the book of Scripture underscores Andy's exit from the years of misery he has been made to endure. The Bible certainly aids him in this quest, but *literally* even more than spiritually.

Andy's use of the Bible in this scene actually highlights Kermode's embrace of religious elements in *Shawshank* that includes the sacred and the profane, both often operating simultaneously. Indeed, he especially sees these planes coexisting through what he calls "the church of the cinema," those "secular nods which Darabont seems to make toward Christian myth matched by a reverence for film and its icons ... a place where dreams take flight, and where miracles become a reality rather than an abstraction" (34–6). While Kermode's argument proceeds to focus on film in general as a transcendent art form, it is just as important to emphasize that *Shawshank* borrows heavily from specific film genres in its allusions to earlier cinematic work. Although Hollywood's prison genre is frequently cited by film scholars writing about *Shawshank* (Browning mentions *Birdman of Alcatraz*, *The Great Escape*, and *Papillon* [152]; Ulin discusses *The Defiant Ones*; while Kermode also references *Birdman* [51]), only Ulin's work on *The Defiant Ones* probes to any degree the relationship that *Shawshank* shares with any previous prison movies. For Ulin, *The Defiant Ones* provided *Shawshank* with the model for a biracial prison film where a mutual racism is overcome as a result of common struggles that the protagonists share and must confront together. Black and white "shed their prejudices and discover a common bond of humanity" stronger than even the literal chain that binds them to one another (5). What each of these earlier prison films have in common with *Shawshank*, to a greater or lesser degree, is that they are all examinations of long-term incarceration, eliciting audience sympathy and identification towards prisoners seeking either to escape their confinement or to assert their dignity in the face of vicious penal systems that work to take it away. These films, then, like *Shawshank*, are paeans to the virtues of defiance in the face of a corrupt or vile prison organization that would seek to deny prisoners their humanity in addition to their freedom. In her critique of *Shawshank* as an unrealistic examination of incarceration, Michelle Brown goes so far to argue that "the 'real' that *Shawshank* imitates is not real at all but a celluloid fantasy—built upon the memories and conventions of past prison films" (61).

In Darabont's film adaptation, Andy provides the first explicit intertextual reference to another fictional prison narrative when he encourages Heywood to read Alexandre Dumas' novel *The Count of Monte Cristo* because "You'll like it. It's about a prison break." Although Andy's allusion is to Dumas' novel, *The Count of Monte Cristo* has undergone multiple film versions beginning in 1934 and at least six other cinematic remakes, including a television program (1954) and a TV miniseries (1998). Like Andy, the protagonist in *Cristo*, Edmond Dantes, is unjustly convicted of a crime against the state and sent to prison for life. He likewise takes justice into his own hands as a consequence of being abused by a corrupt criminal justice system. Once Dufresne escapes from Shawshank, he goes on to punish Warden Norton and Hadley for their illegalities and their efforts to undermine a review of Andy's case by murdering Tommy, who would potentially serve as the review's chief witness. Similarly, when Edmond escapes he lays out an elaborate design to punish the three men responsible for his false imprisonment. Dantes' revenge on Danglars, one of the men responsible for his incarceration, particularly resembles Andy's revenge against Norton because the payback targets his financial status; as Dufresne drains the false accounts he has established under Randall Stevens' pseudonym for the warden's retirement, Edmond exploits his enemy's greed by opening various counterfeit credit accounts that end up bankrupting Danglars. Dantes possesses, like Dufresne, an insider's knowledge of how the financial system operates, and he uses this knowledge to exploit and abuse both the system and the personal finances of his enemies. And just as the warden departs the film baffled by "how Andy ever got the best of him," Danglars suffers his financial ruin without an understanding of why or how it occurs. The two texts also explore the psychological changes that occur to their protagonists during their unjust incarcerations and after their eventual escapes. Dantes breaks out of prison by plunging into the ocean, experiencing a kind of baptism that resembles Andy's symbolic rebirth in the creek and rainstorm on the night of his escape from Shawshank. Both men have suffered metaphorical deaths while in prison, and they are both reborn in waters that lead to redemption.

Of all the Hollywood prison narratives to exert an influence on Darabont's *The Shawshank Redemption, Birdman of Alcatraz* may arguably be the most extensive and most profound. The main character, Robert Stroud (played by Burt Lancaster in an Oscar-nominated performance) shares a number of the personality traits identified with several of the major protagonists in *Shawshank*. He initially strikes the most obvious parallel with Brooks Hatlen: both men help to pass their time in prison caring for birds. While Stroud nurses his sick birds through bouts of septic fever, Hatlen nurtures Jake into an adult crow. Both prisoners come to view their birds as metaphors that underscore their own caged suffering, humanity, and fantasy projections. After a lifetime of incarceration, Stroud revels vicariously in his sparrow's freedom: "You don't want to be a jailbird all your life. Go out there and bite the stars for me." Although Hatlen likewise sets Jake free before his own parole from Shawshank, it actually signals the start of his social alienation, as he is left alone with only the human world as an inadequate substitute. Stroud, however, never suffers the degree of institutionalization that drives Brooks to suicide; his birds and self-determination keep him from despair. Indeed, this is where

Stroud's parallels with Hatlen's character stops and his greater connection to Dufresne takes over.

The Birdman's forty-three years in solitary confinement have turned him, much like Andy, into an articulate and assertive figure of defiance. As Andy is a student of geology, Stroud, despite having only a third grade education, becomes a renowned ornithologist. Stroud also emerges as a relentless "thorn in [the warden's] side." His aggressive campaign to preserve his right to keep birds in his cell and to market his serums for bird lovers outside of jail forces prison authorities to reconsider and expand their rigid rules for prisoner conduct, and this allows Stroud the opportunity to reinvent his life, at least for a little while. Like Red and Andy, the longer Stroud is kept in prison, the more assertive he becomes, eventually writing a book that eviscerates current American penology, "a blast at the entire penal system," as Warden Shoemaker complains. Warden Shoemaker in *Birdman* shares some of the same arrogant complacency we find in *Shawshank*'s Norton, the former convinced that his career has been successful because he thinks he has supplied prisoners with a chance at rehabilitation. Shroud, however, continually deflates this notion with sarcasm and barbed criticism, reminding the warden that there is nothing progressive in a philosophy based on the belief that prisoners must "conform to [your] ideas on how to behave ... I won't lick your hand and that's what eats you, ain't it, Keeper." At the end of the film, the warden's use of excessive force, including the deployment of machine guns and bazookas, to quell a virtually unarmed uprising at Alcatraz is the truest indictment of his commitment to penal reform. Red's last parole hearing bears a close resemblance to the final scene that Stroud shares with Shoemaker before being transferred to Alcatraz; Darabont even invests Red's assertive diction with some of Stroud's language and anti-bureaucratic sarcasm. Both diatribes attack the penal system and its fraudulent inability to foster "rehabilitation" because of its failure to recognize prisoners as individuals. In the end, *Birdman* most closely resembles *Shawshank* in their mutually uplifting emphasis on prisoner self-determination and defiance as the sole means for preserving human dignity and respect in the face of the state's determined acts of oppression. As is the case in *Shawshank*, the prisoner-protagonists inspire audiences with their heroic acts of bravery and endurance; the best that can be said about the wardens, on the other hand, is that they both remain blinded by their sanctimoniousness.

Although set in a Nazi prison camp near the end of World War II, *The Great Escape* revolves around Allied soldiers who refuse to sit out the war in resort-like comfort replete with a constant supply of clean clothes, Christmas caroling, hot running water, a still for making vodka, collusion with prison guards, and amounts of leisure time so vast that the Allies are able to construct three escape tunnels underneath the barbed-wire walls encircling the camp. There is a highly unrealistic and sanitized atmosphere to this film that is far less recognizable in *Shawshank*, although as we have discussed elsewhere, Darabont's movie also provides the inmates of Shawshank with unrealistic access to physical movement and social interaction. The brutal violence that is a consequence of the mass escape attempt in *Escape* actually surprises the viewer because it is awkwardly offset by the environment of the prison camp itself; the guards and prison commandant appear more like characters from the television sit-com "Hogan's Heroes," bumbling and indifferent colleagues rather than the hardened creators of Dachau and Auschwitz. Although ultimately a less optimistic and more spiritually frustrating picture than *Shawshank*—only one prisoner manages to escape Germany and cross the border into Spain; the others are either shot or returned to the camp—*Escape* features Steve McQueen as the American pilot Hilts in a role that anticipates Dufresne as an intrepid risk-taker and self-determined individual. And, like Andy, he spends more time than any of his fellow prisoners sitting in solitary confinement. In a more obvious and direct borrowing, the prisoners in *Escape* deposit the dirt from the tunnels they are constructing into gardens kept inside the Nazi prison yard by employing hidden pouches under their pants that anticipate Andy's preferred method of carrying the concrete detritus from his cellblock wall and depositing it out into Shawshank's exercise yard.

Two years after making *The Great Escape*, Steve McQueen returned to the role of a restive prisoner, only this time with none of the amenities that he was provided as a captured American pilot. Of all the prison films to influence the making of *Shawshank*, *Papillon* offers the harshest perspective on incarceration and is best summed up early in the picture when its warden advises, "Make the best of what we offer you, and you will suffer less than you deserve." What the French penal colony offers are horrific conditions in rain and mud, constant physical labor, and no pretense at prisoner rehabilitation. "We're processors here," the warden explains in describing that the purpose of the camp is to break a man's mind and spirit, or else turn him over to the guillotine, which stands in the middle of the prison as a reminder of the system's way of "dealing with more serious offenses." *Papillon* is one of the vilest movies ever made, and likely provided inspiration for the darkest moments of physical punishment in *Shawshank*: Andy's time alone in the hole, his rapes and beatings at the hands of the sisters, Hadley's acts of sadistic violence, Red's assertion that "prison is no fairy-tale world." Papillon understands early and all too well Andy's feeling of being unjustly incarcerated for a crime he did not commit, "caught in the path of the tornado," most especially when he is betrayed by the Mother Superior of a convent during one of his bids for freedom. She steals his pearls and then turns him over to soldiers she knows will torture Papillon and return him to the infamous prison; her duplicitous actions are based on the film's discredited belief that "if you are innocent, God will protect you." Indeed, Papillon's final words in the movie, "I'm still here," are as much an existential rail against an unjust universe as they are a last defiant assertion of his individuality in the face of a penal system that has deployed its resources in an effort to destroy him. Yet, like Andy, Papillon's resolve to escape remains steadfast; his refusal to be broken, physically or spiritually, despite years of solitary confinement in darkness with reduced rations and the system's indifference to the condition of his deteriorating health, anticipates Andy's unwavering self-resolve. Both films are also testaments to male friendship, as Papillon and Dega form a loyal bond that is as long lasting and protective as the one Andy establishes with Red. And at the end, the plots of the two films parallel one another when Papillon and Dega are rejoined to complete their sentences on a bucolic island beach. Dega, however, has had enough: he surrenders to institutionalization, whereas Papillon's desire for freedom is now so much a part of his identity that even life on a beautiful island remains a prison because it is not his choice; he is again compelled to risk his life on a raft made of coconut shells, despite his advanced age and the lifetime of suffering he has endured.

Sharing a great deal in common with both *Papillon* and *Shawshank*, *Cool Hand Luke* was released in 1967, the year that Andy Dufresne escaped from Shawshank Prison. Set on a southern prison farm in the 1950s, the film's protagonist foreshadows Andy's character as both a Christ figure and a man capable of enduring tremendous levels of physical punishment and psychological cruelty. Like Andy, Luke is a character that spends most of the film refusing to acquiesce to prison authorities. And his spirit of rebellion becomes a contagious and inspiring influence on other prisoners, as Luke, like Andy, uses his sense of humor and wits to thwart the captain and the guards. Luke's successful effort to lead a work crew in completing a road-paving job in less than a day anticipates Andy and his inmate crew tarring the license-plate factory roof, and both men share a constant need to prove their independence amidst great risk and omnipresent levels of imposed violence and bondage. Even some of the filming shots in *Shawshank* appear indebted to *Cool Hand Luke*; for example, the aerial tracking sequence when the fresh fish arrive at Shawshank and the way in which they then emerge from the transport bus joined together as members of a chain gang bear noteworthy affinities to similar scenes and camera work found in the earlier film. Andy and Luke spend vast amounts of time enduring punishment in solitary confinement boxes and each man gambles his life to escape. In the end, however, the parallel figures part ways: Andy manages a successful escape, thus justifying his faith in hope and the likelihood of a happy future in a "place without memory," while Luke fails at successive escape attempts and is forced into greater levels of physical persecution. Luke's chances for survival appear doomed because he is defeated by the penal system; in the end his death is as much a kind of suicide as it a murder because of his inability to find a psychological space similar to Andy's. While Luke and Andy bear close similarities—their actions, for example, throw the respective prison systems' corruption into sharp relief—the hopelessness that attends Luke's situation stands in marked contrast to the optimism that ultimately guides Andy's.

On June 6, 2015, David Sweat and Richard Matt tunneled out from under a maximum-security prison in upstate New York. Both men were serving long prison terms for first-degree murder, and their escape was aided by elaborate trickery—including dummies made to appear as sleeping inmates and a woman employee of the facility who was lured by romantic sophistry into aiding the prisoners—that went undetected until the next day. Almost immediately after the men were discovered missing, newspapers, televised newscasts, the Internet, and the general populace began referring to their escape as a *Shawshank*-style prison break. Some pundits even speculated that the ultimate destination of the inmates might well be Mexico, as Matt possessed a "Mexico Forever" tattoo. Their escape, however, proved to be less well planned (the inmates ended up walking north towards Canada instead of south towards Mexico, and were more concerned about getting drunk than avoiding recapture) or as fortuitous as Andy's, since after three weeks of wandering through the Adirondack wilderness, Matt ended up killed while Sweat was shot by a state trooper and subsequently returned to incarceration. As Darabont's film once employed earlier Hollywood prison movies as references that influenced or at the least echoed through its own storyline, *Shawshank* has now become the reference point not only for other prison films but for many real-life prison escapes as well. The upstate New York break is not the first, only the most recent illustration of how *Shawshank* has turned into a touchstone for the popular imagination's understanding of prison and prison escapes—both real and fictional.

THE WOMEN OF *SHAWSHANK*

Had he lived long enough to see it, it is tempting to wonder what American cultural critic Leslie Fiedler might have thought of *The Shawshank Redemption*, most notably its film adaptation, as it re-imagines the central tropes featured in Fiedler's seminal book, *Love and Death in the American Novel* (1960): that true love and liberty between men is possible only far from the world of women, and that the myth of interethnic male bonding is a recurring archetype in the American cultural experience. Fiedler commented extensively on *Huck Finn*, scandalizing the literati and high school English teachers everywhere, when he posited that Huck and Jim establish a homoerotic bond in the course of their river journey. He also recognized that the prison film *The Defiant Ones* closely approximated the same recurring cultural archetype that he was tracing in the Huck-Jim myth in the movie's white and black prisoners who escape from a chain gang handcuffed to one another: "Though they are captured at the end, they have learned to love each other with a love pure enough to transcend their mutual prejudices and bitterness ... As the myth sinks deeper and deeper into the national mind ... it comes to seem truer than the reality of headlines" (Fiedler 388). Within this cultural paradigm, *Shawshank* would appear to fit right in with the books and films that occupied Fiedler's attention throughout his career because *Shawshank* manages to bridge a highly popular, sentimental lowbrow narrative with highbrow art.[11]

What might eventually disqualify *Shawshank* from inclusion in Fiedler's cultural-mythic paradigm, however, are the starlet posters of women from American cinema that adorn Andy's cell, bringing the feminine into a text that, with the exceptions of three or four brief cameos, is devoid of any "living females." While Fiedler traced male freedom as possible only in realms and arenas that excluded women—sport, war, spiritual retreat, prison—it is impossible to separate Andy's own quest for freedom from icons of a disruptive feminine. Andy might have chosen any subject of poster art—a famous athlete or historical figure (like his smaller magazine photograph of Albert Einstein), even a placid landscape or painting—to disguise the years of excavation work on his tunnel. Or his choice might have included less powerful representations of women instead of well-known stars who were simultaneously sexual and transgressive (it is worth noting that these three posters are the sole female representations present in Andy's cell). At one point in the film, Red refers to the women actresses as "Andy's fantasy girls," and they are certainly that: inspiring Andy's sexual imagination at the same time that they are hiding the literal path of his escape dream. But Red's assessment is only half right. In addition to being escapist projections in terms of what they hide as well as in their very presence inside a male prison, these women become frames of reference that Andy identifies with during his incarceration, serving as both metatextual projections and an affirmation of his subversive persona as it evolves at Shawshank.

Film scholarship has examined the Hollywood star's body as a semiotic marker through which it is possible to render a matrix of meanings about sex, culture, race, gender, ideology, and class. In his book *Heavenly Bodies*, Richard Dyer suggests that stardom seldom signifies a single, unambiguous connotation; instead, the star's image is a kind of canvas displaying multiple and contradictory elements, such as the hyperinflated signs of femininity coded in *Shawshank*'s glamour shots of Rita Hayworth and Marilyn Monroe that are complicated and even undercut by the transgressive characters these actresses portray in their respective films. Thus, for Dyer, stardom provides us with barometers for measuring social conflict and the slippages and disruptions of social configurations. The star's image on the screen (or, in the case of *Shawshank*, a movie still) must be read and interpreted in order for it to be properly understood. The star's body is not merely a representative image, but an emerging force that creates a dynamic between fan and celebrity, an affective interplay between performer and spectator. Susan Haywood argues that we respond to "the star body as material force, as vibration, resonance, and movement," and that this intersection between performer and audience brings together "two distinct bodies" creating an entirely new dynamic: a synthesis between spectator and star (qtd. in Mizejewski 215). It is therefore no stagnant relationship that exists between Andy and the Hollywood women featured in his poster art, but a collaborative bond that affirms daily Andy's response to the women actresses that share his living space. Their presence inspires Andy not only because of their resplendent beauty and insolence in a dark place but also because, like him, their conflicting identities—as women and as character actresses—are immersed in the act of becoming. While the women who appear in Andy's cell are meant to aid the narrative by disguising his tunnel as well as signaling the passage of historical time at Shawshank, it is important to pay attention both to the specific actresses selected and the cinematic contexts in which they appear. It is no accident that these iconic women provide a resonant correspondence to Andy's assertive efforts to maintain his own individuality by flaunting his rejection of (penal) authority. They come to serve Andy as a door to a literal escape portal as well as metaphoric mirrors that reflect back the self he is becoming or wishes to be. Their personae offer a unique variance on Nietzsche's speculation about gazing too long into the abyss: during the many years that Andy stares at the photographic images sharing his cell, over time, these images also stare back into Andy.

Stephen King included Rita Hayworth's name in the original title of the novella, but he chose not to reference her most famous film, *Gilda*, in the course of his narrative. And while the starlet's name is excluded in the title of Darabont's adaptation, references to *Gilda* gain added weight and metatextual resonance throughout *Shawshank*. The inclusion of *Gilda* in Darabont's film turned out to be a fortuitous accident that occurred when Billy Wilder's *The Lost Weekend*, cited in both King's novella and Darabont's original screenplay, proved unavailable because of high reproduction costs. Castle Rock approached Columbia Pictures, as the latter controlled the domestic distribution rights to *Shawshank*, and received a list of lower-priced features, including *Gilda*, which worked as an obviously appropriate link back to King's original title (Kermode 36–7). *Gilda* was released in 1946; Red informs us that Andy arrives at Shawshank in 1947. Thus, it is likely that Dufresne would have been acquainted with this film and perhaps even viewed it prior to the three occasions in the same month that he watches it when incarcerated. Throughout the movie *Gilda*, Rita Hayworth herself is a reminder to Andy of feminine beauty, a defiant and anti-patriarchal figure, and the literal way out of Shawshank prison. In this way, she forms a connection with the Mozart sopranos whose subversive actions, as we have seen, inspire and parallel Andy's own transgressive behavior.

While its plot is elaborately contrived and mired in excessive melodrama, *Gilda* still manages to hold the attention of a contemporary audience because of the dynamism of its title character. Hayworth not only lives up to her sex goddess reputation in this film, she also engages us because of her quick wit and insolent demeanor, which certainly would have distinguished her as a woman in 1946. On her way to acknowledging her commitment to Johnny Farrell, her true love, Gilda is simultaneously

elusive and seductive towards the plethora of men who vie for her attention. Like Andy in *Shawshank*, she is the center of her film's universe
around whom all the other characters and action revolves. And while she
is often deliberately costumed in sexualized outfits—a masked cowgirl
complete with rodeo whip, lacquered hair and heavy makeup, and various
tight evening gowns fraught with complicated zippers—she is always true
to herself; her identity is never compromised despite her highly feminized
personae. This is not to say that any of her male suitors ever comes to
understand her, but her mysteriousness and risqué language—"If I were a
ranch, I'd be called 'The Bar None'"—are reasons why she is so ardently
pursued. She really doesn't care what men think of her. Hayworth's character melds sex and sarcasm in a package designed to undermine the patriarchy, linking Gilda to other "fast talking dames" from her own era—Mae
West and Carol Lombard, for example—and Tina Fey, Sarah Silverman,
and Amy Schumer in the postfeminist present (Fig. 3.4).

Gilda is a text that is frequently associated with film noir, and Hayworth
plays the role of the classic femme fatale: a mercurial, difficult-to-control
woman who takes what she wants from men, particularly their adoration
and money. In his discussion of *Gilda* as a noir text, Richard Dyer argues

Fig. 3.4 Andy and the first of his movie posters, Rita Hayworth in *Gilda*

that Hayworth's singing and dancing emerge as a source of "defiance, not just of a trapped wife against her husband, but of a woman against the male system" (119). Similarly, Deborah Jermyn notes that the territory of film noir features "feisty women, female deception, fear of women, [and] the 'threat' of female sexuality" (159). Although on screen only in the opening of *Shawshank*, Andy Dufresne's wife, Linda, should be viewed similarly, as a femme fatale who rebels against the strictures of a traditionally patriarchal marriage to a banker who is frustrated by her independence. Thus, Gilda and Mrs. Dufresne are linked together in a bond that will, ironically, eventually include Andy himself in the course of his "gender rehabilitation" at Shawshank. Like Andy, Gilda is another of Red's "exotic birds" whose "feathers are just too bright" to remain trapped in a cage constructed by males who seek simultaneously to exploit and control her. *Gilda* specifically alludes to its title character as a "caged canary" the first time she is introduced, and she is also cast in the role of a cabaret singer. Her singing and dancing throughout the movie stand out as rebellious expressions of the personal frustration she experiences with both the males and the situation in which she finds herself and further connect her to the aria's defiance in *Figaro*.

Hayworth's movie poster is the first to hang over Andy's tunnel. This is appropriate because of all the celluloid females that share space with Andy during his time at Shawshank, he comes to mirror most Gilda's insolent behavior. Although Dufresne seeks to discourage all romantic and sexual encounters, his male beauty still manages to draw constant male attention. But more importantly, it is Gilda's ability to use her charismatic personality to seduce men that finds a close parallel in Andy. He also remains a mystery to the men at Shawshank; his impressive business acumen, his persistence in getting what he wants for his library project and the prisoners he tutors, his self-composure at moments of high emotion (e.g., when Hadley is about to throw him off a roof) are all traits that distinguish Andy from the less educated, less self-confident men at Shawshank. Even Bogs, the aptly named leader of the sisters, is mystified in Andy's presence, left wondering "Where do you get this shit?" when Andy baffles him verbally despite the threat of being stabbed while performing oral sex. Bogs' face at the moment when Andy explains to him "the bite reflex"—its mixture of confusion, frustration, bewilderment, and awe—mirrors the conflicted response shared by Ballin, Gilda's new husband, and Johnny Farrell, her former lover, in their various encounters with Gilda. While she takes special delight in humiliating Farrell, neither man garners much respect from her. As the unruly femme fatale in noir resists relegation to gender passivity, Andy assumes many of her character traits in his struggle against Bogs and the sisters and, later, the warden himself, who has his own moment of linguistic bewilderment when Andy dares to call him "obtuse." Like Andy, Gilda employs language that is just too quick-witted for any man to keep up; in the end, she gets her way around them, just as Andy often does, operating under the mantra, "I'm going to do exactly what I want, when I please."

Midway through *Shawshank*, Hayworth's sharp-tongued introduction is literally being screened in the background for the Shawshank convicts in the audience—featuring the scene where Gilda encounters Farrell and Ballin in the same room for the first time together—when Bogs and the sisters choose to assault Andy. At this moment, *Gilda* provides a celluloid simulacrum of Andy's real-time sexualization; *Gilda*'s soundtrack interfaces with *Shawshank*'s as the two movies are juxtaposed: Hayworth's character confronts a gendered tension on screen (cutting diegetically into *Shawshank*'s soundtrack) at the literal moment that Andy encounters Bogs and the sisters. As Gilda interacts with two men who view her as a sexual prize, the audience of *Shawshank* views Andy caught in a similar feminized position. On his knees, Andy initially poses the ruse that he wishes to "get this [the rape] over with," but, in truth, he refuses to participate in his own subjugation, employing a duplicitous posture of submission in order to put the sisters off guard. At the same time, up on the other movie screen, Ballin wishes to impress Farrell with his beautiful new trophy wife who is clad in a tight satin nightgown, but the introduction doesn't go very smoothly because Gilda fails to cooperate.

As the juxtaposed scenes unfold, the screen provides alternating medium and close-ups shots of Dufresne and Bogs, the latter appearing against a completely black background. The darkness in the frame behind him reflects the darkness that engulfs Bogs' psyche. In contrast, the mise-en-scène behind Andy includes several silver film canisters containing the actual film of *Gilda*; they are stacked on the table behind him and appear illuminated. Compared with the dank darkness that surrounds the rest of the projection room, the movie reels appear glowing, suffused in silver-blue light. Like Hayworth's costumes and resplendent hair and makeup throughout *Gilda* that elicit such an overwhelming male reaction from the inmate audience at Shawshank, the film canisters on the desk behind Andy project an unearthly, nearly chimerical presence; moreover, one of *Gilda*'s film reels literally helps Andy in combat against the sisters when he uses it to break Rooster's nose and to defend himself against Bogs.

At the moment where Hayworth is systematically deflating the male arousal of Ballin and Johnny Farrell in spite of her sexually charged presence inside her bedroom, Andy's response to Bogs' demand for fellatio is countered with the sobering retort, "Anything you put in my mouth you're going to lose." While Andy subverts the power dynamic Bogs imposes by promising the thug's emasculation should he continue to pursue his oral goal, Gilda is castrating linguistically the two male leads in *Gilda*, driving them towards each other into what Kermode calls "a strangely sexual bond ... homosocial if not homosexual" (37). Gilda's smoking cigarette becomes the symbolic phallus she appropriates all through this scene as she strips both men of their gendered privilege and assumes its power herself. Indeed, both scenes from these respective pictures appear joined by their mutual emphases on orality: attention is called to Andy's mouth as a sexualized orifice just as Gilda's heavily lipsticked mouth and smoking draws the male gaze to her lips. Yet, in each film these feminized orifices subvert their intended sexual objectification; each scene results in an entirely unexpected utilization of orality. Gilda and Andy simultaneously employ their adroit and insolent language skills to deflate male arousal by humiliating it. While the physical threat to Gilda taking place in her movie is less immediate than what Andy faces alone in the Shawshank projection room, she also finds herself trapped by the male gaze of Ballin and Farrell. However, like the soprano duet from *The Marriage of Figaro*, she and Andy make use their acerbic wit to transform a subordinate position into one of dominance; they refuse to be intimidated by males who, at least initially, appear to exercise power over them.

As the film and novella take us deeper into Andy's life at Shawshank, his various acts of institutional rebellion are affiliated consistently with feminine representation and resistance. Warden Norton is unconsciously disturbed by this cross-gendered nexus—although perhaps cognizant of its seditious potentiality—when he notices the poster of Rita Hayworth at his first meeting with Dufresne during the cell toss and comments, "I can't say I approve of this." Later, after Andy is reported missing from his cell, the warden's consternation is directed at the poster of Raquel Welch, "that cupcake on the wall." He goes on later to implicate "Miss Fuzzy Britches" for aiding and abetting Andy's disappearance even prior to discovering the tunnel; only after Welch's poster remains mute to the frustrated warden's demand for information from her about Dufresne's whereabouts is the escape tunnel revealed accidentally. That the warden twice verbalizes his distaste for the posters of the cinematic women on Andy's wall and hurls several of Andy's rock carvings at the movie still of "the lovely Raquel" (he also displays the same furious reaction to the voices of the sopranos when Andy plays the aria from *Figaro*) underscores Norton's morally puritanical misogyny. But the warden's response also bears immediate relevancy back to Andy, as Norton's reactions reinforce the role of women in this film as subversive agents undermining an authoritarian male domain. The warden senses—even unconsciously—that these are "immoral" women who exist outside his comprehension, beyond his capacity to control. He intuits that they resist compartmentalization not only because they are women but also that they are women who incline towards disorder and disruption. In other words, the warden is repulsed by the "fantasy girl" posters for the same reasons that Andy is attracted to them. As Linda Mizejewski posits, "pop culture is especially dangerous to right-wing ideologies because of the subversive potential of any performance or performer with intense emotional appeal that opens up channels of desire welcoming contradiction and incoherency" (215).

Warden Norton's disapproval of the movie women up on Dufresne's wall and the female aria from Mozart is informed by an essential prudishness that must be distinguished from the lyrical eroticism of Andy's operatic selection and candidly sexualized poster art. Just as the starlet posters (and the secret they maintain) are an enticement to Andy—literally and metaphorically—of a future life beyond Shawshank, the wall safe in Norton's office, which is likewise linked to *his* destiny, maintains its own hidden secret behind his wife's crocheted religious sampler: "His Judgment Cometh and That Right Soon." This foreboding prognostication, produced by a Christian wife and her church group whose level of religious dogma and timidity stand in sharp contrast to the self-confident secular women displayed on Andy's wall, points the way to Norton's fate just as Andy's poster girls simultaneously inspire, disguise, and facilitate his own. Moreover, the needlepoint of the warden's wife suggests a fear of the patriarchy—that the implicit punishment attendant to Jehovah's masculine judgment remains outside human control, is imminent, and can neither be avoided nor mollified. The movie starlets, on the other hand, portray females that revel in their own self-divinity, undaunted by patriarchal evaluation and condemnation. Andy finds redemptive freedom through the symbolic birth canal located behind the successive females pictured on his wall, whereas the safe behind Mrs. Norton's sampler is anything but "safe," as its contents eventually produce the warden's doom. These respective holes within the walls of Shawshank (as well as the contrasting feminine artistry that fronts them) reveal a great deal about each of the men who pay nightly homage to them. Andy's poster women display their feminine beauty brazenly even as they hide his portal to freedom; the biblical sampler in Norton's office is more evidence of the religious hypocrisy that the warden hides behind, as it is used to disguise the evidence (even from Norton's own wife?) of the rapacious crony capitalism in which the warden engages, as evinced in the scene with the road construction crew where Norton receives an apple pie that contains a bribe from a desperate competitor. Andy's tunnel represents the start of a visionary pipeline that extends all the way down to Mexico and will include his self-reinvention as a hotel manager and a repairer of boats. Contrastingly, the depth of Norton's small and shallow safe repository is meant to suggest the level of his paranoia (in one scene the warden looks over his shoulder to make sure Andy is not watching him dial in the lock combination), his lack of confidence and imagination, and it remains as terribly finite as a suicide. Andy's hole, like the concrete interior wall film viewers witness break apart to make way for the new prison library, is actually a tunnel of light with unlimited potential; the warden's safe, on the other hand, is a small grave—a locked box without an exit, containing illicit financial resources that Norton will never get to enjoy.

The warden's character is, of course, far more morally debased than the "pornographic" poster art he decries. Because all three actresses (including Jayne Mansfield and Linda Ronstadt, "looking back over her shoulder, her hands tucked into the back pockets of a very tight pair of fawn-colored slacks" [91] in King's novella) are so intimately tied to Andy and the magic of the movies, projected as they are up on the screen of Andy's cell wall, their provocative poses appear less immoral than mystical, less promiscuous than majestic. At one point Andy is filmed seated on the floor of his cell staring up dreamily at Marilyn Monroe pictured in a still from *The Seven Year Itch* (1955). Kermode reads this as another illustration of *Shawshank*'s fascination with the allure of cinema, but the scene belies such simplicity for at this point in the movie the audience is yet unaware that Monroe's iconic legs and white billowing dress hide the escape dream that is literally concealed beneath her skirt. Thus, it is the merging of Monroe's transgressive sexuality with the subversive tunnel that Andy knows resides directly behind her that produces Andy's look of quiet transfiguration. Similar to the simulacrum that takes place when Andy is assaulted and Hayworth is introduced in *Gilda*, this is another image packed with gendered implications, as it combines Andy's cell tunnel leading to Mexico with the erotic flirtation of Marilyn's mock surprise at the very instant she purportedly becomes aware of the subway tunnel blowing up air from a passing train beneath her. The result produces the equivalent of Andy's own Mozart experience and its affect on the inmates in the prison yard: just as the feminine beauty of the sopranos' voices forces the prisoners into a condition of silent contemplation, Andy appears lost in similar state of aesthetic meditation while gazing up at Monroe's alluring photograph. In both scenes, Darabont projects the sublime power of women to inspire awe in heterosexual men who have been separated from their company, verbal as well as visual. In addition to disguising his escape hatch, Monroe is also a constant reminder to Andy of all that is visually encoded in her photograph—a siren's call back to a perfumed realm from which he has been deprived access: the sweet lure of femininity and its accompanying array of white summer dresses, high heels, cleavage, the softness of a girl's bare arms and legs, and perhaps most important given the exclusively male domain in which Andy has been incarcerated, the lilting sound of a woman's laugh that shines through her surface glamour. In contrast to the dour aspects of prison life that the Shawshank inmates project throughout the film, Monroe's picture reveals a paragon of sensual self-presentation, a beautiful woman delighted in and by her own self-abandonment and unconcerned about whatever judgments others may make regarding her provocative body language and attitude. Marilyn's face and body depict all this—a tease as well as a promise to Andy of what awaits at the other end of his tunnel beyond the perimeters of Shawshank. No wonder Kermode chooses to describe Andy's transfixed response to her presence in religious terms, as a "Christ-like pose, eyes wide open in awe" (58).[12]

Kermode's attention to the importance of cinema as a holy art is a fine generalization about Darabont's *Shawshank*, but it is also an observation that is in need of some refinement. While he notes that "Andy's ultimate escape, in which he will literally step through a movie poster to freedom, suggests that the escapist possibilities of the medium are powerful enough to transcend reality" (38), Kermode carves out too broad a thesis regarding Andy's relationship to film. It is not simply cinema as a medium or art in general that is responsible for sparking Andy's escapist fantasies. As we have argued in comparing Gilda's gendered situation to Andy's, audiences must pay attention to the fact that Andy is inspired by *female* actresses occupying *specific* roles in *specific* movies that are both as deliberately seditious as they are "escapist." This also allows for inclusion of the Mozart sopranos in establishing a collusion with the three actresses on Andy's wall: all these women artists inspire Andy to embrace nontraditional gender configurations by modeling his own behavior after the women who inspire him from Hollywood as well as opera.

The last poster Andy deploys, featuring "the lovely Raquel," is a still from *One Million Years B.C.*, another film that, like *Gilda*, creates potent reference points to Dufresne's own circumstances. In *One Million*, Caveman Tumak is a rebel figure banished by his own father from a savage, phallocentric tribe. After days of wandering alone in a bleak prehistoric landscape, replete with dinosaurs and other giant reptiles (historical accuracy as well as special effects are grossly inadequate in this adventure film), he is rescued and nursed back to health by several female members of another human tribe, including Loana (Welch's character) who falls in love with him. The women in the tribe that adopt Tumak make use of language skills, are agrarian farmers as well as carnivores, raise children, and are apparently several steps advanced on the evolutionary ladder beyond the tribe that initially banished Tumak. Loana is not only the most verbally adroit member of her tribe, she's also independent enough to forgo its security and take off with Tumak when he is again expelled from her tribe for fighting. During the course of the film, Loana teaches Tumak many values that he is sorely in need of learning and that distinguish her from the other characters, male and female, in this primitive world. She is capable of soliciting sympathy from him when she cries upon leaving her tribe, Tumak discovers loyalty to another person when he pursues her after she is carried away by a hungry mother pterodactyl, and, most important, she teaches him through her own example the value of showing empathy for vanquished enemies instead of always killing them. The bond that Loana forms with Tumak is similar to the one that Andy maintains with Red; it develops into a kind of marriage. Loana also embodies several personality traits that we likewise associate with Andy in prison: maternal and independent, she's both a teacher and an iconoclast who distinguishes herself as more intelligent and compassionate than the violent world in which she finds herself.

Thus, Andy's most defiant moment in *Shawshank*, his escape attempt, is again linked to and ultimately enabled by female artistic representation; Loana's character and Dufresne's tunnel are both aligned with acts of blatant patriarchal subversion, undermining male authority figures and the oppressive violence of their established caste systems. In this context, it is thus appropriate that the warden indicts Loana/Welch for a role in Andy's disappearance even before finding the tunnel, sensing that she and

Dufresne are bound together in a "damn conspiracy and everyone's in on it, including her." In King's novella, the Welch poster turns out to be Red's favorite, not so much because of the movie or the actress herself, but more for the natural environment pictured in the poster's background. Even before Andy's escape or revelation of Mexico as his future port of call, Red makes an unconscious connection between Welch/Loana, Andy, and a Mexican beach: "I guess that's why I always liked Raquel Welch the best. It wasn't just her; it was that beach she was standing on. Looked like she was down in Mexico somewhere" (*RHSR*, 46).

As discussed earlier in this chapter, Andy becomes as much an object of the "male gaze" in Shawshank prison as Rita Hayworth, Marilyn Monroe, and Raquel Welch were fetishized on the theatrical screen. But Dufresne's bond with these women involves more than simply reversing the gendered focus of sexual objectification (Neale 14–15). Rather, Andy likewise rises to his own level of celebrity status during and after his tenure at Shawshank. Over the years, the warden grows totally dependent on his money-laundering skills and the fabricated identity of Randall Stevens (which of course underscores ironically the warden's final thought regarding "How Andy ever got the best of him"). Each of the women associated with Andy's tunnel operates within the idealized myth of her own celebrity status, particularly Hayworth and Monroe, and through the medium of film and Hollywood publicity and fandom they consequently became larger than life, just as Andy's prison history enters into the inmate folklore of Shawshank after his escape. The other convicts talk about Andy's tenure with the same tone of awe and enthusiasm that they summon collectively in the scene when they are watching Hayworth in *Gilda*. Andy's acts of defiance that culminate in his escape inspire the other prisoners with a collective myth and dreams of their own, much like Hayworth's presence in *Gilda* surely provides the inmates with inspiration for romantic and sexual fantasies. Further, it is worth noting that his friends who remain in Shawshank after Andy's successful escape are pictured reminiscing over those specific moments when he was at his most subversive. In other words, if Andy is motivated by and comes to mirror the behavior of the artistic women who come into his cell at Shawshank, the memory of Andy's behavior, especially as exemplified in Red, similarly inspires the men he has left behind.

Andy comes ironically to empathize with his wife's disgruntled marital situation. His identification with her and the imposed feminization he undergoes as a prisoner and sexual abuse victim deepens his cross-gendered affiliation to the point where it transcends victimization and embraces the rebellious spirit inherent in his wife's desire for freedom from a stultifying marriage and the personae of the assertive women actresses whose posters adorn his wall. The women of *Shawshank* share in common the example of disrupting the status quo, constructing new identities out of what is possible for women, and wrestling power away from both men and narrow definitions of appropriate femininity. Dufresne is no more a typical Shawshank lifer than are his poster women traditional gender representations of their times. As models for seditious behavior, the women with whom Dufresne identifies provide alternatives to traditional femininity, crossing over into the realm of female empowerment, and thus parallel Andy's difference from the other males at Shawshank. That this occurs in a male prison drama literally devoid of women characters accentuates the genius of *Shawshank* and helps to differentiate it from the Hollywood prison genre while connecting it to the celebrated tradition of rebellious cinematic females from film noir to the present day.

The American prison film genre contains few examples of male-to-female gender cross-identification. Those infrequent moments when the genre does allow for such gender transgression tend to center on homoeroticism, relying on pornographic display and transforming the movie into some hybridization of the genre.[13] While often focused on male-to-male bonding, mainstream prison films assiduously avoid both cross-gendered affiliation and explicit evidence of homoeroticism; while they promote male bonding, the topic is framed, as it is in team sports movies, in terms of masculine friendship and goal-orientated cooperation among men that excludes any taint of feminine cross-representation. When women are present in prison and sports films, as well as other kinds of male-buddy films, they exist only at the movies' perimeters—as sidelined wives, girlfriends, and cheerleaders.

The horror film, on the other hand, often relies on gender ambiguity in the construction of its male monsters, creating, in the words of Judith Butler, "abjected beings who do not appear properly gendered; it is their very humanness that comes into question" (8). The horror monster is tortured by his in-between-ness, by his inability to identify satisfactorily with either gender. From Dracula to Norman Bates (*Psycho*) to Leatherface (*Texas Chainsaw Massacre*) to the "Bobbie" half of the schizophrenic Dr. Elliot (*Dressed to Kill*) to Buffalo Bill (*The Silence of the Lambs*), horror art has tended to view its frequent disruptions in male heteronormative gender and sexuality as abject, especially since such gender bending tends to manifest itself through various displays of violent psychopathology. As Judith Halberstam recognizes in her discussion of Buffalo Bill, "he hates identity, he is simply at odds with any identity whatsoever; no body, no gender will do … he constructs a postmodern gender, a gender beyond the body, beyond the human, and a veritable carnage of identity" (164).[14]

This is what makes *Shawshank* such a unique movie. It is a classic prison film that while freely acknowledging male-cross identification with the feminine still manages to keep the issue of homosexuality at the periphery of the picture, restricted to Bogs and the sisters, who are relegated to the first quarter of the movie, and a last-ditch manipulation threat from Warden Norton late in the film. While *Shawshank* likewise shares a connection to horror's paradigm by associating female representation with the film's male hero, instead of transforming him into a monstrous abjection, his adoption of the feminine defines and enlightens Andy's characterization. Indeed, Andy's identification with women in *Shawshank* helps to make him more human, not less. Andy's appreciation for and appropriation of the feminine thereby link him more to characters such as Tootsie, Mrs. Doubtfire, and Steve/Amanda in *Switch*—film comedies where heterosexual men come to empathize and appreciate women only after being forced to inhabit feminized bodies—rather than the murderous transvestitism associated with Norman Bates or Buffalo Bill. The horror genre ultimately views the feminine misogynistically, as the source for male gender distress and the compulsion to pursue violence (ironically, against women). It is interesting that Hollywood typically permits heterosexual men to identify with and assume aspects of overt femininity only in comedies, and that this association is presented more through a factitious physical transvestitism than a serious challenge to gender identity. Heterosexual male identification with femaleness is thereby made more reductive or at least less threatening to heteronormative society because it appears in a comic context. Without this context, male-to-female identification comes dangerously close to crossing the border into homosexuality or permanent gender realignment, as is the case in a film such as *The Danish Girl*. The subtle but consistent male-to-female bond that Andy Dufresne maintains, however, is centered on the transference of artistic representation, positive heterosexual attraction, and rebellion against conformity and authority, thereby skirting completely issues of crossdressing, homosexuality, and gender antagonism, which explains why *Shawshank* remains transgressive and empowering without also being comedic or abject.

Notes

1. *Gump* was nominated for thirteen Academy Awards for films released in 1994; it collected six.
   In addition to Best Picture, it also won in the following categories: Best Actor, Best Director, Best Adapted Screenplay, Best Sound, Best Film Editing, and Best Visual Effects. *The Shawshank Redemption* was nominated for Best Picture, Morgan Freeman for Best Actor, Best Adapted Screenplay, Best Sound, Best Cinematography, Best Film Editing, and Best Original Score.

2. Of all *The Shining* adaptations, King's 1997 version made for ABC Television supplies the most graphic illustration of this familial breakdown. Wendy Torrance (Rebecca De Mornay) appears in a scene wearing a revealing white satin negligee in an attempt to summon the amorous attention of her husband, Jack (Steven Weber), who is distracted by Overlook memorabilia. She promises him something "you're not going to find in any of those boxes." Jack's obvious lack of interest in her sexual invitation is really the first moment in the miniseries that signals his psychic deterioration, his preference for the hotel in place of his wife.

3. The characterization of Elmo Blatch, the actual murderer of Andy's "tasty bitch" wife and Glen Quinton, her golf pro lover, emerges from out of the shadows to become the film's most gothic figure. His exaggerated facial features, particularly his unwholesome mouth sporting large yellowing teeth, make him resemble a gothic grotesquerie from early horror films, recalling Charles Laughton as Quasimodo in *The Hunchback of Notre Dame* or bearing a similar set of shark-like dentures as Lon Chaney in *London After Midnight*. Blatch's blessedly short screen time is barely tolerable as he pants his way through a boastful confession of the double homicide because his victims "gave [him] shit." For those who consider *Shawshank* too sentimental or unrealistic a picture, they would do well to remember that the power of Blatch's scene is such to encourage the inference that this Hyde-like beast has killed before and, if given the chance, will probably kill again, since he is disturbingly proud of his murders going undetected. Little wonder that Tommy immediately appears so at home once he is transferred to Shawshank; after sharing a cell with Elmo, incarceration at Shawshank Prison must have felt like redemption.

4. Rape and the threat of rape are omnipresent conditions for women throughout the gothic. In De Sade's *Philosophy of the Bedroom* (1795), he asserts that men have the "undeniable right to enjoy [women sexually], and I do have the right to force her if she rejects me for whatever reason" (128). As Ambrosio's sexual propensities become ever more violently perverse in Lewis' *The Monk* (1795), a titillating psychosexual tragedy, the once pious

but corrupted holy man kidnaps, rapes, and then murders his own sister. While in Stoker's *Dracula* (1897), the Count's vamping of both Lucy and Mina always occurs forcefully against the volition of each woman and assumes the form of sexual rape.

5. Technically, Red's journey into the natural world commences with his poetic appreciation of the soprano duet from *The Marriage of Figaro*. Wye Allanbrook discusses the aria as an example of one of the opera's five pastorals used to represent a "green world," wherein Mozart and other eighteenth-century musicians provided countrified music for the entertainment of urban-bound aristocrats (84–5).

6. Much of King's work references a regional truth that Frost, his fellow New Englander, also exposed in "Mending Wall." According to King, "Maine is different. People keep to themselves, and they take the outsiders' money, and on the surface, at least, they're polite about it. But they keep themselves to themselves" (Underwood and Miller 137).

7. Full Disclosure: In personal email conversation, Stephen King has expressed his disagreement with our interpretation of the institutionalization theme in *Shawshank* extending into a reading of Frost's poem. Perhaps reflecting his sparse development of the topic in his novella, King, who adheres to a more literal and systemic construction of institutionalization, opines that our pursuit of the term into "Mending Wall" "reaches too far. Certainly it makes a connection that wasn't in my conscious mind." However, as postmodern criticism would argue, the critic's interpretation may differ from what the novelist intended—such is the nature of art. We would counter that applying the theme of institutionalization to Frost's poem is applicable, regardless of whether or not King consciously referenced "Mending Wall" with this parallel in mind (King, "Question").

8. As King informs us in the novella: "The blueprints might have told him how big the pipe's bore was, but a blueprint couldn't tell him what it would be like inside that pipe—if he would be able to breathe without choking, if the rats were big enough and mean enough to fight instead of retreating ... and a blueprint couldn't have told him what he'd find at the end of the pipe, when and if he got there" (*RHSR*, 92).

9. Andy's period of incarceration would have corresponded with the emergence of Second Wave feminism, named to recognize the development and popularization of feminism in the 1960s and 1970s. Second Wave feminism centered on legal issues, such as equality in the workplace and reproductive rights for women. But most relevant to our discussion of Andy Dufresne and the identifying bond he establishes with women throughout the movie, Second Wave feminism also campaigned for dramatic shifts in normative gender roles, encouraging women *and men* to challenge and expand their identification beyond traditional constructions of gender.

10. The two men never do play chess in the film, although in his letter to Red, Andy promises to "keep the chess board ready," presumably leaving to Red the option in Mexico to resume playing checkers or, perhaps, to learn how to play chess. Red's preference for the simplicity of checkers over chess may well symbolize his black-and-white resignation to long-term incarceration. The reductive nature of the prison world is challenged after Red's parole: the uncomplicated nature of checkers turns into the more complicated "mystery" of chess once he is alone on the outside. Andy, on the hand, befitting his appreciation for the game, plays a kind of grandiose unconventional chess match all through the movie, maneuvering, for example, his "white queen" across the board of the license plate factory roof against Hadley's black tarred "knight."

11. What made Leslie Fiedler's critical work so original and fun to ponder was his career-long commitment to "stranger" figures—from women and Jews in Shakespeare, to carnival freaks, and Hollywood monsters. Fiedler also understood intuitively that the art of popular culture—its literature and media, but likewise its comics and pornography—supplied the opportunity for unique insights to understanding the fantasies and anxieties of a culture often unexpressed in the renderings of its highest art forms. The interracial, class-defying bond that is established between Andy and Red in *Shawshank* confirms Fiedler's core theses about both popular art and American culture insofar as theirs remains an illicit relationship that can only be acknowledged in a prison or on the run. In this sense, *The Defiant Ones* is yet another prison film that closely parallels *Shawshank* in its premise that humans share the capacity to overcome racism even in the face of an omnipotent penal system.

12. Repeat viewers of *Shawshank* are encouraged to wonder the degree to which Monroe's playful sexuality revealed in this iconic movie portrait remains in competition with the secreted tunnels located both beneath and behind her that no doubt serve over time to stimulate and haunt Andy's imagination. *The Seven Year Itch* features Monroe as the fantasy object of a New York husband who finds himself alone in the city for the summer. Monroe plays the role of The Girl, a character without a name, which implies that her presence is primarily to enflame male desire. She does that, of course, but in the process also reveals herself to be highly self-possessed, comfortable with both her own sexuality and in the ability to help the husband control his. So, while The Girl is, in part, an extension of masculine fantasy (and thus perfectly suited to Monroe's image as a sex goddess), her character's context in *Shawshank* appears again to parallel the other women with whom Andy is affiliated—particularly Gilda and the Mozart sopranos—in emphasizing her ability to thwart male desire.

13. The 1985 Brazilian-American film, *Kiss of the Spider Woman*, is a good example where love between two male inmates is eventually sexualized. The film thus morphs into a romance-love story, a cinematic hybrid that comes

eventually to rely on a level of explicit homoeroticism typically missing from the more conservative prison genre.

14. Jeffrey Jerome Cohen, in his far-ranging exploration of what constitutes monstrosity, includes "the acceptance of new subjectivities unfixed by binary gender ... and resistance to integration" (5, 7). For more discussion on the association between monsters and the collapsing gender boundaries, see Linda Williams, "When the Woman Looks," 17–36, Barbara Creed, *The Monstrous Feminine*, 10–15, and Carol Clover, *Men, Women, and Chainsaws*, 42–64.

CHAPTER 4

Fandom and the *Shawshank* Trail (research contributions by Richard Roberson, Jr.)

I still think there's no substitute for going to a live event, being with your fan community and friends right there and then seeing the stars who are also on site. I don't believe anything electronic can ever replace that. Our lives are increasingly complicated and it's expensive, there are so many types of entertainment possibilities that we all have to be discriminatory and pick and choose.

(Adam Malin, qtd. in Zubernis and Larsen 21)

Let's return for a moment to the last chapter's comparison between *Shawshank* and *Forrest Gump*, two of the most celebrated pictures released in 1994, a munificent year for Hollywood. As we discussed then, both films have generated enormous fan bases that continue to grow as the movies are replayed on cable and streaming services to new generations of viewers. *Gump* and *Shawshank* have obviously forged a mysterious and personal connection with their fans, one that clearly demarcates these two pictures, as only a very small percentage of films ever inspire this level of sustained audience attention. Their fans also share much in common: in addition to a deeply emotional attachment to each respective film, many likewise share a desire to visit the various locations where these movies were made. Like Gump, who finds himself spliced into specific black and white photographs detailing moments in American history, a fan touring the shooting sites

© The Author(s) 2016
M. Grady, T. Magistrale, *The Shawshank Experience*,
DOI 10.1057/978-1-137-53165-0_4

of *Gump* and *Shawshank* enters filmic space—creating a kind of personal simulacrum—when visiting a meaningful site from either film. However, Forrest's southern mansion, the place where he lives with his mother and, later in the movie, with Jenny and their son—purportedly situated in Alabama, but actually constructed on an eight thousand-acre plantation filmed in Beaufort, South Carolina—no longer exists; the house was torn down after the movie was made. *Gump* fans still journey to tour the grounds of this South Carolina plantation as well as to the town square/bus stop box of chocolates scene filmed in Savannah, Georgia, but it is apparent that, these two sites notwithstanding, the movie's fan base lacks a central physical place to congregate and resuscitate moments from this film. This stands in marked contrast to what is available for aficionados of *Shawshank*, where the Ohio State Reformatory and several of the other satellite locations used in the film have coalesced to form the *Shawshank* Trail. Essentially, the *Gump* fan base exists primarily in cyberspace, while *Shawshank* fans, as evinced from the websites and other Internet locations listed at the end of this chapter, connect with one another both online and through events that are held periodically at OSR and at other primary locations featured along the Trail.

This chapter explores another bequest of *Shawshank*. It is about what happened after the movie was completed and sent out into the world. It is about the process that enabled the movie's production—its choice of location sites, people, and artifacts that shaped a concept (Darabont's screenplay and King's novella) and turned it into a visual reality, a process common to the making of movies and the creation of most art forms, regardless of their medium. But this part of the book also centers on several of the individuals the film left behind in Ohio; like a torrid love affair, they were transformed and enchanted, and then left to return to their everyday lives, albeit in possession of cherished relics and deeply felt memories. And while this chapter is about the past—highlighting the local recollections of those who worked as extras on the *Shawshank* set, spent time with its Hollywood stars in 1993 as they interacted daily within the Mansfield community, and sustained the production itself as construction workers, caterers, and support personnel—it is likewise about the movie's post-production legacy and future: its continued influence and impact on the community where it was made, and those millions of fans who live outside of Ohio still affected by it.

The *Shawshank* Trail,[1] a drive-it-yourself tour of filming sites, consists of fourteen locations in Mansfield and its neighboring communities that were used in the creation of *The Shawshank Redemption*. Some of these places appeared only briefly as cameos in the picture, such as the pawnshop window where Red chooses between a gun and a compass, while others were of vital importance to the film, such as the oak tree that connects Red to Andy's past and future. The fourteen sites featured on the Trail (along with their current affiliations) are the *Shawshank* Woodshop (Upper Sandusky, Ohio); Andy's Trial Courthouse (Wyandot County Courthouse, Upper Sandusky, Ohio); the Trailways Bus station (Revivals 2 Thrift Shop, Ashland, Ohio); Maine National Bank (Crosby Advisory Group LLC, Ashland, Ohio); Glen Quentin's House (Pugh Cabin at Malabar Farm State Park, Lucas, Ohio); the *Shawshank* oak tree (Lucas, Ohio); Red's bus route to Texas (Rte. 95, Butler, Ohio); Red's road to Buxton (Snyder & Hagerman Rd, Butler, Ohio); Brooks' bench (Mansfield's Central Park, Mansfield, Ohio); Red's pawnshop window (Carrousel Antiques, Mansfield, Ohio); the Brewer Hotel and offices for *The Portland Daily Bugle* (The Bissman Building, Mansfield, Ohio); the site of *Shawshank*'s 1994 world premier (Renaissance Theatre, Mansfield, Ohio); and, of course, the most important and popular stop on the tour, *Shawshank* State Prison (Ohio State Reformatory, Mansfield, Ohio).

The *Shawshank* Trail offers a set of unique opportunities when compared to most other fan sites, and not only in terms of the plethora of individual locations fans can access or the short distances that separate the individual sites situated around central Ohio. The Trail essentially brings together two intersections of potential fandom: the film-induced tourism interest associated with *Shawshank* the movie and prison tourism linked to OSR. While it is certainly true that *Shawshank* made OSR tourism possible (the prison was scheduled to be demolished prior to filming and the film's popular success aided the local people already working to rescue it), the reformatory has now, decades later, established its own place on the registry of decommissioned American prisons and as the site of Ohio's official State Penal History Museum. Although perhaps not as infamous as Alcatraz or Eastern State Penitentiary in Philadelphia, and while it will forever be impossible to separate the reformatory from *Shawshank* in the popular imagination, as a tourist destination OSR continues to raise the same core question relevant to these other defunct prisons—namely, what motivates people to visit these sites of protracted human punishment and misery, and what do tourists bring to and take away from their experiences? As we discussed in Chap. 2, many tourists are interested in OSR because of its architecture, and this was certainly the major reason why Darabont's scouting crew chose it as the primary location for *Shawshank*'s filming. Michelle Brown expands the range of explanations, however, when she opines that visitors "arrive at the gates of closed prisons for many reasons—to retrace history, to search for ghosts, and to view otherwise prohibited places … most have trouble articulating why they are visiting at all" (90). The Trail, then, brings together two related moments in time—the film history of *Shawshank* established in 1993 and the century-long existence of OSR as a state institution—and on the Trail these two histories intersect and cannot help avoid blurring into one another. In other words, in the course of touring the Trail, it is possible to start out as a fan of *Shawshank* and, after engaging OSR as a physical presence and learning something about its convoluted past, to leave a fan of the reformatory as well.

Visitors to OSR have increased from 80,000 visitors in 2013 to over 110,000 in 2015, and it is projected that this number will continue to increase as greater restoration work is completed on the old facility and more events are held on its grounds. But the prison is not the only draw for *Shawshank* fans to the area. The *Shawshank* Trail has been in operation for several years and coordinates with the individual sites to plan and promote special events, such as a 2013 cast and crew reunion celebrating the filming year anniversary and, especially enticing for the film's larger fan base, a 2014 twentieth anniversary event that commemorated the release of the film. The Trail is now chiefly hosted through the Mansfield Convention and Visitors Bureau in Mansfield, but is a genuine community effort, supported and coordinated by the individual sites, local businesses, and communities. Hundreds of local residents were involved in the 1993 filming, as cast, crew, extras, and support to the production. Though the novella and the film are set in a fictionalized Maine (as are most of King's works), the real history and atmosphere of these Ohio locations, as well as the contributions of the local North Central Ohio communities, had and still exert a real effect on the look and feel of the film; moreover, the production has had a lasting impact on the local area. The *Shawshank* Woodshop in Upper Sandusky (about 46 miles from Mansfield) would seem to be a bit outside the orbit for visitors centered around the sun of OSR, but, in fact, "Upper" (as it's called by the locals) is the birthplace of the *Shawshank* fan tourism industry in Ohio.

BILL AND APRIL MULLEN AND THE *SHAWSHANK* WOODSHOP

Although it has been in existence only since 1994, *The Shawshank Redemption* consistently ranks as one of the most beloved films of all time. Viewers and critics have been putting it at or near the top of "best of" lists for nearly a decade (Heidenry, n.p.). Both Morgan Freeman and Tim Robbins note that this film—more than any of the scores of other films they have done—is the one that prompts the most spontaneous declarations of love from fans they meet (*Shawshank: The Redeeming Feature*). There is a formidable volume of online tributes to *Shawshank* by fans, who have produced and posted hundreds of videos, Tumblr sites, fan pages, and online discussion threads about the movie (see the last section of this chapter). Critics have praised *Shawshank*'s elegant script, pitch-perfect casting, lush cinematography, and stirring score, but there seems to be something greater than the sum of these parts that inspires fans to drop whatever they may be doing and watch the movie whenever it appears on cable television during one of its frequent airings. A true fan of this film doesn't require much prompting to begin discussing it with a total stranger, both typically employing terms of awe and reverence.

While many writers and critics (including the authors of this volume) have taught and analyzed *Shawshank*, there has been relatively little scholarship on the nature of *Shawshank* fandom. Until the organization of a fifteenth anniversary filming reunion event in the small town of Upper Sandusky, Ohio, in 2008, *Shawshank*'s many viewers enjoyed the film in relative isolation, without a central locus linked to the movie or an identifiable fan base. Since that event, however, *Shawshank*'s community of fans has coalesced around the filming locations in North Central Ohio. And this is largely because of the efforts of one person—Bill Mullen—and his love for his town, its history, and a movie that was partially filmed there. In 2000, Bill and his wife April Mullen purchased the lumber building which served as the location for several scenes set in the *Shawshank* Prison's Woodshop, where Red was employed when not helping Andy file tax returns. After filming, the building was sold along with most of the woodworking equipment. When the Mullens bought the building, they worked to track down as much of the original equipment as possible. More than that—they got a lot of it working again, not just as a point of pride but to make the experience of visiting the Woodshop as authentic as possible a reproduction of being on the set.

The Mullens are the owners of a heating and cooling supply business in Upper Sandusky. Bill has never met a stranger—he possesses a warm, engaging, and calming presence; he manages to put everyone who meets him at ease with his open expression and quiet enthusiasm. He's the type of person who inspires people to do things for him, such as dress up as inmates and stage a reenactment of the beloved "opera scene" from

Shawshank in the Mullen woodshop as a fund-raiser. Bill conceived of a fan event—a reenactment of the pivotal "opera sequence" in the film, where Andy Dufresne locks himself in the warden's office to play a selection from *Le Nozze di Figaro* over the prison's PA system. Apart from the high angle shots of the prison yard, emphasizing the point-of-view of the loudspeaker above the prison population below, the sequence features the woodshop location prominently; Red is pictured working there at the moment when he hears the music. In this sequence, the camera lingers on Morgan Freeman in front of a distinctive wood saw. The saw was made by HB Smith Company, headquartered in Smithville, New Jersey, originally called Shreveville. HB Smith bought the town and named it Smithville. According to the Mullens, the company was responsible for producing most of the woodworking machinery used in mid-twentieth-century America.

The event, which brought extras and crew associated with the 1993 production back to the community to reminisce, raised $10,000. Frank Darabont himself sent a donation of $1000 along with some memorabilia from the film that was then auctioned off. Aside from the joy inherent in restaging an integral part of this beloved film, the collected funds were allocated towards the restoration of a bronze statue of Lady Justice (a cost of $23,000) located on the roof of the Wyandot County Courthouse, the film site of Andy Dufresne's trial and sentencing in *Shawshank*. In his commentary to the fifteenth anniversary DVD, Darabont described the location as "a wonderful courtroom … a beautiful courtroom" supported by a local population "that really did welcome" the production. Darabont further recalled being "really very taken by that." Knowing that more repairs would be needed for a full restoration of the courthouse, built in 1899 and badly in need of renovation at an estimated cost of $1.4 million, the nonprofit formed for the reunion transferred its momentum to the *Shawshank* Woodshop. The Mullen-owned Woodshop, in turn, became a permanent *Shawshank* exhibit with all funds going to the courthouse. The community felt some urgency to get a capital campaign under way quickly to avoid suffering the doomed fate of a courthouse in neighboring Seneca County, which at the time was likewise threatened with demolition because funds could not be raised to repair it (and it was duly razed in 2012). In an interview, Mullen asserted that Ohio's old courthouses "are an asset that can't be duplicated. Ours is quite beautiful" (Feehan "*Shawshank*"). The beauty of the building and its historic ambiance is what initially attracted the *Shawshank* film crew to Upper Sandusky in

1993, since Mansfield's old court building was demolished in 1969 and replaced with a striking, yet clearly more modern, structure. According to a 1993 interview with former Wyandot County Court reporter Carolyn Law, the filmmakers "fell in love" with the courtroom because it "still has the 1900s décor. We have the old judge's chair. The seats in the jury box are the old leather chairs. We have a stained glass dome that they just loved" (Feehan "*Shawshank*").

Unlike some more well-known fandom communities usually associated with genre fiction, film, and television, *Shawshank*'s fandom has had a slower, more organic build-up, springing to life from the nondescript and post-industrial communities in Ohio where *Shawshank* was filmed. Had it not been for both *Shawshank* and a renewal of local pride and ingenuity, these communities might well have remained obscure towns, easily missed by a traveler passing through the state on her way to Columbus or Cleveland. Bill Mullen hit upon the idea of using enthusiasm for *Shawshank* to garner community support for a fundraising campaign. The work of Bill, April, and others not only raised the initial $10,000 necessary for refurbishing the courthouse statue, but further proceeds from the *Shawshank* Woodshop and its associated nonprofit as well as other *Shawshank*-related events helped to convince lawmakers and citizens in 2013 to generate a six-year bond issue for $2.25 million that will complete the rest of the courthouse's restoration work (Feehan "*Shawshank*").

Describing the courthouse's condition in the 2000s, Bill remembers, "from the roof level and up it was falling apart and 'Lady Justice' on top sounded the alarm bell." "Lady Justice," the 10-foot-tall copper representation of the Roman goddess of justice, manufactured by the W.H. Mullins Company of Salem, Ohio, sat atop the courthouse's 132-foot copper dome since 1899 and was showing wear after a century of being subject to the elements, pigeons, and even bullets. The scales she once held in her hand had been removed by the wind, half of her sword of justice was gone, part of the skirt by her hip was missing, and birds would fly into her (Feehan, "Lady Justice"). Though some makeshift repairs had been attempted over the years, they hadn't held up. Bill recalls that one evening in 2007, a group of friends met at a local watering hole and talk turned to the courthouse—the general sentiment was that "no one [local politicians] seemed to want to do anything about fixing her up," and since Bill's business supplied the county with its HVAC needs and he was acquainted with several of the commissioners at the state and local levels, it was determined that he should serve as the group's point guard in finding a solution. The response he received from the commissioners was one that is often heard in cash-strapped small towns: the state had placed so many unfunded mandates on the county that the latter was "lucky to keep the lights on here" (Mullen, Bill). The commissioners informed Bill that a recent study had estimated that repairs would cost well over a million dollars, if the goal was to return the building to good working condition. The dollar figure was thought to be simply impossible, given the other commitments of the county government, so the Mullens and their neighbors steeled themselves to battle with the roof without municipal assistance.

Bill and April decided to do what they could to begin to raise the funds themselves. "We had this asset—*Shawshank*," Bill says, "and that could get everyone excited." They brainstormed ways to get as many people involved as possible, and since *Shawshank* carried the greatest and most obvious cachet, they hit on the idea to hold a reunion for cast, extras, and crewmembers to celebrate the film's fifteenth anniversary and stage a reenactment of the opera scene using the same extras who had appeared in the film originally, as well as other volunteers. "We thought of something that would get people involved. Bill wanted the machinery to work. He said what better thing to do than recreate the scene from the woodshop in the movie? Instead of just having people look around," which didn't sound nearly as compelling. "Being so far away from everything [in Mansfield], we knew that we'd have to have one of those moments here" (Mullen, April). But at this point the Mullens also began to establish connections with the other locations in Mansfield to coordinate a more elaborate celebration. They invited Darabont to return to Ohio; they contacted a number of the actors from the production. April recalls, "We sold tour buses for people to go from here to Mansfield. The tour guides were people who had been in the movie. Our guides ended up attracting people who weren't in our group," as OSR didn't have enough guides to accommodate the increased number of visitors over that weekend. The Mullens visited the prison three times before the [2008] reunion, and according to Bill, "They brought us in [to OSR] personally with their best tour guide and we went everywhere" in the building, even locations not on the official tour. OSR recognized the potential value in cooperation—as they benefitted directly and measurably from the publicity of Upper's event. As Bill recalled, "We had 100-plus people at our site [in Upper] and they had 400 [at OSR]." Knowing that the prison would always represent the bigger draw, April added, "That's why we had to do something to get them to come to Upper. We had a band and Stroh's beer," the latter was featured in the film.

The former Stephen Lumber Company building came into the Mullens' possession as a site for a branch warehouse/office for their business wholesaler. The space was larger than they needed, so they were able to set aside the woodshop's area for use outside of the business' heating and cooling equipment supply needs. "April and I knew they had filmed the woodshop scenes from *Shawshank* there, but little was left as far as equipment and what was left wouldn't work" (Mullen, Bill). Bill and April surveyed further damage after taking possession, including evidence that local kids had used the glass windows as target practice for their stone-throwing activities. They rented out some of the additional space to other businesses, including a real estate appraisal firm that had initially asked the Mullens to demolish the old brick mill part of the building (i.e., including the woodshop), but Bill and April "dismissed the idea" due to their "love of everything and everybody old." They worked on bringing the building into working order—new windows, new paint, new gutters, all brick cleaned and tuck pointed—until, as Bill put it, "the old girl was really looking good."

Bill and April painstakingly tracked down as much of the original woodworking equipment as they could find and were determined to get it working for the reunion, reasoning that seeing and hearing it in operation would add to the fan experience. They produced their first web video to promote the fifteenth anniversary event, in which they sought to entice *Shawshank* fans to visit by asking: "How'd you like to walk where they walked, touch what they touched, be in the scene? You're going to hear what they heard; you're going to see what they saw. There's an element of danger here, too! Something could happen. This is old stuff" (Mullen, Bill). A local resident, an extra in the movie, and regular *Shawshank* Woodshop volunteer, Bob Wachtman, told us that "part of that belt-driven power train was still there [at the reunion] and the one [large planing] machine so characteristic of that time was still operating" (Wachtman). This equipment is seen in the film when Tommy teases his fellow inmates by calling them, "old-timers moving like molasses [making him] look bad." In addition to obtaining the woodworking equipment, Bill and April sent out the word that they were looking for any object connected to *Shawshank* to showcase at the reunion for the fans and film participants. Bill recalled, "Other than re-enacting the scene, people wanted to see things from the movie [such as] costumes; a lot of that belonged to other people." April added, "When we were planning it, [we] wanted to get the people that were movie extras involved, even people that had cars, or whatever." The Mullens not only found and restored the same woodworking equipment and vehicles used in the film, they have also curated a collection of costumes, props, and original photographs from the set. Local extras were invited to autograph pictures of themselves in costume. While the assumption might be that fans are most interested in big stars, devoted fans are often equally excited about "lesser" characters and extras because including them in events offers fans the opportunity to connect with the film on a level not available to the broader public or the casual viewer (Zubernis and Larsen 209). In other words, meeting anyone connected with the film helps fans feel as if they have gained access to something special, a more personalized experience associated with a movie they love.

Since the reunion, the Mullens have tracked down several vehicles from the film—including the bus that brings Andy to *Shawshank* Prison in 1947 and later ferries Brooks Hatlen out of jail and back into town. They even got the bus engine running again ("She purrs like a kitten," says Bill) and put it on display at the 2015's *Shawshank* Hustle 7K race, which drew over 5000 runners from around the country to OSR. Also at the Woodshop is the ambulance that removes Bogs from *Shawshank* when he is transferred to a medical prison facility following his beating by Hadley. Much of the treasure hunting for *Shawshank* artifacts takes place online. "It's how we found the bus and I think that's probably how [Bill] found the ambulance. [The ambulance] is sitting back there. We drove down to West Virginia to get that from a collector down there. Twenty years takes its toll … it's gonna be a job to restore it. But Bill can do it. I'm too old to have that kind of gumption in me!" (Wachtman). The restoration of the vehicles and the woodworking equipment gives visitors a full sensory experience when they visit the Woodshop. The smell of wood shavings greets fans the moment they enter, as do the sounds of the woodworking equipment and the engines of the old vehicles. These are long-time passions for Bill: "Always been into old cars. Old cars, old buildings, old people." When we suggested that *Shawshank* is the perfect excuse to bring all of the things he loves together, Bill concurred enthusiastically: "It is! It is! I think what I like is what a lot of other people like. We have our group, our following. We're seeing a lot of young people come to the Trail and that's great." The Mullens documented everything they did for the 2008 reunion and sent a video copy to Frank Darabont in Hollywood. "Frank was blown away by it—he sent [us back] a video. We [also] sent all the actors a packet with a t-shirt and poster we put out, and a video of Lady Justice. We sent it to all the stars" (Mullen, Bill). The Mullens distributed these *Shawshank* care packages as both a thank you and a sort of invitation, "to see if it would spark something so if maybe we could try this in five years [to commemorate the twentieth anniversary of the film's release], the stars might decide to visit then" (Mullen, April).

The Woodshop's choice to feature the "opera sequence" was a clever one—a scene wholly invented by Darabont for the film, it's a favorite for many fans of the movie. The sequence resonates in particular with fans from Ohio. In the pre-CGI days of 1994, hundreds of extras were needed to form an audience for the music in the prison yard; the sequence couldn't be created digitally. For prison yard scenes such as this one and the stunning aerial sequence that announces the arrival of Andy and the fresh fish to *Shawshank*, hundreds of extras were required—most were unemployed locals who had the time to spend a full month on the film set—and a number of these same people gathered again for the fifteenth anniversary reunion to recreate the iconic operatic moment. The opera scene reenactment is now a regular feature at the woodshop, performed for visiting groups whenever possible. In an effort to reproduce the film's sound of a scratchy recording coming out of a PA system, the reenactment plays the music through a modified speaker so that the cracks and pops are emphasized as they are in the film. "We knew it had to be authentic. [That first time in 2008], we did the best job we could with our local talent," Bill said with a grin. Local identification and enthusiasm are key factors in stimulating and maintaining interest in the film and tourism events. In our research for this and other projects related to *Shawshank*, each person we spoke with residing in the three filming counties of Ashland, Mansfield, and Wyandot was either personally involved with making the film or knows someone who was. A part-time volunteer at the Ashland University library, for example, still carries with him on his phone a photograph of the check he received from Castle Rock Entertainment (for a film production then titled *Rita Hayworth and Shawshank Redemption*) paying him to rent his vintage car and to appear as an extra in the "Portland Bank" scene at the end of the film, which was produced in Ashland. He noted wryly that his car got paid twice as much as he did.

Fans visiting the *Shawshank* Woodshop are quickly impressed by Bill and April Mullens' passion for the film. The Mullens are genuine fans themselves—their location site during the 2014 anniversary event was more like an open house, where everyone could take their time looking at

Fig. 4.1   Bill and April Mullen with Red (Morgan Freeman) at a charity event

the exhibited objects and chatting with the actors, and less like a standard fan convention or Harry Potter experience-type attraction. It was a far more organic experience, like the fan base itself, grown out of the desire for people to share a love of the movie in the exact location where it was made. Fans report they know that proceeds benefit the restoration of the Woodshop and the courthouse, but don't seem solely motivated by this when they purchase merchandise. However, it probably helps sales that they know they are supporting a good cause. By 2014, April had put together a full gift shop with t-shirts, posters, key chains, and other souvenirs for visiting fans. Roberson and Grady's data from the 2013 reunion survey indicated that fans wanted an even greater selection of merchandise than had already been available at the Woodshop, OSR, and other locations along the Trail. The locations responded, adding a wider variety of items and in 2014, merchandise sales went up correspondingly (Roberson and Grady 57, 59). During the 2013 weekend, the Woodshop sold out of stock quickly and hit upon the idea to burn the official *Shawshank*

Woodshop logo into scraps of wood and sell those for a dollar apiece as souvenirs. The Roberson and Grady study, as well as other research on fan spending, indicates that fans are willing to support nonprofits, such as the Woodshop and OSR, which are dedicated to the upkeep of the film's buildings, because fans want these locations to be preserved either for themselves to visit again or for others because they value *Shawshank* as a significant historical and cultural object. *Shawshank* fans seemed particularly happy to support the locations knowing that they are owned by independent operators. They viewed themselves as not making "charity" purchases: they were buying what they wanted and bought more when they were provided with a bigger and better selection of merchandise. Overwhelmingly, fans commented that these experiences are far superior to other filming sites they have visited due to the personal attention and the unique, non-corporate, local feel of each location. These are not franchises and they cannot be recreated anywhere else because these locations are where the scenes were actually filmed (Fig. 4.1).

THE *SHAWSHANK* TRAIL

When Castle Rock and the production crew for *The Shawshank Redemption* came to central Ohio in the summer of 1993 to film, the community welcomed them enthusiastically. At that time, all these communities were down on their luck—financially and spiritually. It was only in 2014 that Mansfield was officially removed from a state of fiscal emergency, a status it had held for more than three years as a result of decades of economic decline coming to a crisis point in the 2007 recession (Grazier). In the late nineteenth and early twentieth century, when construction occurred for most of the buildings featured in *Shawshank*'s city scenes—Brooks carrying his one suitcase along the streets to his lodgings and sitting on the park bench, Red walking to the pawnshop, and both men working at the Foodway supermarket—Mansfield was a prosperous city, its growth bolstered first by a connection via railroad in 1846 to Sandusky, not to be confused with Upper Sandusky ("Mansfield, Ohio"). The city had a population of 2330, twenty-three stores, seven churches, and two newspapers. Over the next four decades, Mansfield continued to grow, adding population, retail and manufacturing, and trade. Its prominence was due largely to its situation as a crossroads at the convergence of four railroad lines. Dozens of manufacturing businesses set up shop at this strategic location, producing doors, brass fittings, linseed oil, paper boxes, and cigars ("Mansfield, Ohio"). By 1888, the year the city broke ground at OSR, Mansfield had around 13,000 residents.

In its heyday, a city of beautifully built structures rose up. Several of these are featured prominently in the film and have become central stops on the *Shawshank* Trail. The Bissman Building (the exteriors of the Brewer Hotel where both Brooks and Red reside after being paroled; its interior also served as the headquarters of the *Portland Daily Bugle* which receives the postal package from Andy containing Warden Norton's ledger) is a stunning example of late nineteenth-century urban architecture. Still owned by the Bissman family, the 50,000 square foot building was commissioned in 1886 by Peter Bissman and designed by the architectural firm Alexander and Dow. It was engineered and constructed by the same group of contractors that built OSR and served as a store representing wholesale grocers until the recession of the 1970s. Prior to that time, the business supplied the local area with a variety of goods, including hand-rolled cigars, Bissman's Red Band coffee, canned goods, and bottled alcoholic beverages. Locals strolling by could smell roasting coffee and peanuts.[2] The current owner is Ben Bissman, and though much of its square footage is not utilized, the building is home to several Bissman family businesses, including Pirate Printing, a screen-printing and embroidery business, which, among other things, produces original *Shawshank* t-shirts. The building is a popular stop for enthusiasts of "Haunted Mansfield" and a site of frequent organized ghost hunts. Visitors climbing the front stairs to the building are immediately struck by the deep grooves worn in the marble steps from years of repeated use. Ben Bissman, a tall and jovial man with a goatee beard and curly head of hair tied in a ponytail, proudly shows visitors around his building with an air of a curator sharing a treasured family legacy. He regales tourists with stories of his family's business, the city's past in commerce and grocery distribution, the purported ghosts, and his family's personal history. He describes playing in the building—having the run of the place—as a small child and points out many of its architectural features. He and his wife appeared as extras in the film (their framed photographs are on prominent display) and they share with great alacrity their conversations with James Whitmore (Brooks Hatlen), whom they made feel comfortable inside their building during breaks in the filming. The glass window display that announced the location of the editorial offices for *The Portland Daily Bugle* near the end of *Shawshank* still resides in a wood-paneled room inside the Bissman Building that also displays movie memorabilia for visiting fans, including one of the bottles of Stroh's Bohemian beer used in the film, now enclosed in a clear display case. By coincidence, Bissman Grocers was once the distributer for Stroh's in the area.

As was the case with many other urban manufacturing centers in the Midwest, the 1970s started Mansfield on a period of economic decline. The steel recession and the loss of manufacturing jobs, first to automation and eventually overseas, required a cheaper (and nonunionized) labor force and made it difficult for Mansfield to compete. The city consequently lost a number of large employers: Mansfield Tire & Rubber, Ohio Brass, Westinghouse, and others. A General Motors metal stamping plant held out until GM's troubles in 2009 led to the plant's closure in 2010 (Samavati), its loss summed up in the hard-hearted death knell that "these big box stamping plants are a relic of the past" (Christ). Castle Rock's decision to locate their production in Mansfield meant not only the global attention of a Hollywood movie starring recognizable actors but also an economic boost to the area during filming. The actors and crew needed living accommodations, warehouse space was rented for Terence Marsh's elaborate prison cellblock set, goods and services were purchased, and locals were employed as extras, actors, and production support staff.

Being chosen by Hollywood not only provided work and income to local residents, businesses, and governments, it made the community feel *viable* again. As Lee Tasseff, President of the Mansfield/Richland County Convention and Visitors Bureau since 1990, recounts, "All the stars had houses in the country or rented within the city, and eventually the crew and other cast members found apartments or houses. They moved in" (Kane). Locals still recollect how the film's stars settled into the area and enjoyed themselves during the long shoot. Bob Gunton bought a bicycle and often went for long rides in the country and through the town (Gunton). Not surprisingly, Morgan Freeman emerged as a town favorite. Tasseff relates, "Morgan Freeman was interactive and accessible to people. I remember seeing him eating lunch with his family and the crew when they were shooting in Central Park" (Kane).

The production brought in approximately $11 million to the Mansfield economy in 1993, and though that initial boost has since dissipated, more than twenty years later the city is again benefiting from its moment in the cinematic sun. "We got lucky, because it could have been a bad movie. It could have had no legs," Tasseff commented: "It was well-written, Frank Darabont did a great job. The thing took on a life of its own, and we're known for it across the world" (Kane). This isn't bragging—since

2013, the *Shawshank* Trail has gained global media coverage. The Trail is coordinated through the Convention and Visitors' Bureau (CVB), whose headquarters is located across the street from the Bissman Building in downtown Mansfield. After the 2008 reunion in Upper Sandusky, the Mansfield CVB recognized the potential in catering to film fans; further, an ever-increasing number of inquiries from fans outside of the region inspired the CVB to assemble something more permanent to draw fans to the area.

What has become the *Shawshank* Trail evolved in response to requests by fans for information on the filming sites of *The Shawshank Redemption*. Jodie Puster-Snavely, Group Tour/Media Director for the Mansfield/Richland CVB, notes that the Trail grew out of the CVB's desire to help fans find what they wanted to see. Eventually, fourteen sites were added to the Trail, a brochure, website, and Facebook page were developed, along with unique products available for purchase at selected sites. These locations are marked with a distinctive logo and podcasts are available online for a self-guided audio tour. Jodie is the current linchpin of the *Shawshank* Trail and the central conduit for communication among the Trail's individual sites. When we interviewed her in 2013, she recalled that the origins of what is now the *Shawshank* Trail began "probably eight years ago [when] we had a gentleman from overseas that came into our office at the Convention and Visitors' Bureau and he wanted to know where the oak tree was—the *Shawshank* oak tree. And we said, 'Well, we think it's near Malabar Farms, you know, it's somewhere there ...'" Jodie remembers that the CVB sent this tourist on his way without much thought at this point, "But then people *kept coming* into our office wanting to know 'where was this filmed?' or 'where was that filmed?' Mostly the tree and mostly the prison were the things that people wanted to see. And one day, my boss [CVB Director Lee Tasseff] said to me, 'we need to put together something that has all of the sites.' Basically we went about researching where everything was filmed ... I watched the movie over and over and over again to make sure we had everything" (Puster-Snavely) (Fig. 4.2).

Jodie reports that they made use of licensed imagery warily, alert to the rumor that Warner Brothers often asked for images to be taken down from websites and advertising. Consequently, they used no photos of the actors or stills from the film and instead chose to showcase the actual Ohio locations. As a result, while the Trail provides a tour of the filming locations, it also highlights the local sites, their history, and architecture. Over time, the Trail inspired businesses to design specialty products for fans to

Fig. 4.2   The *Shawshank* oak tree after a 2011 windstorm, shorn but still standing. The tree finally fell on July 22, 2016

purchase while on the tour. Ed Pickens Café in Mansfield, for example, features the $5.95 "*Shawshankwich*" and "The Warden's Wrap," containing Brooks' Roast Beef, Red's Onion, and Andy's Aioli. Additionally, other local products emerged, such as a "Reformatory Red" wine from Cypress Hill Winery[3] and Redemption IPA and Rooftop Bohemian Style Lager from Phoenix Brewing Company, which opened in Mansfield in 2014. For many of the town's businesses involved in some capacity with the Trail, it is as if the town has become a living movie set, a testimonial to the power of this film. Even beyond the locations that are featured in the film, *Shawshank* has affected Mansfield in a way that is perhaps similar to how

baseball has shaped the town of Cooperstown, or horse racing the community of Saratoga, New York. Jodie told us, "We've started a Facebook page
and we have a website ... we just try to make it really easy for the fans to
find what they want to see." The Mansfield CVB continues to improve the
website, linking to individual vendors from their "Shank Mall" page—the
items featured can be purchased online and clicking on them leads to the
CVB page featuring businesses with greater descriptions of the products
and maps to their locations. "We didn't realize how big it was until all these
people kept coming into the [CVB's downtown] office." When Jodie talks
with fans who come to visit and they tell her why this movie is so meaningful to them, "It really gives me chills because I've met so many people from
all over that tell me why they're so attached to this movie, and it is because
it is a movie of hope. It really just gives them hope" (Puster-Snavely).

The CVB uses the term "superfan" to describe individuals who seem
extra-dedicated to the film; superfans view it not just as a favorite movie
but as a source of spiritual sustenance. Jodie described one example: a
"gentleman from Canada" who said he was the world's biggest *Shawshank*
fan. He traveled to Ohio where he went to the CVB for guidance. He
told Jodie that he typically watches the movie 2–4 times per week, and
it was helping him through a difficult period in his life: "He had a lot of
health problems and he was not getting better. The movie gave him hope
... it was really touching to be with this person, knowing how he felt and
watching him during the two days when I took him around to the sites.
And I'll just never forget it. You can't go to the oak tree [without permission from the private owner of the land] but you can look at it from the
road, and, I mean, we were there for two hours. And he just kept saying,
'I just can't believe how much this means to me. This has changed my
life to actually see this. This whole thing is coming true.' He just had this
mindset: life's going to get better now that I've seen all the *Shawshank*
sites" (Puster-Snavely). The experience of viewing the tree with this vulnerable fan became a transformative moment for Jodie as well; she began
to see this the production sites in a more serious context, to appreciate
their degree of importance, especially for those who view the film if not as
a quasi-religious experience, then at least as an intensely personal one. "It
changed *my* life too, and made me just realize how important this movie
is for fans." Jodie described a "young man who came in from Michigan
[in 2012] in his early twenties, and he had a tattoo of the *Shawshank* oak
tree on his calf featuring Red walking up to the tree. It was a beautiful tattoo." The man was only "a baby when this film came out. And he goes,

'Well, I've been watching it with my grandfather, and it meant a lot to my grandfather … I felt it was very important to get this tattoo on my leg.' It was almost like a spiritual awakening for him in a way. We've met people like that. It's amazing" (Puster-Snavely).

The *Shawshank* oak tree was one of the first location sites to attract national media to the area and to form a nexus between *Shawshank* and Ohio in the public's consciousness. In 2011, National Public Radio's Cory Turner visited Mansfield to do a feature on *Shawshank* for the series "On Location," and a year later posted an update that the tree had been damaged in a windstorm. Following the airing of both stories, fans began calling Mansfield's CVB to ask where to view the tree and other sites. The tree remained a powerful symbol to fans, even if it no longer looked as it did during filming. In fact, the tree's resilience—part of it still stood and still grew, even after half of it was sheared off in high winds—has itself transformed into a metaphor for the film's themes of struggle and endurance, even after it finally fell in 2016. The tree was located on land adjacent to the Malabar Farm State Park. This park was the former farm and home of Pulitzer Prize winning American author Louis Bromfield. According to Jayne Waterman, Bromfield's writing spanned multiple genres and formats: literary, commercial, and agricultural, from 1920–1956. But, despite early "accolades such as the Pulitzer Prize (1927), the O Henry Memorial Short Story Award (1927), nomination to *Vanity Fair*'s Hall of Fame (1927), and membership to America's National Institute of Arts and Letters (1928), Bromfield started to lose critical favour in the 1930s. However, he continued to write prolifically, in both fiction and non-fiction, commanding a large readership and best-selling status," but he was neglected critically and thus his work is not widely known today. Waterman notes his rejection by critics may have been "due, in part, to scathing reviews such as Edmund Wilson's 'What Became of Louis Bromfield' for *The New Yorker* in 1944" (Waterman).

Bromfield purchased the Lucas, Ohio, farm in 1939 as well as adjacent farms in subsequent years, eventually totaling the 595 acres that now constitutes the park. In the 1940s and 1950s, the farm was a favorite retreat for the Hollywood elite—some local residents still reminisce about seeing James Cagney, Clark Gable, George and Gracie Burns, Errol Flynn, and Dorothy Lamour come and go from the secluded and picturesque farm property. Humphrey Bogart was a personal friend of Bromfield and married Lauren Bacall in Bromfield's house in May, 1945. The Pugh Cabin, a log cabin built by neighbor Jim Pugh in the 1940s, was selected as the location for *Shawshank*'s opening scene, where Andy waits outside the home of golf pro Glenn Quentin (Scott Mann), knowing Quentin is inside with Andy's wife (Renee Blaine). The interior of the cabin was used as well for the passionate scene between the two lovers and is currently a popular site on the *Shawshank* Trail. In 2013 and 2014 Scott Mann, now a professional photographer living in Cleveland, returned to Mansfield to greet fans and tell stories about shooting in the location during the summer of 1993. As is the case with the Woodshop, the Pugh Cabin greets visitors with a distinctive smell—of pine and woodsmoke—and offers a cool refuge from the summer heat because the structure is tucked beneath a grove of evergreens. Mann recalls, however, that it was anything but cool on the day they were filming his scene, as the lights and the vintage fabrics of the costumes raised the temperature to nearly 100 degrees. Moreover, though Darabont edited the opening sequence in an effort to maintain R-rated film standards (both actors keep their clothes on in the finished cut), the original choreography was far more risqué. According to Mann: "Do you know what it's like to have simulated sex in front of about a dozen people with cameras and lights? Nerve wracking! Do you know what it's like to have simulated sex in front of about a dozen people with cameras and lights … and Tim Robbins? Terrifying!" Though he doesn't appear onscreen with the lovers, Tim Robbins, a method actor, had stopped by to watch the scene being filmed. Mann recalled that Robbins said, "He was sorry for barging in on us knowing how hard it is to shoot scenes like that. He told us he just wanted to see and get a feel of what all the 'turmoil he was in' for his character. The only thing I told him was that he scared the crap out of me!" (Mann).

Following his first time attendance at a *Shawshank* event in 2013, Mann admitted to being a bit nervous introducing himself to fans. At the time he auditioned for the Glenn Quentin role, Mann was working primarily as a model, not as an actor—*Shawshank* was his first billed film role—and he wasn't sure how much fans would care about meeting him, especially since his part in the movie was so small. But they surprised him.

> I didn't know that what I was about to experience would have a major impact on me. "Scott, can we take a picture with you?" "Mr. Mann, would you mind signing this?" "Who [what celebrities] did you get to meet?" "What's it like being in a movie?" It was overwhelming! I never thought people would be that interested in my role for the movie. I think a lot of the appreciation was that I was *the reason* Andy Dufresne went to prison. It was my fault! Another factor may have been having my scene shot at Pugh Cabin, being the only scene shot there. That was *my home*, Glenn Quentin's house! My house complete with the original [vintage] car parked outside,

which I never knew I had at the time of filming until I recently watched the opening scene closer and saw a car parked in the driveway. (Mann)

Mann provided visitors to the Pugh Cabin with details about precisely where the scene's action took place, where the crew stood, and where the cameras were positioned. And he told them about how he and Renee (both models at the time) had gotten their parts. Mann's agent told him they were casting for people willing to do a nude sex scene that was initially advertised to Mann as "B-movie horror flick" (Mann). Mann went along and was paired up with Renee to read for the scene; they noticed that a number of the other "couples" were rehearsing in a way Mann thought looked wrong:

> I noticed other couples rehearsing, all giggly and kissy-kissy. So I read the script:

> *The door bursts open. A MAN and WOMAN enter, drunk and giggling, horny as hell. No sooner is the door shut than they're all over each other, ripping at clothes, pawing at flesh, mouths locked together …* (Darabont)

> I was then introduced to Renee Blaine, my partner for the audition. Even though everyone auditioning was from the same talent agency, I didn't know any of them, and that included Renee. Renee and I discussed how we were going to do this. I finally told her, "I don't know you, you don't know me, so I think we should do it just like the script … come in drunk and just go at it!"

It was clearly the right approach, as both were cast. Scott and his family enjoyed themselves so much at the 2013 event that they contacted Renee Blaine, who joined him for the 2014 event. Mann told us: "It was the first time I had seen Renee in 20 years! We had such a great time recanting tales of our 'love scene.' We greeted fans at Pugh Cabin and would be mildly entertained by the few couples that would try to re-enact our scene in front of the door. There were also the few who would ask if Renee or I would re-enact with them! Ah, … the door at Pugh Cabin, if it could only talk" (Mann). In terms of the fan response, Mann found himself amused that he was positioned as a veteran in helping Blaine find her way as an object of fans' attention.

> It was funny watching Renee's first reaction when being approached by fans. She looked perplexed as to why people wanted her autograph and [to] take pictures of her. She acted very much like I did in 2013 … "Why me? I didn't

do *that* much in the movie." I told her, "You have to understand that you are Andy's wife in *The Shawshank Redemption*. You are the reason he goes to prison … *We* are the reason he goes to prison. These are die-hard fans of the movie and you're just going to have to get used to it." It was always funny how people would slowly approach me and ask if it was okay to sign something or take a picture with them. I'm sure major celebrities get tired of it, but I'm *not* a major celebrity, so I loved it. Plus, that's the whole reason why I'm there, to meet and greet the fans of the movie. (Mann)

The 2013 and 2014 reunions also featured the Maine National Bank location in Ashland, Ohio. This building, which now houses a private investment consulting company, was constructed in 1917 to be the home of Farmers Bank (founded in 1874). The majestic Romanesque building was designed by architect Vernon Redding (born in Ashland in 1866), a man with no formal architectural training who nonetheless designed a number of prominent local buildings, including the town's high school built in 1914 (Plank 32). Jim Kisicki, a veteran professional actor, was hired by Castle Rock to portray the bank manager who provides Andy with his cashier's check. Kisicki, a Cleveland resident, met with fans and posed for photographs in front of the beautiful and distinctive circular vault door. In an email interview in 2016, Kisicki recollected warmly:

> I can say without hesitation that being able to meet with fans of *Shawshank* during the reunions in 2013 and 2014 was an absolute delight. It is both exciting and interesting to meet so many people who are ardent fans of a movie that has become a classic and is assured of a respected presence in the list of all-time great films. While making the film, most people involved with it knew that it was a very good script. I doubt, however, that anyone could have guessed at the immense popularity it would enjoy as the years passed.

Kisicki's sonorous voice is used on the *Shawshank* Trail podcasts which comment on each of the available sites and can be downloaded for free at the Trail's website. He further noted, "By the time the twenty-year reunion took place, the host of folks who descended upon Mansfield, Ashland, and all the film sites in the area gave testimony to the enduring affection fans have for the film and anything, anyone, or anyplace related to its production" (Kisicki). By invitation from Bill and April Mullen, another actor joined the party in 2014—Frank Medrano. A veteran character actor with an impressive list of credits, including *Parks and Recreation*, *Law and Order*, *NYPD Blue*, *Entourage*, and others, Medrano was credited only as "Fat Ass" in the film (the unfortunate new fish who is beaten by Captain

Hadley on Andy's first night in *Shawshank*). Hailed as visiting royalty, Medrano was given the key to Upper Sandusky, and he told us the respectful and warm welcome from the fans and local residents had deeply moved him. At the formal cocktail reception held in the guardroom at OSR on Saturday night during the twentieth anniversary weekend, he delighted assembled fans by shouting his plaintive line, "I'm not supposed to be here!" which sounded through the cellblock in a haunting echo (Fig. 4.3).

Fig. 4.3   Scott Mann's poster for the Twentieth Anniversary's celebration of the release of *The Shawshank Redemption*. The 24×36 mosaic is made up of 20,636 tiles, using 765 different images consisting of poster and DVD covers in 29 languages, photos, and movie stills pulled by Scott from the movie (yumanngallery.com)

Perhaps the biggest thrill for fans in 2013 and 2014 was the chance to meet Bob Gunton (Warden Norton), whose appearance on both occasions was due to the personal connections he had established with Bill and April Mullen. In a personal conversation with the authors at the 2014 Anniversary Event, Gunton expressed his desire to meet with *Shawshank*'s fan base because of the latter's enthusiasm and obvious connection with the film. "[Fans] have helped provide the movie with a deeper meaning for me," he acknowledged (Gunton). What was perhaps most interesting in watching *Shawshank* fans interact with all these actors was that regardless of the significance of their roles in the film, it didn't seem to matter. Other "cult films" have similarly enthusiastic followers, but it is unlikely that minor characters from these other films receive the same level of fan appreciation. Of course Bob Gunton held a special status for all in attendance, no doubt because of the resonant evil in his portrayal of Warden Norton. It was also clear that these actors who had traveled from Cleveland and Los Angeles for these commemorative events were being appreciated not only for their cinematic work but likewise for caring enough to come back to Mansfield and make themselves so accessible to strangers. The degree of popularity and critical success of *Shawshank* turned out to be a slow-building surprise for everyone, its cast included.

Fandom and Nostalgia

A large part of *Shawshank*'s appeal is based in nostalgia: nostalgia for America's lost past, so authentically represented by the Ohio locations; nostalgia for the type of slowed-down character-focused melodrama that Hollywood doesn't often make anymore; nostalgia for absent family and friends with whom we have shared repeated viewings of *Shawshank* (as in the example of the young man with the oak tree tattoo and the memory of his grandfather); nostalgia for the music, clothes, and automobiles from the era that the movie captures so authentically; nostalgia for location-based shooting. Nostalgia, like a fan tour, is about recreating the past, reliving memory. The flip side of nostalgia is that *Shawshank* has often been criticized for its sentimentality, a charge typically leveled at melodramatic "womens' pictures" of classic Hollywood—films often derided, we suspect, largely because of their popularity with women. The irony of *Shawshank*, however, is that its level of sentimentality affects men as much or more than women; it remains one of those few movies where men give themselves permission to cry.

In examining the role nostalgia plays not just in the appeal of *The Shawshank Redemption* but in the tourism it currently inspires, we pursue a broad definition of the concept that moves us beyond understanding it as a simple affection for the trappings of a past we may (or may not) have personally experienced. Seventeenth-century doctors believed nostalgia was a disease with possible cures, including travel to the Swiss Alps (as well as opium and leeches). We know now that nostalgia is not a medical condition, but we still seek out some kind of healing for it. *Shawshank* fans have embraced the balm of travel to satisfy their longing—but their travel is motivated by a desire to commune with the reality of a film they love, as well as with their fellow nostalgics. In her book, *The Future of Nostalgia*, Svetlana Boym explores the concept of nostalgia as it relates to a cinematic "image of nostalgia [as] a double exposure, or a superimposition of two images—of home and abroad, past and present, dream and everyday life" (xiv). Boym writes that nostalgia is "[t]he border zone between longing and reflection, between native land and exile." She notes that nostalgia "opens up spaces of freedom. Freedom in this case is not a freedom from memory but a freedom to remember, to choose the narratives of the past and remake them" (354). Her definition is particularly applicable to *Shawshank*, a story and film focused on themes of exile, freedom, loss, old friendships, memory and the burden of past mistakes, as well as on the passage of time. For Boym, nostalgia "had not only to do with dislocation in space but also with the changing conception of time" (7). Red's meditations remind us that the inmates' understanding of time is irrevocably altered by the terms of their imprisonment. Andy and Red reflect on this after Red is again rejected for parole, Red noting "Thirty years. Jesus, when you say it like that ..." and Andy completes the thought with, "You wonder where it went. I wonder where 10 years went" before giving Red a "parole rejection present" of a harmonica, the latter another reference to Red's past life.

As discussed in Chap. 2, the prison life depicted in *Shawshank* has moments when it mirrors the real history of the Ohio State Reformatory, but, on the other hand, also departs significantly from this reality when privileging its narrative. Yet, the story's location and history, although fictional, *feel* real to viewers, perhaps even more real than history itself. Boym alludes to this sensation as "a yearning for a different time—the time of our childhood, the slower rhythm of our dreams" (xv). One reason this is applicable to *Shawshank* is because Mansfield itself is a town that feels somewhat lost in time; it is a throwback to small town,

Midwestern America, a time and place where things moved at a slower pace and in retrospect appeared more coherent. Although a post-parole Brooks complains that "the world went and got itself in a big damn hurry," in comparison to other parts of postmodern America, Mansfield still feels like a place caught in an envelope of time. This is another example of Boym's nostalgia, "a longing for a home that no longer exists or has never existed. Nostalgia is a sentiment of loss and displacement, but it is also a romance with one's own fantasy" (xiii). There are many elements in *Shawshank* that feed various elements of nostalgia associated with the film: the sense of being in a place that exists outside the realm of the postmodern via television screens and telephones—Andy writes letters—the sense of being back in the forties and fifties that Mansfield can still deliver in its Midwestern ambiance, the way in which *Shawshank* references the earlier tradition of the prison film genre, a sense of the prison experience as less alienated and solitary than it is now, as Red and his friends form a kind of social club at *Shawshank* that would never be possible in contemporary penal America (as it was seldom possible in the real history of OSR).

Contributing to the film's pervasive sense of nostalgia is its musical score. Many of the songs that appear on the *Shawshank* soundtrack—including the Ink Spots' opening "If I Didn't Care" and *Gilda*'s "put the Blame on Mame"—take the audience directly back to the forties, when these songs were composed and the film is partially set. The Academy Awards recognized the importance of music to *Shawshank* in nominating the film for the Best Music: Original Score category as well as the Best Sound category. But it is not merely the nostalgic songs that transport us back to an earlier era in America; Thomas Newman, who composed the movie's score, produced unspoken instrumental work that is just as effective in helping to create *Shawshank*'s emotive atmosphere. "The *Shawshank* Theme," for example, composed of orchestral strings, piano, and a solo oboe when Red arrives in Buxton, adds a pensive harmonica solo as he walks the rock wall towards Andy's tree, and ends the film with soaring strings and kettle drum as the camera pulls away from Andy and Red embracing on the Mexican beachfront. The music, then, is aligned seamlessly with events in the sequence as it unfolds; when Red is most alone, the soft-spoken oboe and solo harmonica predominate, when he is reunited with Andy, the stirring strings take over. The score establishes a resonate musical structure for the audience to reinforce the film's most evocative moments. Newman highlights this point in his comment that

"*Shawshank* elicited such strong emotions without any music at all ... the challenge was to create a score that elevated scenes without getting in their way" (Adams). OSR, well aware of the power of Newman's score, frequently has it playing through speakers on tour days.

There is, moreover, a brooding sadness that pervades *Shawshank* and is only mollified by the film's good-natured humor and larger themes of hope and endurance. The theme of institutionalization that results in Hatlen's suicide and Red's post-parole acknowledgement that it is a "terrible thing to live in fear," Andy's years of grieving over the loss of his wife and his role in her death, the waste of years that all the inmates must sacrifice for their mistakes, the unwarranted cruelties of Warden Norton, the palpable loneliness that surrounds Red after Andy's escape—these are the melodramatic features of *Shawshank* that solicit deeply poignant responses from viewers. This emotional construction of nostalgic-like pathos features the one-sided economy of suffering and the film embraces and stages this spectacle in order to create a pitying affect upon the viewer that is further heightened by the harsh and often arbitrary violence doled out by the sisters, Captain Hadley, and the warden.

But perhaps most important: this is a film that is a nostalgic paean to friendship and commitment. Every time we watch it, we think of our own (real or imagined) best friend of twenty years. We might be willing to travel to Mexico to see that person anytime, but especially after not being together for a long spell. It's the anticipation of reconnecting that we also see in Red missing his friend and longing to be with him again, and this sense of nostalgia immediately connects the viewer to his own friendships, especially those that are long standing and long distance. The movie sustains its bittersweet tone in its resolute belief that while we may be forced to suffer and die alone, there remains the possibility for love in between. In the end, the film's elements of pathos are counterpointed by its energy of hope—and the affect of these oppositional extremes resonates within the audience, pulling us in different directions, ranging from melancholic nostalgia, to comedy, to transcendence, exhausting us emotionally as the picture's melancholia finally tilts and is overcome by its spiritual exultation. Similarly, *Shawshank* manages to construct the brutality of prison life as it certainly existed at the OSR, while at the same time also inspiring viewers with the deep bond that Red and Andy share, their quests for dignity, and their acts of rebellion. Is the film balanced equally between these two perspectives? Which parts of this polemic do most film viewers end up taking away with them?

Shawshank proffers a different kind of cinematic experience, one that is sweeping and holistic at the same time that it meditative and challenging. There is danger in projecting too much of our own fantasy onto celluloid—we risk glamorizing elements of it that do not stand up to close scrutiny, leading us to conflate fantasy and reality: "The danger of nostalgia is that it tends to confuse the actual home and the imaginary one" (Boym xvi). Film tourism and other related businesses that capitalize on a shared cultural past, tapping into the place where individual biography intersects with the biography of groups or nation (e.g., the idealized America found in colonial Williamsburg, Virginia, songs from bygone eras such as the twenties or fifties, even portraits of a middle class childhood peppered throughout the Disneyworld experience), tend always to emphasize the positive over the negative, the utopian over the real. *Shawshank* shares much in common with this phenomenon, idealizing above all else, male friendship bonds and the hope they help to sustain. As such, it is a quint-essentially *American* film; as we discussed in Chap. 3, the narrative neatly sidesteps problematic issues associated with class and race because these issues would necessarily compromise the purity of the friendship that Red and Andy establish and the film's optimistic trajectory.

Those who feel compelled to rewatch *Shawshank* periodically are drawn to such repetition for reasons that are both inimitably personal and universally shared. Boym believes "nostalgia tantalizes us with its fundamental ambivalence; it is about repetition of the unrepeatable, materialization of the immaterial" (xvii). While the film's ending provides us with a sense of closure, there is also a longing associated with this film, a desire for more. The film of course can have no possible sequel—there could never be a *Shawshank 2* that attempts to follow Red and Andy while they lead charter-fishing expeditions in Zihautanejo—yet among most fans there is still a wish for *more Shawshank*, as if the act of watching the film again, connecting with these two immensely likeable men, stimulates the desire for even more contact. Perhaps this is another reason why the film's aficionados seek out the *Shawshank* Trail—so that they can continue to dialogue with the film, enlarging their experience beyond the act of merely watching its plot unfold passively. Much like Civil War enthusiasts feel an almost palpable connection to the history that fascinates them when they visit Gettysburg, St. Albans, or Fort Sumter, *Shawshank* fans touring the Trail learn about the history associated with each site, reading and hearing about the location and filming while seeing, smelling, and touching the minutiae of a place they recognize intimately—if only in their imaginations. Such recognition brings an immediate sense of pleasure. As Boym specifies, "the nostalgic has an amazing capacity for remembering sensations, tastes, sounds, smells, the minutiae, and trivial that those who remain home never noticed" (4).

The *Shawshank* Trail's authenticity goes beyond providing access to the locations of the filming. The real histories of the locations themselves are fascinating in their own right and visiting fans can see how the genuine atmosphere created by the sites adds to the film's "lived-in" feeling. Those visiting OSR discover that the main cellblock featured in *Shawshank* was a set built in a Mansfield warehouse (the film's cell block has long been dismantled), but in its place fans get to tour OSR's actual cellblock and a dozen other interior locations (including the solitary confinement cells at OSR) that were used in the film. It matters to the veracity of their experience that they are actually standing in the actual locations where the film was made. Fan interviews indicate that they do not care that some movie magic was employed; in fact, for some, this makes the tour all the more interesting. Tourism research indicates that fan visitors make a distinction between different kinds of authenticity (Wang 351), and Roberson and Grady's survey data suggest that this can be extended to describe fan film tourists. "Objective authenticity" involves the authenticity of the historical objects (e.g., the real OSR cellblock), and "staged authenticity" involves the recreation of locations to resemble their expected appearance, such as their appearance in the movie (e.g., the manufactured cellblock built inside a Mansfield warehouse). Norton's office location was never used as the real historical warden's office at OSR. However, the reformatory has since arranged the room to look as it did in the film—with a desk, a phone, office supplies and books, as well as the actual wall safe where Norton conceals the ledger and Andy hides the Bible during his escape. The safe, which was built specifically for the filming, was sold off after filming, but the manufacturer of it returned it to the building once it became a historical site. Fans perceive this room as "real" even as they may consciously understand it was staged for the film and now is being staged again for their benefit. During the tour, they are told the historical function of the room and get to appreciate both its objective authenticity and its staged authenticity. Moreover, fans have an "authentic experience" at the location, as they are encouraged to sit at the warden's desk and take pictures of themselves, thereby projecting themselves into the film. As we will explore in the following section, research strongly indicates that interacting with, touching, manipulating objects, and posing for photographs in front of recognizable backdrops from the film are extremely satisfying activities for fans touring film locations. Fans tell us that being in the "real place" where they know the film was made is very important to them, especially since many of the last decade's most popular movie locations were fabricated with the assistance of digital technology and therefore cannot be duplicated to look again as they did on film. While it may seem odd that fans of *Shawshank* long to be part of this fiction's harsh, gray, and monotonous world, this may reflect a general fascination about the prison experience, even as most would prefer not to experience it personally. And while filmgoers may wonder about the sensations associated with prison life, they are also seeking something beyond *Shawshank*'s surface subject matter; they seek to experience a fiction that "feels" real, that revels in human complexity and a compelling, believable story line. The longing from fans that identify with this film is for human contact, self-determination, and art—the very elements of life that we watch Andy and Red struggle to sustain.

Thus, *Shawshank* Prison is able to create the illusion that it was real, even though it never existed. Its ancestry belongs more to the movies than to history. It reinforces an image of prisons past in a way wholly invented to serve contemporary nostalgic needs. The film's conjuring of a "*Shawshank* Prison" through the magic of filmmaking "both induces nostalgia and offers a tranquilizer; instead of disquieting ambivalence and paradoxical dialectic" (Boym 33); it sparks the imagined horror most of us associate with penitentiary life, while calming our trepidations regarding the inhumanity of imprisonment. The injustices that occur at *Shawshank* Prison are unambiguous, vicious, and unredeemable. What is fascinating is why viewers are still drawn to the image of a *Shawshank* Prison, especially during a time when real prison populations have exploded and punishments meted out are so often punitive. Perhaps it is related to the fact that the place ultimately provides an unrealistic portrait of prison life, transcending images of cold mortar and stone, blood and violence, to provide viewers with a nostalgic oasis of racial harmony, roomy solitary cells, and (once the sisters are dispatched) relative autonomy and solidarity among prisoners. A visit to Ohio State Reformatory is a similar exercise in penal nostalgia: on display are both the efforts to produce humane reform via the reformatory and the horror represented by those tiny, rusted cells that once housed two human beings uncomfortably.

The American penal landscape is a perilous wasteland of men adrift and clawing their way towards survival. And it is a place of benumbed consciousness, of men worn down by the process of bureaucratic institutionalization. Yet the movie is also a paean to hope that springs eternal, balancing decades of incarceration with best friendships capable of easing the burden of prison loneliness. Part of *Shawshank*'s artistic achievement is its ability to complicate the viewer's response to a variety of criminal justice issues: the value of penitentiary incarceration juxtaposed with shifting definitions of good and evil, right and wrong. And while the film questions the extent to which a character shapes his environment (Andy) or to which the environment shapes him (institutionalization), it ultimately ends up supplying an affirmative answer. Fans find the film's message of hope inspirational, and while there are surely other films with hopeful messages, the expression here is one that seems to resonate more profoundly than most others.

FILM-INDUCED TOURISM AND *SHAWSHANK*

In an increasingly fragmented media environment, audiences for individual entertainment products have likewise fractured into smaller and smaller niche markets. The term "cult film" is no longer reserved for low-budget output screened at midnight theaters but instead is often applied to any media with a devoted and growing fan following. Rather than be defined by genre, budget, or rating, the "cult" is determined by the nature of fan behavior. As *Cultographies* notes in its definition of cult cinema, a cult film can be broadly "characterized by its lively and active communal following" ("Cultographies"), but more narrowly by factors such as the art form's features, style, genre, and content, as well as its fan consumption, practices, and celebrations. Attendances at celebratory gatherings, such as conventions and anniversary reunions, represent long-standing rituals for fan communities. And even though fan communities have multiplied and fragmented with amazing speed via online iterations, fans continue to value personal interactions with other fans, and the opportunity to engage in semi-public, ritualized activities, such as trivia contests and costume competitions, wherein their dedication to fandom can be openly displayed in a forum where they are immediately welcomed, establish an instant feeling of belonging, and receive immediate feedback from appreciative audiences. Fellow-fan recognition such as this often enhances the pleasure already found in the media product itself.

The study of groups and their travel patterns has been of interest to those in the fields of hospitality and tourism since the 1990s, when hospitality stakeholders began more fully to appreciate the substantial impact movies, television, and other media exert on exposing people to new destinations and creating demand to visit sites associated with the creation of these media. But more specialized interest in film-induced tourism has exploded in the last decade, largely because of one film trilogy: Peter Jackson's *Lord of the Rings*. *Lord of the Rings*, released in three installments in 2001, 2002, and 2003, was credited with bringing in over 33 million dollars (USD) to boost New Zealand's already considerable tourism economy ("Film Tourism Fast Facts"). With this undeniable impact, hospitality professionals have taken note and pursue other media products that might well tap into similar fan communities possessing the financial wherewithal and interest to travel. Fandom scholarship, however, has been hesitant to intersect with fans in explicitly commercialized spaces. Instead, film-induced tourism studies have largely been conducted and sponsored by researchers in the fields of hospitality, consumer studies, and other disciplines; they have focused on the financial impact of film tourism patterns. Chiefly, this research has centered on fan visits to filming locations. Consequently, traditional hospitality and tourism research has identified a need to understand more clearly the motivators for the film-induced tourist (Connell), but researchers, in turn, have opined that a more complete profile on these travelers is only possible with additional information gleaned from outside the hospitality industry.

Using a very broad brush, "film-induced tourism" refers both to the visitation of sites where movies (and television programs) have been filmed, with particular attention paid to tourist activity associated with the film industry (Beeton) and those sites that may only have association with a film, movie, or program. The fans seeking out these places do so for a wide range of personal and cultural reasons. The film-induced tourist is not simply responding to media influences but is seeking physical representation of cultural value (Busby and Klug). This leads to one of the significant differences of film fans from other types of fandom. As opposed to other types of fans (e.g., music or sports), the film fan is participating in a fictional, or at least fictionalized world, instead of following real people or occurrences (Karpovich 17). The recreated world that fans tour, while obviously part of the "real" world, is actually an imaginary one. When *Lord of the Rings* fans travel to New Zealand, they aren't just touring filming locations; they feel present in Middle Earth. Art creates different constructions of reality, and cinema is uniquely capable of providing these different realities with a palpable sense of truth and life. At its core, fandom is seen in film-induced tourism as the emotional connection between the fan (viewer) and their fan object (viewed) (Connell). Film tourism enthusiasm often depends on proximity to site locations, to celebrity, and to the desire for authentic experiences (Lee, Scott, & Kim and Couldry). Cinema presents a unique relationship that is both personal yet universally recognized.

"Fan" is a shortened form of the word "fanatic." And while most would shrink from describing themselves as a "fanatic" (due to the word's association with wild, out-of-control behavior and stereotyped portraits of stalking), almost everyone is a "fan" of something. As fandom scholar Matt Hills notes: "Everyone knows what a 'fan' is. It's somebody who is obsessed with a particular star celebrity, film, TV program, band; somebody who can produce reams of information on their object of fandom, and can quote their favored line or lyrics, chapter and verse. Fans are often highly articulate. Fans interpret media texts in a variety of interesting and perhaps unexpected ways. And fans participate in communal activities—they are not 'socially atomized' or isolated viewers/readers" (ix). Hills attempts to solidify an academic definition of "fan" that goes deeper than the popular understanding of the concept. The term "fan" is so widely used in American culture that most people have never taken the time to question its precise definition. Finding a definition is further complicated by the negative tinge associated with the word fan and the stereotyped image of fans in popular culture—that of the immature, awkward, antisocial misfit out of touch with reality—to which Hills counters with the assertion that fans are not fragmented or cut off from the rest of the culture (i.e., "socially atomized"). Images persist of "nerds" and "geeks" obsessing over minutiae from their favorite sci-fi show and overlap with crazed football fans painting themselves the team colors and going shirtless to a home game in subzero temperatures, but these are extreme examples of fandom. Indeed, fans come with a variety of behavioral dispositions. The majority are neither obsessed nor psychologically unbalanced; for whatever their reasons, they seek greater contact with a media product or personality that has stimulated their interest. Often, fandom is the simple desire to learn more about the object of their attraction.

But some case studies of fan cultures have tended to perpetuate a negative understanding of fans and fan practices by categorizing these groups into hierarchies according to behaviors and practices (MacKellar, Abercrombie and Longhurst, Tulloch and Jenkins) or have viewed fans as an "audience commodity" (Stiernstedt). Fans generally resist being viewed as a target market waiting to be exploited for others' profit, since they generally see themselves not as mere consumers but instead as devotees of a particular text, film, or program and don't want their passion to be reduced to a mere commercial interaction. Individual fan communities have been studied and profiled by dozens of scholars (see Hills for an extensive list, "Preface," x). But Hills argues that fandom cannot be seen "simply as a 'thing' to be picked over analytically. It is also always performative," meaning that it "performs cultural work" (xi). Many fans and the scholars who study them would choose to define their participation in fan culture "in terms of active consumption of information about their fanned objects and the people who contribute to its creation" because "this kind of interaction with the text involves obtaining a wide ranging knowledge of the fanned object and requires a significant amount of time and effort and a specific set of technical skills" (Zubernis and Larsen 16). Such skills can be categorized in accordance to a range of typical fan practices.

Why should fans and their behaviors be treated seriously? Because fans matter. They are passionate. They are enthusiastic. They spend money on things they enjoy. They will travel to participate in fan activities. And they perpetuate art. Service providers—from regional owners of hotels and restaurants to proprietors of sites where fans congregate—must understand fan mentalities to avoid missing out. Communities that wish to induce fans to visit their film tourism locations and events should consider what sets fans apart from other travelers and what makes for a satisfying film tourism experience. While most film-induced tourism studies focus on individual visits to filming locations, there are also other kinds of fan gatherings taking place at or alongside the tourism destinations which may differ from events such as the fan convention (which typically takes place at a hotel or convention center and features celebrity guests, merchandise dealers, and other specifically related elements). Such gatherings of fan-authors, fan-filmmakers, and other fan-producers are not new, but needs to be distinguished from community-focused film tourism, featuring destinations such as the *Shawshank* Trail and The Christmas Story House (both in Ohio). The Trail and Christmas Story House are unique additions to these options, combining real filming locations with museums, interactive experiences, and gift shops. These locations, for example, offer the rare opportunity to study enthusiasts who are willing to travel to a new city, perhaps on multiple occasions, in order to celebrate their beloved film object with fellow fans and to interact with locals who are in the same way connected to the filming and/or location site(s). The impact of tourism on the fan experience at these localized events and sites is new and therefore has not been fully examined. More importantly, a look at how helping tourism professionals understand the needs and desires of fans has not been widely examined.[4]

In 2015, Roberson and Grady published "The '*Shawshank* Trail': A Cross Disciplinary Study in Film Induced Tourism and Fan Culture." The authors solicited survey data from fans at various locations along the *Shawshank* Trail during the 2013 and 2014 *Shawshank* reunion and twentieth anniversary celebration, respectively. Fans in attendance were asked questions relevant to both *The Shawshank Redemption* and the tour sites they were visiting. They were queried to rate and comment on the significance of the following topics:

1. The ability to interact with the creators or participants involved in the production of the fan object
2. The ability to visit and see iconic filming locations
3. The opportunity for and importance of interacting with other *Shawshank* fans
4. Satisfaction with available merchandise themed to the film
5. Opportunities for self-directed creation or interaction with the film object

The results of this survey (see Roberson and Grady source publication for statistical details) conducted with 200 participants over two three-day periods indicated that fans rated the two most important factors that had enhanced their visit were visiting iconic locations and the ability to interact with props and set locations. The least important consideration for those in attendance at these two *Shawshank* events was the ability to interact with other fans, while the opportunity to interact with the creators (actors, director, etc.) of the film was of moderate value, the one area where the level of satisfaction was actually lower than the importance fans assigned to it.

While interested in ways in which fan behavior might be generalized and categorized, Roberson and Grady's study was most concerned with measuring whether the Ohio tourism providers had "accomplished their job" of giving *Shawshank* fans a satisfying experience on the Trail. Both the authors of this study and the owners of the Trail wanted to know how the statistical data could contribute to answering questions such as: What mattered the most—and least—for fans while touring the Trail? Were expectations the same for fans that traveled from out of town compared with locals? Did their experiences leave them wanting something more? Could fans articulate those desires in a way that would help influence future work by the Mansfield tourism planners and Trail providers? What is important to glean from other fan base studies, such as those conducted by Abercrombie and Longhurst, towards helping Trail sponsors to realize that fans spending money and traveling weren't just taking a trip but seeking something more specific by visiting a film site? Displays of fan enthusiasm may risk ridicule in other contexts by singling out individual fans, but this occurs much less frequently during a film tourism event. What makes the difference here, and how can it best be highlighted? As Zubernis and Larsen point out, when fans feel that their love of the object is respected—when they are encouraged to engage the site, to take photographs, to touch and manipulate important objects, and when they gather with groups of other fan tourists to share experiences—then they feel that their love is being appreciated and encouraged, and the risk of being ostracized for a display of affection diminishes accordingly.

Because fan practices and means of participation are as diverse as fans and fan communities themselves, Roberson and Grady worked closely with the organizers of the Trail locations to obtain data and to design questions meant to form a general picture of the fandom for each location. The Trail has a more diffuse product (many locations in different towns, cities, and rural areas) and is linked to an event on a larger scale than anything that had previously been examined by tourism research. Roberson and Grady worked with Trail organizers in order to determine how their promotional dollars might best be spent in the future. Perhaps most important, they also wanted to obtain insights into why this film held such a strong meaning for the fans who visited, and to understand how to ensure these fan-travelers were satisfied with their experience. After analyzing the data they accumulated from the 2013 and 2014 *Shawshank* events, Roberson and Grady were able to provide the operators of the Trail with the following observations and recommendations that have subsequently shaped the promotion and focus of the Trail itself:

1. Participants were defined in this study as people who were in any way connected to the production of the film. These included the most obviously visible of those sometimes called "producers" in fan studies (e.g., leading actors, directors, screenwriters, or source-text authors) but also include film extras, location scouts, prop managers, assistant set designers, and actors (whether leading, supporting, or featured). The researchers were concerned with whether interaction with participants would be a motivating and/or satisfactory element for fans visiting the tourism sites. Fan conventions, both

bigger celebrity-centered, for-profit events and smaller, fan-only gatherings are "one of the most commonly utilized (and least-studied) in-person fan spaces" (Zubernis and Larsen, 21). Zubernis and Larsen discuss in detail the ways in which for-profit conventions—even those that offer an unprecedented level of intimacy—nonetheless maintain boundaries between fans and "producers." Roberson and Grady theorized that fans might choose to travel in order to interact with "participants," to get closer to those involved in producing the fan object. For example, the twentieth anniversary of *Shawshank*'s release in 2014 went beyond advertising the Trail to include speculation about which "producers" would be in attendance. Roberson and Grady had suggested in 2013 to organizers some experiences that would resonate with fans looking for more analysis and conversation. Dr. Anthony Magistrale was invited to provide an interpretative film lecture. A panel discussion for fans, similar to those held at large events, like San Diego's Comic Con, was also suggested. Organizers knew that several "producers" from the film—e.g., Scott Mann and Renee Blaine, Ernie Malik from Castle Rock, and Eve Lapolla (the Ohio Film Commissioner at the time *Shawshank* was produced)—would join Magistrale as part of a roundtable discussion and autograph session at the Renaissance Theatre. But it was not certain until a week or so before this event who else would join these others. There was speculation that Frank Darabont would fly in for part of the festivities, and perhaps even Morgan Freeman. As it turned out, everyone present at the reunion was delighted when Bob Gunton chose to return to Ohio because he had had such an enjoyable experience interacting with fans in 2013. It was this speculation among fans—i.e., which "producers" would be there?—that helped to fuel the excitement associated with the twentieth reunion. In the end, such speculation both inspired some fans to travel to Mansfield while it heightened the enthusiasm of those already committed to attending. By traveling to participate in these events, fans had the opportunity to interact in a "neutral space where fans and celebrities can come together ... facilitating closer connection than fans could otherwise gain" (Zubenis and Larsen, 22). As Roberson and Grady explained to *Shawshank* Trail organizers, fans travel to experience something that they cannot find at home and that the organizers could provide—a way to get closer to their fan object by meeting some of the people intimately involved in its production.

2. Place is defined as the location(s) that are featured in the tourism attraction. Fans engage in participatory culture by traveling to filming locations as a way to get close to the fan object. The appeal is the opportunity to interact tactually with the fan object: fans stand where they know the actors and crew stood, they can replicate scenes from the film or fan object by taking photographs, and they can touch and interact with the location in a more intimate way than can be done by watching a DVD or looking at photographs. In *Film Induced Tourism*, Sue Beeton stresses the importance of visiting an iconic location or at least a "tangible representation," of the film (91) when she refers to a location or installation representing a recognizably identifiable location in the series or the film fans are visiting. This might be a *Braveheart* statue in Stirling, Scotland; a statue of Gollum in Wellington, New Zealand; a recreation of Andy Griffith's Mayberry in Mount Airy, North Carolina; or the warden's office at OSR. Often, some sort of map or guidebook is essential, such as Ian Brodie's guides to *The Lord of the Rings* locations in New Zealand or the website and brochure for the *Shawshank* Trail.[5] A place may provide the fan with a physical representation of their emotional attachment to the fan object (Beeton 5). Fans' desires to reenact or recreate the film through visiting the locations are a powerful form of participation. Thus, Roberson and Grady sought to measure whether the fans' expectations for encountering the location were met, not met, or exceeded. The survey results indicated that the fan experience associated with the *Shawshank* Trail far exceeded expectations. Moreover, for those fans who had visited other movie sites, the Trail was rated as vastly superior in comparison (Roberson and Grady 58).

3. Fan community is typically defined as an environment composed of fellow fans, in this case, a measurement to what extent fan groups valued meeting other fans of the same object as part of their experience. Fans often seek out gatherings of fellow fans to realize the benefits of being in a space where fan shame is minimized (i.e., there is safety in numbers—no one will question an individual's devotion to their beloved film, TV show, or sports team in a fan-filled space, in contrast to what they might experience in the larger culture) and to have their fandom recognized and validated by others who share

it (Zubernis and Larsen; henryjenkins.org). For the organizers of the *Shawshank* Trail, this question was particularly interesting. The Trail is open year-round to visit as a "drive-it-yourself" experience, but the filming reunion event (2013) and twentieth anniversary event (2014), as well as later events such as 2015's *Shawshank* Hustle 7K Race brought many fans to the locations and planned events at the same time, offering the opportunity for fan-to-fan interaction in addition to the usual fan-to-location interaction available at other times. Trail organizers were interested to know whether meeting and mingling with other fans would be of interest to this fan community. Perhaps surprisingly, the Roberson and Grady survey demonstrated that this issue was much less paramount to fan expectations than might have initially been assumed (57, 59).

4. Fans are often collectors—of merchandise, of photographs, of autographs, and other memorabilia. Collecting such objects can represent the connection with an imagined, larger community or can stand in for sites of cultural production (henryjenkins.org). In one of the first studies into *why* tourists purchase souvenirs, Wilkins observed that tourists see souvenirs as "a facilitator of memory," while others commented on the need for a "tangible evidence to re-live the experience" or simply as "evidence" of their experience to show others that they had participated in the experience (Wilkins 1). Wilkins has also noted that women tend to purchase more souvenirs than men. Although the Trail's organizers have been limited by Warner Bros. studio in their ability to sell licensed merchandise, Trail location owners (OSR, the *Shawshank* Woodshop, Malabar Farms, CVB, Olivesburg General Store, and the *Shawshank* oak tree) and the CVB members in Ashland and Mansfield (Squirrel's Den, Ed Pickens on Main, Two Cousins Pizza, Relax! It's Just Coffee, Cyprus Hill Winery, Richland Carousel Park, Nothing Bundt Cakes, Blueberry Patch Coffee Roasters, and Phoenix Brewing Company) have created a variety of unique *Shawshank*-related merchandise for fans to purchase. Trail organizers were interested to discover whether their merchandise would hit the mark with fans visiting the Trail. The fan data indicated that Trail merchandising was not highly regarded by those participating in the survey, as it ranked just above the lowest category, that of fan interaction (57). It was unclear whether tourists simply did not value the *type* of merchandise available for sale along the Trail or if *Shawshank*

souvenirs in general were not considered very important. Roberson and Grady were able to conclude that enough satisfaction with the available merchandise affected an intention for fans to return.

5. The survey measured the opportunities available for fans to interact with the physical location and/or recreate favorite moments from the film. Fans participate in a number of practices that might be called interactive. This is referred to by many as "participatory culture" (henryjenkins.org) and can encompass a wide range of practices, such as creating fan videos, writing fan fiction, making and wearing costumes, wearing t-shirts identifying or affiliated with the fan object itself, and creating fan art, or other products such as themed foods, dolls, games, or other objects, chiefly for the enjoyment of themselves and their fellow fans. When these objects are sold, it is seen more often as a service to fans than as a moneymaking enterprise, since any profits realized are often miniscule. Their purpose is simply to enable fans to procure souvenirs and share their enthusiasm with other fans. Part of the participation involves the fan imagining herself in the world of the fan object. In this way, many of the practices already named are related to the ability for fans to go into the locations and touch objects and parts of the locations (walls, props, furniture), as well as stand in the locations and take photographs. The *Shawshank* Trail offers the fan the rare opportunity to interact physically with the location(s), and fans acknowledged their awareness of this opportunity by reporting their highest satisfaction ratings with this aspect of the tour (57, 59).

We have argued elsewhere in this book that *The Shawshank Redemption* is a film that continually bends traditional constructions of both gender and genre. It also bends consistent audience expectations of atmosphere and tone—juxtaposing scenes of melodrama and despair with those of anticipation and triumph. Most interestingly, the dramatic spectrum of emotions the film elicits from filmgoers increases in frequency and depth in the second half of the picture. Consider, for example, the sequence where Red must choose between the compass and a gun in the pawnshop window display. On the one hand, *Shawshank* has supplied us with reasons why a man might contemplate breaking parole in order to "be back where things make sense, where [he] won't have to be afraid all of the time." Yet, Andy's legacy of beauty and freedom counters continually Red's urge to capitulate to institutionalization. By the end of the film, then, the audience is prepared to accept the dramatic shift the film makes from the dark moment in Red's squalid apartment, where he sits alone in a t-shirt surrounded by fear and despair, to the very next scene as he descends from the back of a red pickup truck and enters the bucolic hayfields of Buxton. The spirit of the film, as well as Red's perspective, completely and abruptly shifts in accordance with its change in settings—from a chiaroscuro interior to a summer afternoon's outside light, from Mansfield's corseted concrete streets and buildings to Ohio's yawning countryside and open sky. Moreover, once again the musical score cues in the filmgoer to this change in the movie's ambiance and perspective.

This shift in tone and atmosphere is similar to what one experiences touring the Trail. There is a world of difference that distinguishes a fan's short journey through OSR's labyrinth of cells and confined corridors and into the serenity of nature that surrounds the *Shawshank* oak tree or the Pugh Cabin. Like Red's experience at the end of the film, the Trail presents a range of tone and vision—inside versus outside—from an empathic contemplation of the suffering men endured at OSR to the recreation of Red's delight when he espies Andy's oak tree for the first time. Because the Trail features so many different locations, a fan's journey is not limited to a single emotion. Like the film itself, the Trail encourages a broad range of fan responses—some of which present a need to be shared with the people who are accompanying you on the tour (even strangers, strangely enough), while others are best kept to oneself, in appreciation of the way in which *The Shawshank Redemption* is ultimately a meditative and highly personal experience.

New Media Fandom

Emily Pugh, a 22-year-old "superfan," journeyed with her mom from Austin, Texas, in 2013 to visit the *Shawshank* sites. She's the creator of a Tumblr site packed with *Shawshank* videos, GIFs, photos, and blog posts. A veteran film tourist who has traveled to see dozens of filming locations, she told us: "I've never been to anything like the Trail. A lot of the movie sites I've been to featured me, alone, with no one to guide me. Or I've been on the tours of Warner Bros. and Universal studios—and it was not personal at all: 'Here sit in this trolley, we'll take you to the backlot, the same experience for everybody and you can't take your time with it.' [With] the Trail you can spend as long as you want with anything you want. I felt special [touring the Trail] because

I knew so much about this movie that everyone was there for" (Pugh). Emily's experience has now reached beyond simply visiting the Trail. Her documentation of her trip—designed for online sharing with other fans—included printing out screenshots from the film, which she then held up against each real location on the Trail and photographed again, layering the "reel" against the "real." She posted these to her Tumblr (http://fyeahshawshankredemption.tumblr.com/) and the Mansfield CVB obtained her permission to use these photos in their promotional materials, helping to illustrate to fans the interactive experience available to them along the Trail (Fig. 4.4).

Emily returned in 2014 as a celebrated guest, this time with her father in tow, and also joined a contingent of *Shawshank*-affiliated Ohio attendees to the twentieth anniversary screening of the film in Los Angeles, on November 18, 2014. At this latter event, host Max Brooks (author of *World War Z, The Zombie Survival Guide* and son of Mel Brooks and Anne Bancroft) welcomed Darabont, Freeman, and Robbins to the stage of the

Fig. 4.4 One of Emily Pugh's layered screenshots, Tommy and the *Shawshank* Woodshop

Samuel Goldwyn Theater to reminisce. Also in attendance were a number of other artists associated with the film, including many cast and crew (http://www.oscars.org/events/shawshank-redemption). At the LA event, the authors made the acquaintance of Pete George, an Ohio native who appeared in *Shawshank* as an extra and who is currently a comedian and performer based in Los Angeles.[6] In an interview following the event, George shared some of the memories that he felt illustrated the magic of the *Shawshank* experience:

[In 1993], I was in LA staying with some friends, trying to get some acting work. I participated in some Tony Robbins goal-setting workshops, right? And I really visualized it. I was off for six weeks in the summer from my stand-up cause I'm always touring, [thinking] what am I going to do for six weeks? Here [my agent's] telling me I need more SAG, you know, I need more credits. I said to myself, "I am going to work on a film in Ohio for six weeks during that time frame." What were the chances there was even a film [production] anywhere close? What were the chances for me, even as an extra, to be on it for 6 weeks? I didn't care. I was going to be very intentional and focused, and I felt it, and I just let it well up. [And then] my agent says "hey, they're doing this film [near Cleveland]." And I get there and they say, "We can use you for six weeks." (George)

George told us that he is often introduced for his stand-up act with the factoid that he appeared in *Shawshank* (savvy viewers can spot him in several key scenes) and that many people approach him after the show to tell him how important the film is to them. George reflected on why he thinks attention surrounding this film has grown so steadily over the years: "I really think because it's a movie that's a reflection of the human condition. People have struggles in their life and it's great to see somebody go through such an *intense* struggle for *so* long and more or less be an underdog for so long and then the end result is really what every single person wants—it's that freedom. And that last shot, [DP Roger Deakins] does it so vast and wide, it's like pure oxygen for the soul" (George). Arguably, the best way to participate in *Shawshank* fandom is to tour the Trail itself, preferably during one of its anniversary reunions (the twenty fifth is scheduled for 2019). Aside from joining the Ohio tour, the Internet has made it possible to share information, experiences, pictures, and insights with other fans, cinephiles, OSR personnel, and those directly associated with many of the various sites along the Trail. Listed below are several of the

Fig. 4.5   The authors at the entrance to the Ohio State Reformatory

available online iterations, sites, chat rooms, and fan clubs affiliated with both *The Shawshank Redemption* and the *Shawshank* Trail (Fig. 4.5).

Film Locations:

Mansfield Convention and Visitors Bureau: www.mansfieldtourism.com
Ashland Convention and Visitors Bureau: http://www.visitashlandohio.com/
The *Shawshank* Trail (information on all sites): www.shawshanktrail.com
Ohio State Reformatory (*Shawshank* Prison): http://www.mrps.org/
ShawshankWoodshop(PrisonWoodshop)andWyandotCountyCourthouse (Andy's trial): https://www.facebook.com/Shawshank-Woodshop-429512630465198/
The Bissman Building: http://www.hauntedbissmanbuilding.com/The_Bissman_Building/Welcome.html
Malabar Farm State Park: http://www.malabarfarm.org/
Shawshank Oak Tree: www.theShawshankOakTree.com

Carousel Antiques (Pawn Shop window): www.ohioantiques.com/carrousel

Crosby Advisory Group, LLC (Maine National Bank): http://www.crosbyadvisory.com/

Revivals 2 Thrift Store (Trailways Bus Station): http://www.pumphouseministries.com/ministries/revivals-2-thrift-store

Fan Art:

https://www.etsy.com/market/shawshank_redemption

http://fineartamerica.com/art/shawshank+redemption

http://ohiostatereformatory.deviantart.com/gallery/31127557/The-Shawshank-Redemption

http://www.fanpop.com/clubs/the-shawshank-redemption/fanart

https://www.behance.net/gallery/22614037/The-Shawshank-Redemption-20th-Anniversary-Fan-Art

http://geektyrant.com/news/2012/8/19/the-shawshank-redemption-awesome-fan-art.html

http://www.comicbookmovie.com/fan_fic/fan-art-stephen-king-stories-starring-comic-book-characters-a67733

http://www.fanart-central.net/pictures/user/RaggleTaggleGypsy/846324/The-Shawshank-Redemption-Rooftop-Scene

http://www.fanpop.com/clubs/the-shawshank-redemption

Fan Video:

https://www.youtube.com/watch?v=ia14dZ00jTM

http://www.dailymotion.com/video/x33a1cm

http://www.gamespot.com/articles/the-shawshank-redemption-if-it-were-an-8-bit-video/1100-6427657/ (8 bit video game style)

http://www.digitalspy.com/fun/news/a574092/shawshank-redemption-pivotal-scene-gets-smash-mouth-remix-video/ (smashmouth)

Fan Fiction:

https://www.fanfiction.net/movie/Shawshank-Redemption/

https://www.wattpad.com/story/22244199-freedom-a-shawshank-redemption-fan-fiction-yep

http://archiveofourown.org/tags/Shawshank%20Redemption%20-%20All%20Media%20Types/works

Slash Fiction:

http://movies.adult-fanfiction.org/main.php?list=1181
http://irisbleufic.livejournal.com/86579.html

Reenactment:

https://www.youtube.com/watch?v=5PyyT8zwLj4&list=PL98C88670
2A8F3950&index=3

Questions About the OSR:

http://www.answers.com/topic/reformatory

Andy was Guilty:

https://www.inverse.com/article/7029-fan-theory-101-the-shawshank-
redemption-s-andy-dufresne-was-guilty
http://moviepilot.com/posts/2641122
https://sorryneverheardofit.wordpress.com/2015/08/29/keeping-it-
reel-shawshank-redemptions-andy-is-guilty/

Meme:

https://www.google.com/search?q=shawshank+meme&safe=off&sourc
e=lnms&tbm=isch&sa=X&ved=0ahUKEwjX7Je1ooLLAhXFqB4KHW
mVA2cQ_AUIBygB&biw=1920&bih=947
http://ryanestrada.livejournal.com/33144.html (*Shawshank* as a 1980s
cartoon)

Notes

1. www.shawshanktrail.com
2. http://www.mansfieldtourism.com/what-to-do/attractions/haunted-
   bissman-building
3. cypresscellars.com
4. There has been some research done, chiefly helmed by cultural geographer
   Derek Alderman, examining Mount Airy, North Carolina's celebration of Andy
   Griffith's fictional "Mayberry." A number of articles explore the difficulty of

sustaining smaller film tourism events if community involvement is insufficient (Benjamin, Schneider, Alderman, and Alderman, Benjamin, Schneider).
5. http://www.mansfieldtourism.com/what-to-do/the-shawshank-trail
6. http://www.therockstarofcomedy.com/

WORKS CITED

Abercrombie, Nicholas, and Brian J. Longhurst. 1998. *Audiences: A Sociological Theory of Performance and Imagination.* London: Sage. Print.

Adams, Russell. 2014. How Thomas Newman Scored *The Shawshank Redemption.* *The Wall Street Journal,* 20 June. Web. 24 Feb. 2016. http://blogs.wsj.com/speakeasy/2014/06/20/how-thomas-newman-scored-the-shawshank-redemption/

Alber, Jan. 2007. *Narrating the Prison: Role and Representation in Charles Dickens' Novels, Twentieth-Century Fiction, and Film.* Youngstown, NY: Cambria Press, Print.

Alexander, Michelle. The New Jim Crow. New York: The New Press, 2012. Print.

Allanbrook, Wye. 1993. Human Nature in the Unnatural Garden: *Figaro* as Pastoral. *Current Musicology* 51: 82–93. Print.

Angels with Dirty Faces. 1938. Dir. Michael Curtiz. Screenplay by John Wexley and Warren Duff. Warner Brothers. DVD.

Baxter, John. 2015. Kubrick in Hell. In *The Shining: Studies in the Horror Film,* ed. Daniel Olson, 15–54. Lakewood, CO: Centipede Press. Print.

Beahm, George. 2015. *The Stephen King Companion: Four Decades of Fear from the Master of Horror.* New York: St. Martin's. Print.

Beaumont, Gustave de, and Alexis de Tocqueville. 1833. *On the Penitentiary System in the United States, and Its Application in France.* Philadelphia: Carey, Lea & Blanchard. Print.

Beeton, Sue. 2010. The Advance of Film Tourism. *Tourism and Hospitality Planning & Development* 7 (1): 1–6. Web. 28 Feb. 2016.

———. 2005. *Film Induced Tourism.* Clevedon (UK): Channel View Publications. Print.

© The Author(s) 2016   217
M. Grady, T. Magistrale, *The Shawshank Experience,*
DOI 10.1057/978-1-137-53165-0

Bentham, Jeremy. 1791. *"Panopticon": Or, the Inspection-House: Containing the Idea of a New Principle of Construction Applicable to Any Sort of Establishment, in Which Persons of Any Description are to be Kept Under Inspection.* London: T. Payne. Print.

The Big Sleep. 1946. Dir. Howard Hawks. Screenplay by William Faulkner, Leigh Brackett, and Jules Furthman. Warner Brothers. DVD.

Binelli, Mark. 2015. A Landmark Lawsuit Reaches Inside the Walls of America's Toughest Federal Prison. *The New York Times Magazine*, 29 March, Natl. ed., 37+. Print.

Birdman of Alcatraz. 1962. Dir. John Frankenheimer. Screenplay by Guy Trosper. United Artists. DVD.

Bishir, Catherine W. 2009. Levi Tucker Scofield. *North Carolina Architects & Builders: A Biographical Dictionary.* NCSU Libraries. Web. 4 Nov. 2015. http://ncarchitects.lib.ncsu.edu/people/P000138

Blake, William. 1968. London. In *Songs of Innocence and Experience. The Portable Blake*, 112. New York: Viking. Print.

The Blob. 1988. Dir. Chuck Russell. Screenplay by Frank Darabont and Chuck Russell. TriStar Pictures.

Bloom, Harold. 2007. Introduction. In *Bloom's Modern Critical Views: Stephen King*, ed. Harold Bloom, 1–3. Philadelphia: Chelsea House. Print.

Boym, Svetlana. 2001. *The Future of Nostalgia.* New York: Basic Books. Print.

Brake, Sherri. 2010. *The Haunted History of the Ohio State Reformatory.* Charleston, SC: The History Press. Print.

Briefel, Aviva. 2011. Shop Til You Drop: Consumerism and Horror. In *Horror After 9/11*, eds. Aviva Breifel and Sam J. Miller, 141–162. Austin, TX: Texas UP. Print.

Bright, Susie. 1995. *Sexwise.* Pittsburgh, PA: Cleis Press. Print.

Brodie, Ian. 2003. *The Lord of the Rings Location Guidebook.* New York: Harper Collins. Print.

Brown, Michelle. 2009. *The Culture of Punishment: Prison, Society, and Spectacle.* New York: New York University Press. Print.

Browning, Mark. 2009. *Stephen King on the Big Screen.* Chicago: Intellect (U of Chicago P). Print.

Busby, Graham, and Julia Klug. 2001. Movie Induced Tourism: The Challenge of Measurement and Other Issues. *Tourism, Leisure, and Hospitality Measurement* 7 (4): 316–332. October.

Butler, Judith. 1993. Introduction. In *Bodies that Matter: On the Discursive Limits of "Sex".* New York and London: Routledge. Print.

The Buzz. 1995. *The Advocate*, 4 April. Web. 9 Sept. 2015. http://www.advocate.com/search/site/The%2520Shawshank%2520Redemption

Christ, Ginger. 2009. GM Closing Mansfield Plant: Local Facility One of 15 Affected in Company's Restructuring Plan. In *Ashland Times Gazette*, www.times-gazette.com, 2 June. Web. 13 Mar. 2016.

Chua, Daniel K. L. 2011. Listening to the Self: *The Shawshank Redemption* and the Technology of Music. *19th-Century Music* 34: 341–355. Print.

Clover, Carol. 1992. *Men, Women and Chainsaws: Gender in the Modern Horror Film*. Princeton, NJ: Princeton UP. Print.

Cohen, Jeffrey Jerome. 1996. Introduction: Monster Culture (Seven Theses). In *Monster Theory: Reading Culture*, ed. Jeffrey Jerome Cohen, 3–25. Minneapolis, MI: U of Minnesota P. Print.

Connell, Joanne. 2012. *Tourism Management* 33 (5), October: 1007–1029. Web. 8 Mar. 2016.

Cool Hand Luke. 1967. Dir. Stuart Rosenberg. Screenplay by Donn Pierce and Frank Pierson. Jalem Productions. DVD.

Cooper, Bennett. Transcript. An Oral History of Bennett Cooper, First Director of the Ohio Department of Rehabilitation and Corrections. April 2006 by Jeffrey E. Carson. Web. 3 Feb. 2016. http://ohiocjoralhistoryjournal.blogspot.com/2009/11/oral-history-of-dr-bennet-cooper-first.html

Couldry, Nick. 2000. *The Place of Media Power: Pilgrims and Witnesses of the Media Age*. London: Routledge. Print.

Creed, Barbara. 1993. *The Monstrous-Feminine: Film, Feminism, Psychoanalysis*. New York and London: Routledge. Print.

Crook, Clive. 2015. Mass Incarceration is not the Worst Problem of U.S. System. *The Buffalo News*, 16 August: H4. Print.

Cruz, Gilbert. Q & A: Talking with Stephen King. *Time Magazine*, Web. 28 Nov. 2007. http://www.time.com/time/arts/article/0,8599,1687229,00.html

Cultographies Definition of Cult Cinema. *Cultographies.com*, Web. 8 Mar. 2016.

The Danish Girl. 2015. Dir. Tom Hooper. Screenplay Lucinda Coxon. Working Title Films. DVD.

Dante's Inferno. 1935. Dir. Harry Lachman. Screenplay by Philip Klein and Robert M. Yost. Fox Film Corporation. DVD.

Darabont, Frank. 2006. *The Shawshank Redemption: The Shooting Script*. Alexandria, VA: Alexander Street Press. Print.

The Defiant Ones. 1958. Dir. Stanley Kramer. Screenplay by Nedrick Young and Harold Jacob Smith. Metro-Goldwyn-Mayer. DVD.

Dickinson, Emily. 1960. Poem 613. In *The Complete Poems of Emily Dickinson*, ed. Thomas H. Johnson. Boston, MA: Little, Brown and Company. Print.

Doherty, Thomas. 1996. Genre, Gender, and the *Aliens* Trilogy. In *The Dread of Difference: Gender and the Horror Film*, ed. Barry Keith Grant, 181–199. Austin: U of Texas P. Print.

Dressed to Kill. 1980. Dir. Brian DePalma. Screenplay by Brian DePalma. Cinema 77 Films, Filmway Pictures, Warwick Associates. DVD.

Dumas, Alexandre. 1998. *The Count of Monte Cristo*. 1844. New York: Penguin. Print.

Dyer, Richard. 1986. *Heavenly Bodies: Film Stars and Society*. New York: Routledge. Print.

————. 1978/2005. Resistance Through Charisma: Rita Hayworth and *Gilda*. In *Women in Film Noir*, ed. E. Ann Kaplan, 115–122. London: British Film Institute. Print.

Edmundson, Mark. 1997. *Nightmare on Main Street: Angels, Sadomasochism, and the Culture of the Gothic*. Cambridge, MA: Harvard UP. Print.

Elmira. *New York Correction History Society*. Web. 4 Nov. 2015. http://www.correctionhistory.org/html/chronicl/docs2day/elmira.html

The Fall of the House of Usher. 1928. Dir. James Sibley Watson and Melville Webber. No Screenplay.

Farmer's Bank Gets Facelift. *Ashland County Historical Society*. Web. 29 Feb. 2016. http://www.ashlandhistory.org/

Feehan, Jennifer. 2009. Lady Justice Back in Place at Wyandot Country Courthouse. *The Toledo Blade*, 9 June. Web. 8 Mar. 2016.

————. 2008. *Shawshank Redemption* Extras Donate to Wyandot County Courthouse. *The Toledo Blade*, 16 December. Web. 8 Mar. 2016.

Fiddler, Michael. 2007. Projecting the Prison: The Depiction of the Uncanny in *The Shawshank Redemption*. *Crime Media Culture* 3: 192–206. Print.

Fiedler, Leslie. 1960. *Love and Death in the American Novel*. New York: Stein and Day. Print.

Film Tourism Fast Facts New Zealand. 2013. *Tourismnewzealand.com*, 10 April. Web. 15 July 2013. http://www.tourismnewzealand.com/sector-marketing/film-tourism/fast-facts/

Fisher, Benjamin Franklin. 2002. Poe and the Gothic Tradition. In *The Cambridge Companion to Edgar Allan Poe*, ed. Kevin J. Hayes, 72–91. Cambridge: Cambridge UP. Print.

The Fly 2. 1989. Dir. Kurt Neumann. Screenplay by Frank Darabont, Mick Garris, Jim Wheat. Brooksfilms. DVD.

Forrest Gump. 1994. Dir. Robert Zemeckis. Screenplay by Eric Roth. Paramount Pictures. DVD.

Foucault, Michel. 1977. *Discipline and Punish: The Birth of the Prison*. Trans. Alan Sheridan. New York: Vintage Books. Print.

Frankenstein. 1931. Dir. James Whale. Universal Pictures. DVD.

Frost, Robert. 1975. Mending Wall. In *The Poetry of Robert Frost*, ed. Edward Connery Lathem. New York: Holt, Rinehart and Winston. Print.

Futty, John. 1990. A Tale of Two Cities: The Journey from OSR to ManCI. Reprinted with permission from *The Mansfield News Journal*, 9 December. *Ohio Department of Rehabilitation and Correction*. Web. 6 Nov. 2015. http://www.drc.ohio.gov/web/historyosr.htm

George, Pete. 2014. Interview with Maura Grady and Richard Roberson, Jr. 23 December.

Gilda. 1946. Dir. Charles Vidor. Adaptation by Jo Eisinger. Columbia Pictures Corporation. DVD.

Grazier, Steven M. 2013. Mansfield, Like Massillon, Faces Fiscal Emergency. *CantonRep.com*, 19 October. Web. 13 Mar. 2016.

The Great Escape. 1963. Dir. John Sturges. Screenplay by James Clavell. Mirisch Company. DVD.

The Green Mile. 1999. Dir. Frank Darabont. Screenplay by Frank Darabont. Castle Rock Entertainment, Columbia Pictures. DVD.

Guiher, Susan. 2015. Message to Maura Grady. 15 June. E-mail.

Gunton, Bob. 2014. Personal Conversation with Tony Magistrale. 29 August.

Halberstam, Judith. 1995. *Skin Shows: Gothic Horror and the Technology of Monsters*. Durham: Duke UP. Print.

Hallinan, Joseph T. 2003. *Going Up the River*. New York: Random House. Print.

Haynes, Todd. 1974. Introduction. In *Criterion Collection: Fear Eats the Soul*. Dir. R.W. Fassbinder. Filmverlag der Autoren. Criterion DVD, 2003.

Heidenry, Margaret. 2014. The Little-Known Story of How *The Shawshank Redemption* Became One of the Most Beloved Films of All Time. *Vanity Fair. com*, September. Web. 22 Sept. 2014.

Hell Night. 1981. Dir. Tom DeSimone. Screenplay by Randy Feldman. BLT Productions. DVD.

Hills, Matt. 2002. *Fan Cultures*. London and New York: Routledge. Print.

Hinds, Julie. 1989. Get Out Your Handerchiefs. *Burlington Free Press*, 30 November, D13. Print.

Horror Stories from State Prisons. 2015. *New York Times*, 18 December: A34. Print.

House of Usher. 1960. Dir. Roger Corman. Screenplay by Richard Matheson. Alta Vista Productions. DVD.

The Hunchback of Notre Dame. 1939. Dir. William Dieterie. Screenplay by Sonya Levien and Bruno Frank. RKO Radio Pictures. DVD.

Hunter, Mary. 2002. Sentiment and Wit, Feeling and Knowing: *The Shawshank Redemption* and *Prizzi's Honor*. In *Between Opera and Cinema*, eds. Joe Jeongwon and Rose Theresa, 93–120. New York: Routledge. Print.

Incarceration Gap Widens between Whites and Blacks. Pew Research Center. Web. 17 Feb. 2015. www.pewresearch.org/fact-tank/2013/09/06/incarceration-gap-between-whites-and-blacks-widens/

Inmates Speak Out!: Ohio State Reformatory Stories, Thoughts, Ideas & Plots Conceived by Those Who Lived, Worked and Died Behind the Walls. 1998. Mansfield, OH: Mansfield Reformatory Preservation Society. 2016. Print.

Jenkins, Henry. 2012. *Textual Poachers:Television Fans and Participatory Culture*, 2nd ed. New York, NY: Routledge. Print.

Jenkins, Henry. *henryjenkins.org/aboutmehtml*. Web. 9 Aug. 2014.

Jenkins, T. C. *The Ohio State Reformatory Mansfield Ohio: 1896–1934*. State Report 1934. Print.

Jermyn, Deborah. 2005. The Rachel Papers: In Search of *Blade Runner*'s Femme Fatale. In *The Blade Runner Experience*, ed. Will Brooker, 159–172. London: Wallflower Press. Print.

Kane, Dan. 2014. Shawshank Celebrates 20 Years: Prison Saved, History Made. *Canton Rep.Com*, 14 August. Web. 8 Mar. 2016.

Karpovich, Angelina. 2010. Theoretical Approaches to Film-Motivated Tourism. *Tourism and Hospitality Planning & Development* 7 (1), March: 7–20.

Katz, Susan Bullington. 2000. *Conversations with Screenwriters*. Portsmouth, NH: Heinemann. Print.

Kennard, Mary. 2014. *Shawshank* Questions. Message to Maura Grady. 16 April. E-mail.

Kermode, Mark. 2003. *The Shawshank Redemption*. London: British Film Institute. Print.

King, Stephen. 2011. *11/22/63*. New York: Scribner. Print.

———. 1982. *Apt Pupil. Different Seasons*. New York: Viking. Print.

———. 2010. *Big Driver. Full Dark, No Stars*. New York: Scribner. Print.

———. 2006. *Cell*. New York: Scribner. Print.

———. 1981. *Danse Macabre*. New York: Berkley. Print.

———. 1989. *The Dark Half*. New York: Viking. Print.

———. 1982. *The Dark Tower: The Gunslinger*. West Kingston, RI: Donald M. Grant. Print.

———. 2004. *The Dark Tower VII: The Dark Tower*. New York: Simon and Schuster. Print.

———. 1993. The Doctor's Case. In *Nightmares and Dreamscapes*. New York: Viking. Print.

———. 2013. *Doctor Sleep*. New York: Scribner.

———. 1993. *Dolores Claiborne*. New York: Viking. Print.

———. 2015. *Finders Keepers*. New York: Scribner. Print.

———. 1992. *Gerald's Game*. New York: Viking. Print.

———. 2008. The Gingerbread Girl. In *Just After Sunset*. New York: Scribner. Print.

———. 2010. *A Good Marriage. Full Dark, No Stars*. New York: Scribner. Print.

———. 1994. *IT*. New York: Viking. Print.

———. 2013. *Joyland*. London, England: Titan Books. Print.

———. 2006. *Lisey's Story*. New York: Scribner. Print.

———. 2014. *Mr. Mercedes*. New York: Scribner. Print.

———. 1991. *Needful Things*. New York: Viking. Print.

———. 1979. *Night Shift*. New York: New American Library. Print.

———. 2014. Question About *Shawshank*. Message to Tony Magistrale. 24 October. E-mail.

———. 2015. *Revival*. New York: Scribner. Print.

———. 1982. *Rita Hayworth and the Shawshank Redemption. Different Seasons*. New York: Viking. Print.

———. 1975. *'Salem's Lot*. New York: New American Library. Print.

———. 1977. *The Shining*. New York: Doubleday. Print.

———. 1978. *The Stand*. New York: Doubleday. 1990. Print.

———. 1984. *The Tommyknockers*. New York: G.P. Putnam's Sons. Print.

Kisicki, Jim. 2016. E-mail Interview with Maura Grady. 18 January.

Kiss of the Spider Woman. 1985. Dir. Hector Babenco. Screenplay by Leonard Schrader. HB Filmes, FilmDallas Pictures. DVD.

Larsen, Katherine, and Lynn Zubernis. 2012. *Fan Culture: Theory/Practice*. Newcastle Upon Tyne (UK): Cambridge Scholars Publishing. Print.

Lee, Soojin, David Scott, and Hyounggon Kim. 2008. Celebrity Fan Involvement and Destination Perceptions. *Annals of Tourism Research* 35 (3): 809–832. Web. 16 Feb. 2016.

Lewis, Matthew Gregory. 1990. *The Monk*. 1795, ed. Howard Anderson. Oxford: Oxford UP. Print.

Logan, Charles H., and Gerald G. Gaes. 1993. Meta-Analysis and the Rehabilitation of Punishment. *Justice Quarterly* 10: 245–263. Print.

London After Midnight. 1927. Dir. Tod Browning. Screenplay by Tod Browning. Metro-Goldwyn-Mayer. DVD.

Lusk, Shannon. 2013. Interview with Maura Grady and Richard Roberson, Jr. 15 August.

MacKellar, Joanne. 2009. Dabblers, Fans, and Fanatics: Exploring Behavioral Segmentation at a Special-Interest Event. *Tourism Leisure and Hospitality Management* 15 (1): 5–24. Web. 16 Feb. 2016.

Madden, Edward. 2007. Cars are Girls: Sexual Power and Sexual Panic in Stephen King's *Christine*. In *Bloom's Modern Critical Views: Stephen King*, ed. Harold Bloom, 117–194. New York: Chelsea House. Print.

Magistrale, Tony. 1992. The Writer Defines Himself: An Interview with Stephen King. In *Stephen King the Second Decade, Danse Macabre to The Dark Half*, 1–19. New York: Twayne Publishers. Print.

———. 2003. Steve's Take: An Interview with Stephen King. In *Hollywood's Stephen King*, 1–20. New York: Palgrave Macmillan. Print.

Mann, Scott. 2015. E-mail Interview with Maura Grady. 25 March.

Mansfield, Ohio. *Ohio History Central*. Web. 4 Nov. 2015. http://www.ohiohistorycentral.org/w/Mansfield,_Ohio?rec=1968

The Marriage of Figaro. By Wolfgang Amadeus Mozart. Web. 16 Nov. 2014. www.aria-database.com/translations/figaro.txt

Mary Shelley's Frankenstein. 1994. Dir. Kenneth Branagh. Screenplay by Steph Lady and Frank Darabont. TriStar Pictures. DVD.

McElroy, Ethan. Kirkbride Buildings. Web. 20 Feb. 2016. www.kirkbridebuildings.com

McKinley, Jesse. 2015. State-Run Prisons Planning to Take a Punitive Recipe off the Cookbooks. *New York Times*, 18 December: A32+. Print.

McKinnell, Becky. 2009. *Ohio State Reformatory: Curriculum for Teachers and Educational Professionals*. Mansfield, OH: Mansfield Reformatory Preservation Society. Printed Pamphlet.

———. 2015. Interview with Maura Grady. 17 June.

———. 2016. Sewer Pipes at OSR. Message to Maura Grady. 1 January. E-mail.

Meyers, David, and Elise Meyers. 2009. *Images of America: Central Ohio's Historic Prisons*. Charleston, SC: Arcadia Publishing. Print.

Meyers, David, Elise Walker, and James Dailey, Jr. 2013. *Inside the Ohio Penitentiary*. Charleston: The History Press. Print.

Mikhaylova, L. 2012. Star Trek (2009) and the Russian ST Fandom: Too Many Batteries Included. In *Fan Culture: Theory/Practice*, eds. Katherine Larsen and Lynn Zubernis, 148–161. Newcastle-Upon-Thyne: Cambridge Scholars Publishing. Print.

The Mist. 2008. Dir. Frank Darabont. Screenplay by Frank Darabont. Dimension. DVD.

Mizejewski, Linda. 2014. *Pretty Funny: Women Comedians and Body Politics*. Austin, TX: U of Texas P. Print.

Montgomery, Marion. 1962. Robert Frost and His Use of Barriers: Man vs. Nature Toward God. In *Robert Frost: A Collection of Critical Essays*, ed. James M. Cox, 138–150. Englewood Cliffs, NJ: Prentice-Hall. Print.

Moser, John. 2015. Interview with Maura Grady. 5 June.

Mrs. Doubtfire. 1993. Dir. Christopher Columbus. Screenplay by Randi Mayem Singer. Twentieth Century Fox. DVD.

Mullen, April, and Bill Mullen. 2015. Interview with Maura Grady. 24 July.

Mulvey, Laura. 2011. Visual Pleasure and Narrative Cinema. 1975. In *Critical Visions in Film Theory: Classic and Contemporary Readings*, eds. Timothy Corrigan, Patricia White with Meta Mazaj, 715–725. Boston, MA: Bedford/St. Martins. Print.

Neale, Steve. 1983. Masculinity as Spectacle. *Screen* 24: 2–16. Print.

Nero, Charles Isidore. 2004. Diva Traffic and Male Bonding in Film: Teaching Opera, Learning Gender, Race, and Nation. *Camera Obscura* 19: 46–73. Print.

A Nightmare on Elm Street 3: Dream Warriors. 1987. Dir. Chuck Russell. Screenplay by Wes Craven, Bruce Wagner, Frank Darabont. New Line Cinema. DVD.

Nilsen, Sarah. 2008. White Soul: The Magical Negro in the Films of Stephen King. In *The Films of Stephen King*, ed. Tony Magistrale, 129–140. New York: Palgrave Macmillan. Print.

The Ohio State Reformatory. *Forgotten Ohio: Ohio Hauntings*. Web. 4 Nov. 2015. http://www.forgottenoh.com/OSR/osr.html

One Million Years, B. C. 1965. Dir. Don Caffey. Screenplay by George Baker and Joseph Frickert. Hammer Film Productions, Seven Arts Productions. DVD.

Otto, Rudolf. 1938. *The Idea of the Holy*. Trans. John W. Harvey. London: Oxford UP. Print.

Papillon. 1973. Dir. Frank J. Schaffner. Screenplay by Dalton Trumbo and Lorenzo Semple. Allied Artists. DVD.

Perry, Dennis R., and Carl H. Sederholm. 2009. *Poe, "The House of Usher," and the American Gothic.* New York: Palgrave Macmillan. Print.

Plank, Betty. 1987. *Historic Ashland County Vol. 1: A Collection of Local Accounts about People, Places, and Events from 1918–1987.* Ashland, OH: Ashland County Historical Society. Rpt. 2008. Print.

Poe, Edgar Allan. 2010. *The Narrative of Arthur Gordon Pym of Nantucket.* 1838, eds. Frederick Frank and Diane Long Hoeveler. Buffalo, NY: Broadview Editions. Print.

Pratt, John. 2000. *Punishment and Civilization.* London: Sage Publications. Print.

Prisoners in 2007: 1 in 31 American Adults in Prison, Jail or on Parole. The November Coalition. Web. 21 Feb. 2015. www.november.org/resources/studiesreports.html

Pritchard, Anette, and Nigel Morgan. 2013. Hopeful Tourism: a Transformational Perspective. In *Transformational Tourism: Tourist Perspectives,* ed. Yvette Reisinger. Oxfordshire (UK): CAB International. Print.

Psycho. 1960. Dir. Alfred Hitchcock. Screenplay by Joseph Stefano. Shamley Productions. DVD.

The Public Enemy. 1931. Dir. William A. Wellman. Screenplay by Kubec Glasmon, John Bright and Harvey Thew. Warner Brothers. DVD.

Pugh, Emily. 2014. Interview with Maura Grady and Richard Roberson, Jr. 27 January.

Puster-Snavely, Jodie. 2014. Interview with Maura Grady and Richard Roberson, Jr. 28 July.

Real Time: Number 349. 2015. *Real Time with Bill Maher.* HBO, Los Angeles, 10 April. Television.

Restoring Our Local Landmark! The Mansfield Reformatory Preservation Society. Web. 17 Feb. 2015. www.mrps.org/home.htm

Roberson Jr., Richard, and Maura Grady. 2015. The Shawshank Trail: A Cross Disciplinary Study in Film Induced Tourism and Fan Culture. *Almatourism: Journal of Tourism, Culture and Territorial Development* 6 (4): 47–66. Special issue on Film Induced Tourism. Web. 28 Feb. 2016.

Robinson, Frances. 2015. Overcrowding Puts New Strain on Century-Old European Prisons. *The Wall Street Journal,* 3 February, Natl. ed.: A8. Print.

Ross, Jeffrey Ian. 2012. Why a Jail Prison Sentence is Increasingly Like a Death Sentence. *Contemporary Justice Review* 15: 309–321. Print.

Runaway Prison Costs Trash State Budgets. *The Fiscal Times,* Web. 17 Feb. 2015. www.thefiscaltimes.com/Articles/2011/02/09/Runaway-Prison-Costs-Thrash-State-Budgets

Sade, Marquis de. 2006. *Philosophy in the Boudoir.* 1795. Trans. Joachim Neugroschel. New York: Penguin. Print.

Samavati, Shaheen. 2009. Two Ohio Cities, Parma and Ontario, React to News from General Motors. *The Cleveland Plain Dealer*, 1 June. Web. 8 Mar. 2016.

Schiller, Friedrich von. 1967. *On the Aesthetic Education of Man: In a Series of Letters*. Trans. Elizabeth M. Wilkinson, and L. A. Willoughby. Oxford: Clarendon Press. 1985. Print.

Schulz, Bill. 2014. Visiting Shawshank Sites, 20 Years Later. *New York Times*, 7 August. Web. 4 Nov. 2015. http://www.nytimes.com/2014/08/10/travel/visiting-shawshank-sites-20-years-later.html?_r=0

Sciullo, Marisa. Former Prison in Ohio Draws Captive Audience, Thanks to Shawshank Redemption. *Pittsburgh Post-Gazette*. Web. 24 Aug. 2014. http://www.post-gazette.com/ae/movies/2014/08/24/Former-Mansfield-reformatory-in-Ohio-draws-captive-audience-thanks-to-Shawshank-Redemption/stories/201408240010

The Seven Year Itch. 1955. Dir. Billy Wilder. Screenplay by Billy Wilder and George Axelrod. Twentieth Century Fox Film Corporation. DVD.

Shawshank Panel. 2014. A Round-table Discussion at the 2014 Twentieth Anniversary Celebration of *The Shawshank Redemption*. With Bob Gunton, Eve LaPolla, Tony Magistrale, and Ernie Malik. Renaissance Theater, Mansfield, OH. 29 August.

Shawshank: The Redeeming Feature. 2004. Dir. Andrew Abbott. Writer / Perf. Mark Kermode. Documentary featured on Two-Disc Deluxe Limited Edition and Three-Disc Special Edition DVDs. Warner Home Video, 2001. DVD.

The Shawshank Redemption. 1994. Dir. Frank Darabont. Screenplay by Frank Darabont. Castle Rock Entertainment, Columbia Pictures. DVD.

The Shawshank Redemption: Twentieth Anniversary DVD Commentary. 2014. Documentary featured on Two-Disc Deluxe Limited Edition and Three-Disc Special Edition DVDs. Warner Home Video. DVD.

Shawshank Redemption Rare Deleted Scenes. YouTube. Web. 16 July 2015. www.youtube.com/watch?v=5g21fJk-aCo

Sifferlin, Alexandra. 2014. What 28 Years of Solitary Confinement Does to the Mind. *Time*, Time, Inc. 29 July. Web. 4 Nov. 2015.

The Silence of the Lambs. 1991. Dir. Jonathan Demme. Screenplay by Ted Tally. Orion Pictures. DVD.

Stand By Me. 1986. Dir. Rob Reiner. Screenplay by Raynold Gideon and Bruce E. Evans. Columbia Pictures, Act III Productions, Castle Rock Entertainment. DVD.

Stephen King's Rose Red. 2002. Dir. Craig R. Baxley. Teleplay by Stephen King. Greengrass Productions, Victor Television Productions. DVD.

Stephen King's The Shining. 1997. Dir. Mick Garris. Teleplay by Stephen King. Warner Brothers Television, ABC-TV. DVD.

Stephen King's Storm of the Century. 1999. Dir. Craig R. Baxley. Teleplay by Stephen King. ABC-TV. DVD.

Stiernstedt, Frederik. 2008. Maximizing the Power of Entertainment: The Audience Commodity in the Radio Age. *Radio Journal: International Studies in Broadcast & Audio Media* 6 (2–3), December: 113–127. Web. 28 Feb. 2016.

Stoker, Bram. 2002. *Dracula*. 1897. Boston: Bedford/St. Martin's. Print.

Sukel, Scott. 2015. Interview with Maura Grady. 25 July.

Summers, Montague. 1931. Architecture and the Gothic Novel. *Architectural Design and Construction* 2: 78–81. Print.

Switch. 1991. Dir. Blake Edwards. Screenplay by Blake Edwards. Beco Films, Home Box Office. DVD.

Tasseff, Lee. 2015. Interview with Maura Grady. 5 September.

The Texas Chainsaw Massacre. 1974. Dir. Tobe Hooper. Screenplay by Kim Henkel, Tobe Hooper. Vortex. DVD.

Thoreau, Henry David. 1947. *Civil Disobedience*. 1849. In *The Portable Thoreau*, ed. Carl Bode, 109–137. New York: Viking. Print.

Titko, Robert Ernest. 1962. *Reasons Men from the Ohio State Reformatory Stay in or Escape from Honor Assignments*. Master in Social Work Thesis. Ohio State University. Print.

Toobin, Jeffrey. 2015. The Milwaukee Experiment. *The New Yorker* 11, May: 24–32. Print.

Tootsie. 1982. Dir. Sydney Pollack. Screenplay by Larry Gelbart, Murray Schisgal. Columbia Pictures. DVD.

Trilling, Lionel. 1953. *The Liberal Imagination: Essays on Literature and Society*, ed. Anchor Books. Garden City, NY: Doubleday. Print.

Tulloch, John, and Henry Jenkins. 1995. *Science Fiction Audiences: Watching Doctor Who and Star Trek*. London: Routledge. Print.

Twain, Mark. 2003. *Adventures of Huckleberry Finn*. 1877. New York: Penguin. Print.

Ulin, Donald Ingram. 2013. From *Huckleberry Finn* to *The Shawshank Redemption*: Race and the American Imagination in the Biracial Escape Film. *European Journal of American Studies* 8: 2–18. Print.

Underwood, Tim, and Chuck Miller, eds. 1988. *Bare Bones: Conversations on Terror with Stephen King*. New York: McGraw-Hill. Print.

Vance, Chris. (aka Zippy). 2015. Interview with Maura Grady. 25 July.

Wachtman, Bob. 2015. Interview with Maura Grady. 24 July.

The Walking Dead. 2010. Creator Frank Darabont. American Movie Classics. TV.

Wang, Ning. 1999. Rethinking Authenticity in Tourism Experience. *Annals of Tourism Research* 26 (2): 349–370. Web. 28 Feb. 2016.

Warhol, Robyn R. 2003. *Having a Good Cry: Effeminate Feelings and Pop-Culture Forms*. Columbus, OH: Ohio State UP. Print.

Waterman, Jayne. 2004. Louis Bromfield. *The Literary Encyclopedia* 3, June. Web. 18 Jan. 2016. http://www.litencyc.com/php/speople.php?rec=true&UID=5 78January

Weiss, Robert P. 1999. Reflections on Social Justice and the Prisoner Struggle. *Social Justice* 26: 175. Print.

Welch, Michael. 2015. *Escape to Prison: Penal Tourism and the Pull of Punishment.* Oakland, CA: U of California Press. Print.

What Should We Make of Prison Tourism? 2011. Web blog post. *Prison Culture: How the Prison Industrial Complex Structures Our World.* 1 February. Web. 4 Mar. 2016.

What Were You Thinking? 2015. *The Economist,* 24 January: 24. Print.

White Heat. 1949. Dir. Raoul Walsh. Screenplay by Ivan Goff and Ben Roberts. Warner Brothers. DVD.

Wickman, Forrest. Bond Beats Bronte: Who's the Most Adapted Author in Cinema? Web. 2 Oct. 2015. http://www.slate.com/blogs/browbeat/2011/03/11/bond_beats_bront_who_s_the_most_adapted_author_in_cinema.html

Wilkins, Hugh. 2011. Souvenirs: Why and What We Buy. *Journal of Travel Research* 50 (3): 239–247. Web. 28 Feb. 2016.

Williams, Linda. 2015. When a Woman Looks. 1983. In *The Dread of Difference: Gender and the Horror Film,* ed. Barry Keith Grant, 17–36. Austin, Texas: U of Texas P, 1995, 2015.

Wilson, Jacqueline Z. 2008. *Prison: Cultural Memory and Dark Tourism.* New York: Peter Lang. Print.

The Woman in the Room. 1983. Dir. Frank Darabont. Screenplay by Frank Darabont. Simitar Video, Granite Video, Interglobal Video, VCL Communications. DVD.

Zubernis, Lynn, and Katherine Larsen. 2012. *Fandom at the Crossroads: Celebration, Shame and Fan/Producer Relationships.* Newcastle-Upon-Thyne (UK): Cambridge Scholars Publishing. Print.

INDEX

© The Author(s) 2016
M. Grady, T. Magistrale, *The Shawshank Experience*,
DOI 10.1057/978-1-137-53165-0

CPSIA information can be obtained
at www.ICGtesting.com
Printed in the USA
BVHW010149300419
546930BV00005B/97/P